Facilitating Reflective Learning in Higher Education

Facilitating Reflective Learning in Higher Education

Anne Brockbank and
Ian McGill

Society for Research into Higher Education
& Open University Press

Published by SRHE and
Open University Press
Celtic Court
22 Ballmoor
Buckingham
MK18 1XW

email: enquiries@openup.co.uk
world wide web: http://www.openup.co.uk

and
325 Chestnut Street,
Philadelphia, PA 19106, USA

First Published 1998
Reprinted 1999

A catalogue record of this book is available from the British Library

ISBN   0 335 19685 3 (pb)   0 335 19686 1 (hb)

Library of Congress Cataloging-in-Publication Data

Brockbank, Anne, 1943–
    Facilitating reflective learning in higher education / by Anne
Brockbank and Ian McGill.
        p.   cm.
    Includes bibliographical references and index.
    ISBN 0–335–19685–3 (pbk.). — ISBN 0–335–19686–1 (hard)
    1. College teaching. 2. Learning. I. McGill, Ian. II. Title.
LB2331.B676   1998
378.1′2—dc21   97– 47445
                                                                CIP

Typeset by Graphicraft Limited, Hong Kong
Printed in Great Britain by St Edmundsbury Press Ltd, Bury St Edmunds, Suffolk

To Tom, Gerard, James, Alison and Stephen

Contents

Acknowledgements

Our book represents the experience of many years in higher education, living with many of the changes we advocate and convey through our practice.

More recently we owe much deepening of our experience to those at City University and the University of Brighton who trusted us to take risks and innovate where we knew in our bones that it meant moving down the road to learning that was relevant to those learners who travelled with us.

For Ian: it meant being privileged in working with staff in all Faculties at Brighton in a developmental role with the wholehearted support of the Director, David Watson and in particular David House, the Deputy Director, who saw potential for developmental initiatives where I was still tentative. Their support was underpinned by Jon Bareham, Dean of the Business School, who provided continuous encouragement within and beyond the School.

In a very specific way my collaborative work in Brighton with Liz Beaty, in creating the workshop package on Developing Reflective Practice, provided one of the significant sources of the ideas in this book. That collaboration would not have been achieved without the creative work of Martin Hayden and his staff, who made the video to support the material. Linda Lang and Sophie Nicholls provided the live experience of reflecting upon their practice for the video.

At City University I have had the support of Ronnie Lessem of the Business School in being able to work with a very innovative MBA that actually lives critically reflective learning. The students on that programme have worked with me on the challenge of reflective dialogue, so that I too learned and developed my role as a facilitator. Valerie Iles with the Health Management Group at City gave me the opportunity of working with alumni, who in turn, facilitate Masters students.

For Anne: the experience in the Faculty of Management and Business at Manchester Metropolitan University was invaluable in developing ideas about experiential learning and reflective dialogue. The support of Gary Davies enabled me to put some of these innovative ideas into practice, combined with the enthusiasm of colleagues in the Faculty.

Collaboration with Alison Assiter, while at the University of North London, enabled refinements of ideas on reflective learning and supportive colleagues in the Business School kept the flame alive. At City University in the Department of Continuing Education, I had the support of Stella Parker and Caroline Leigh, sharing in the development of an innovative Masters degree in Continuing Education and Training. Working with Julia Carter, enabled me to develop a model of how facilitative methods can be practised in parallel with subject expertise.

Our thanks to participants at our SEDA workshop in December 1995, for their reflections on facilitative practice.

Our readers, Jane Alderton, Bob Sang and Susan Weil did our near final manuscript justice by being critical yet constructive and very supportive of our endeavour. We take full responsibility for the final outcome. Our thanks to Gerard O'Connor for some of the illustrations in Chapter 10 and our thanks to Ewan Ketteman for comments on Chapter 3.

Finally our thanks to John Skelton and Linda Watkins at Open University Press for their patience and understanding as we approached John for yet another extension. John's faith in our idea at the outset and over time has been a huge source of support.

Anne Brockbank and Ian McGill

Part 1

Learning and Reflection

The book is in three parts. Part 1 is about theory. We need to set out the origins of our work in a theoretical stance that underpins and is reflected in our practice. In turn our practice has mediated our values back into our theoretical struggles. Writing this book has itself forced us to engage with theory, both in its history and in relation to the purposes of a significant institution in our society – higher education.

Parts 2 and 3 are about engaging in practice. Part 2 initially sets the contemporary context of practice in higher education. The remainder of Part 2 sets out as clearly as we can the basis of practice in reflective dialogue and facilitation. Here we aim to cut through the language of 'talking about' to the practice of thinking, being and action in reflective dialogue and facilitation.

Part 3 is designed to place reflective dialogue and facilitation in a praxis that takes the 'purity' of how practitioners, teachers, learners and other actors in higher education can engage in facilitating reflective dialogue, and relates it to group learning, supervision and mentoring. These three chosen forms of praxis are not the only means of engagement. We have chosen them as important means of promoting learning which can be adapted to a wide range of situations.

The book is therefore very different in style according to the Part you are reading. Go to Part 2 if you wish to enter immediately into the 'roots' of our practice. The detail given on reflective dialogue and facilitation may support their introduction to colleagues and student learners. If you are familiar with this core of Part 2 you may wish to work with Part 3, and adapt these exemplars to a range of learning contexts in higher education. For the conceptual base of where our stance, values and ideas emanate from we recommend Part 1. Necessarily the style in each Part varies according to our purpose.

Finally, the book is intended not only to enable teachers and learners to promote more effective learning. It is intended to promote learning that is critical, to enable us all as learners to take the risks to move beyond necessary improvement in our capacities to learn and use that learning. In thinking, being and acting as critical learners we can enter and pass through struggles that take us beyond that which is given to move into that which is not yet imagined, explored and journeyed. We are privileged in working with colleagues and student learners who do make the journey beyond themselves.

For each reader we emphasize a choice and responsibility about where they are and how they relate to the journey inherent in the learning that is advocated here. The book recognizes the challenge in this for readers and the need for support for those who challenge themselves in this way.

Higher education need not only be a repository of the necessarily instrumental in society. Continuously claiming and reclaiming that which moves beyond the instrumental is fundamental for society, for all of us who spend our lives in higher education, and for those who live through the experience of higher education and return during their lives.

Chapter 1 explains our own journeys in coming to the writing of this book.

1

Introduction to our Themes

We address the central theme of learning in higher education. Our primary purpose is to suggest *how* learning can be effectively and consciously promoted. However, our purpose cannot be separated from the following questions. What is the purpose of higher education? What kind of learning should higher education be promoting? We review these questions in order to identify the relevance of our approaches to promoting learning.

Higher educational institutions aspire to create the conditions for learning often without articulating those aspirations. A growing number of academic staff, policy makers and writers are now more explicit about the purpose of the institutions in promoting learning that is not merely instrumental. Higher education is rightly endeavouring to ensure that students can realize their aspirations after university as well as providing an enriching experience on the path to graduation and post-graduation. However, beyond the instrumental are explicit aspirations captured in phrases like transformational learning, critical learning, lifelong learning, which we examine later. These aspirations, or purposes of higher education are explored and justified in the context of late twentieth-century understandings of society, knowledge and the relevance of universities in the future. Higher education is having to justify its existence as it is no longer taken as a privilege given by society. Indeed, the pressure to justify causes concern for some in that the traditional qualities of higher education such as academic freedom and autonomy, to pursue knowledge, may be sacrificed.

Given the aspirations for learning that includes, yet goes beyond the instrumental, how can learning be promoted and encouraged that meets these aspirations? The key for us is in the nature of learning and the interactions and relationships between academic staff as teachers and student learners and between learners themselves.

Drawing from our experience as learners and teachers in higher education as well as sources drawn upon and referred to later, we recognize the shift that is taking place in knowledge and understanding about the nature of learning. In some ways the views of what is learning and how it can be achieved when intentionally addressed and the values that lie beneath those views have preoccupied societies for millenia. We draw upon recent inter-pretations of the nature of learning in higher education as well as its pur-poses. We make known our values as these deeply affect the way we work with student learners and colleagues in academia and elsewhere. We set out these ideas briefly below as a prelude to a deeper analysis in the remainder of the book. We will not at this stage become definitional – that we do later. Our purpose here is to provide an overview of our case for the way in which we believe learning in higher education can be realized.

We start from a value position in holding that people are abundant in the resources of their experience which they bring to situations that are inten-tionally about creating learning in learners. This contrasts crudely with the view, often implicitly held, that people are 'empty vessels' to be filled until they are in a position to work within the arena that is created for them. We draw on the work of social constructivism (Berger and Luckman, 1966), in holding that we are deeply influenced by our life experience, that learning contexts in higher education (as elsewhere) are themselves social constructs, that knowledge is socially constructed and that when learners enter and experience higher education they enter a system that is not value free and where power is exercised that can influence the progress and learning of a student learner. The same applies to academic staff who have the respons-ibility, in part, to create the conditions for learning to take place.

We aim to support those in higher education who wish to create the conditions for learning that are at the 'transformational' end of learning, a phrase relating to the effect of the learning potentially in the learner. This phrase, which we explore later, is related to or characterized by phrases like deep as opposed to surface learning. Development of the person is the aspiration, where the capacity to learn is increasingly in the learner as greater autonomy is reached. The learner is able to be critical in relation to the domains of knowledge, self and the world, where the learner is able not only to embrace knowledge but also to bring self, including emotion and action, into the learning process. The learner is effective within her disci-pline, as well as critical of her discipline from without, as well as crossing disciplines in acknowledgement of the relativity of knowledge. She is able to be in a reflexive position about learning how she learns.

However, such learning does not occur in a vacuum. The context in which learning may happen is crucial. Learning is a social process which will influence the degree of 'agency' experienced by the learner. Essen-tially, the context of learning and what the learner perceives, consciously or not, as the ability to think, feel and act in any situation is crucial to the means by which that person becomes a transformational learner.

Learning as a social process is critical to the learning process itself. By the learning process we mean the context and conditions in which learning takes place. Process is about how intentional learning situations are created and undertaken. If learning embraces and integrates, knowledge, self and action, then the means require their inclusion and integration as well.

Moving more closely to our theme, learning as a social process is crucial because transformational or critical learning requires conditions that enable the learner to reflect upon her learning not only by herself, but with others. The ability to become a critical learner, to be able to shift across paradigms of knowledge and self as well as perceive and act in ways that may transcend understandings in the past requires the capacity to be able to reflect on what is known, felt and acted upon. Being able to undertake reflection alone is necessary but not sufficient. The tendency to self-deceive, collude and be unaware is ever present. Moreover, given the socially constructed nature of knowledge and that meaning is created in relation to others, then reflection and the creation of meaning is inevitably a social process.

This leads to the significance of relationship in learning. If the purpose of institutions of higher education is to encourage the move beyond the transmissional to the transformative, then it should be a fundamental condition of the students' experience – whether, diplomate, undergraduate or postgraduate, full or part time – that relationship is crucial to learning. By the term relationship we mean situations are created where teachers and learners (and learners together) can actively reflect upon the issues and material before them, e.g. seminars and tutorials. The substance of the relationship which is created is one of dialogue between teacher and learners. Through dialogue with others which is reflective we create the conditions for critical reflective learning. This is at the core of our purpose.

For reflective dialogue to take place, a particular kind of relationship is required between teacher and learners, and among learners. The relationship is one where learners and teacher engage and work together so that they jointly construct meaning and knowledge with the material. The material and how it is worked on is a product of that relation between those in dialogue. The material is not out there, detached and unconnected. In the conditions of reflective dialogue there is the possibility of moving beyond taken-for-granted assumptions and paradigms of the learner's world, and the possibility also for the teacher to review her meanings within her own scholarship.

For reflective dialogue to happen the teacher relates differently with student learners. The teacher becomes a facilitator of learning. The focus becomes the students' learning and how they may come to understand, appropriate, modify and transcend meanings with the material. The student learners become the centre and focus of the dialogue. For the teacher, the focus moves away from the transmission of the material to how the learners are working with the material in the here and now.

The teacher, as facilitator, takes responsibility for creating the conditions conducive to critical reflective dialogue until student learners are familiar with the process. As students become aware of the process the teacher can enable them not only to reflect critically upon the material before them, but also begin to reflect upon the process by which they are learning. They can begin to reflect upon learning about how they are learning.

We recognize that the move from teaching subject content or demonstrating an experiment, to facilitating reflective dialogue with student learners, is not straightforward. The transition from transmitting content to attending to the learners' needs may be unfamiliar or difficult for both teachers and learners. We cannot assume that teachers are familiar with formal or explicitly created ways of working with reflective dialogue, though, of course, some will be. We have thus created in Chapters 7 and 8 a transition process which begins with teachers and only then moves on to student learners.

We start, then, with teachers engaging with each other in reflective dialogue by recourse to their 'material', or what constitutes their practice, for example: teaching; scholarship; research; course leadership; design and implementation. By working 'live' on their material, teachers can engage in reflective practice through reflective dialogue to enhance and learn about their practice. In the experience they create their own meanings and understandings of reflective dialogue as well as having direct experience of the process.

This experience acts as a precursor to working as facilitators of reflective dialogue with student learners. When students have experienced reflective dialogue to promote their learning and have had the process effectively modelled, they will then be in a position to undertake reflective dialogue themselves. Clearly, some students may already be reflective learners through their life experience or previous development.

By focusing on the idea of reflective dialogue between teacher-as-facilitator and learners, we are aiming to go to a basic form of an emerging relationship that can promote the conditions for transformational learning. This does not mean that academic staff have to set up, in a kind of isolated purity, a reflective dialogue situation on its own. We do recommend explicitly entering into the process of experiencing and coming to understand and work in reflective dialogue with student learners early on in their undergraduate or postgraduate programmes. We are suggesting that once the form of the dialogue is familiar to student learners and teachers, the approach can be brought with effect to more familiar situations, such as seminars, group activities, supervision and mentoring, hence our attention to applications in Part 3.

Having stated our purpose there are other issues we need to declare.

Our rationale

Much is written and spoken about the purposes and approaches to teaching and learning that is intended to encourage critical reflective learning which is transformational, e.g. Harvey and Knight (1996) and Barnett (1992a, 1997). However, there is little that records how such learning may be facilitated. Our aim is to contribute by making the process by which such learning can be achieved more accessible. We have written this book in order that it may be useful for teachers, learners, staff developers, and policy influencers recognizing that each of those roles may be interchangeable.

We aim to set out a model of the process by which reflective dialogue can be facilitated that encourages critical reflective learning. The model first, offers teachers a plan which they can put into use with student learners. Secondly, the model can be used by teachers to reflect on their own professional practice. Thirdly, the explicit recognition and example of reflective dialogue provides a means for student learners to reflect on their practice as well as supporting them in learning about their learning.

We are aware that in addition to the model being practised explicitly in some academic quarters, the model or variants of it will be in use implicitly. By explicitly recognizing and describing how the model may be implemented we may also be providing a basis for reflection on existing practice. Articulating potential practice, provides a means of comparison with existing practice – whatever form the latter takes. There may be those who assert that reflective dialogue and critical reflective learning is already happening. Our model provides a template against which those who assert it is happening can reflect on their practice.

The question can be posited, to whom does transformational learning using facilitated reflective dialogue apply? We would assert that it is applicable to all learners in higher education whatever the discipline base or combinations. It is a form of discourse that is potentially available to all students, a view already taken by others, e.g. (Barnett, 1992a).

We are also aware that in contributing to the greater accessibility of these approaches to teaching and learning, we are taking a philosophical and educational position that can be contested. We accept that contention and are reminded of Webb's (1996) warning of the danger of seeking 'closure upon a foundational position' which we take to mean as: 'this is the only way'. We would not wish to assert such a position and welcome alternative approaches that 'open up' process to make the realization of the learning that is the purpose of higher education more feasible. We do assert that prescription about the form that teaching and learning should take, without being transparent about process, is likely to remain prescription. There is a need for a 'how' discourse in which teachers and learners can take on and create their own meanings and practice.

The form of teaching and learning that we are encouraging would appear to be currently on the margin of usage – the significant form being teaching as transmission. The latter leaves little room for a relationship that creates an interactive discourse. Indeed, the most recent evidence that teaching is still significantly transmissional is apparent in recent findings, e.g. (Dearing, 1997), the teaching methods experienced by the highest proportions of students in their survey were lectures (98 per cent) though there was also recognition that over the last five years staff had been widening their repertiore of teaching methods. The introduction of information technology as a factor in the development of teaching and learning methods has influenced institutional responses to diminishing units of resource.

However, while teaching for transmission may be more efficient through IT methods, the need for interactive learning support remains. The latter is not replaced by IT.

We recognize that higher education institutions have to meet imperatives such as diminishing resources, demands for enhanced research effectiveness while meeting the need and desire to improve the quality of student learning that will justify the award of high standard degrees and postgraduate qualifications. We endeavour to encompass such concerns within the aims of our book.

The plan of the book

Part 1: Learning and Reflection, sets out our theoretical base for engaging in reflective dialogue that promotes learning that is both instrumental and transformational.

Chapters 2 and 3 summarize the history and leading philosophies of learning, theoretical models of learning, research methodologies and current understandings of what constitutes learning. Our purpose in these chapters is to investigate the roots of our 'taken-for-granted' approaches to learning and to lay the foundations for the reflective process by revealing embedded attitudes, stances and values in the theoretical models of learning that exist, often invisibly, in higher education. Subsequent chapters will reveal to readers *our* attitudes, stance and values and why we hold them.

In Chapters 4 and 5 we lay the bases for critically reflective learning and practice by examining the key elements that are necessary to engage in critical reflection. We explore in Chapter 4 concepts including intention, process, modelling and the nature of dialogue. These are some of the conditions for critical reflection. In Chapter 5 we set out what we mean by reflective practice, convey the importance of reflection to learning in higher education in promoting the potential for learning and show how reflection by learners requires to be modelled by teachers. We also show how reflective dialogue requires effective facilitation by teachers.

In Part 2: Facilitating Learning and Reflective Practice, we convey how reflective dialogue can be developed, facilitated and utilized by teachers in enhancing student learning. Before we discuss the practice of reflective dialogue, we examine the context of higher education, existing and potential academic practice, and possible institutional responses in Chapter 6. On the assumption of institutional support at a range of levels we go to the core of our work by examining and setting out the processes by which reflective dialogue can become an integrated part of practice for teachers and learners.

Chapter 7 creates a structured means to develop reflective practice in the teacher. This is followed by teachers skilled in reflective practice facilitating other teachers to engage in reflective practice in a workshop format. The workshop is designed to achieve three purposes, to promote reflective practice, to enhance facilitation skills and to provide a model for a workshop to be undertaken with student learners. Chapter 8 aims to convey how teachers can then facilitate student learners to engage in reflective practice. Finally, we demonstrate how the student learner, can with student colleagues, become self-facilitating to support that reflection engendered by the teacher.

In Chapter 9 we explore the process of becoming a facilitator without losing subject expertise in an academic discipline. The possibility of both of these aspects of a teacher's role in higher education being maintained is discussed and the difficulties and opportunities are assessed. We believe that the journey to becoming a facilitator is not a rapid one, particularly when continuing to be a subject expert, but seek to show why we believe it a journey worthwhile. We show that the rigour of critical reflective learning can be achieved by appropriate facilitative methods.

A range of styles and the key skills of facilitation are described in Chapters 10 and 11, and their overlap with the skills of reflective dialogue emphasized. These chapters connect what the teacher models as reflective practice to student learning, through the shared skills of facilitation and reflective dialogue. We recognize in this chapter that universities may want to equip students with skills and approaches to learning that are as yet not an established part of academic practice.

In Part 3 we introduce exemplars that can be used in higher education which can promote reflective dialogue and learning. All the exemplars have in common approaches to facilitation that embrace reflective dialogue leading to critical reflective learning. Chapter 12 on action learning presents a particular form of group-based learning that supports reflective dialogue. The format provides a structure and process that can be initially facilitated by teachers leading to self-facilitation by student learners. An examination of academic supervision is undertaken in Chapter 13 and the quality of relationship that we suggest is needed for effective supervision is identified. Reflective dialogue which supports such a relationship is the key to the critically reflective learning to which the postgraduate and doctoral student aspires. Chapter 14 explores mentoring as a relationship where the use of reflective dialogue is congruent with creating and maintaining a mentoring relationship. A variety of mentoring situations are considered.

In the remainder of this introductory chapter we convey our own learning journeys, highlighting those key factors that enhanced and inhibited our progress. We particularly emphasize our non-traditional experience of higher education as examples of the issues we will be considering throughout the book. We invite readers to reflect upon their own learning stories as part of the process of critical reflection on practice in higher education.

Our stories

We begin with our personal stories, our experience of learning and education, particularly higher education. We believe that our own learning experience has influenced how we approach our academic work although this denies the traditional positioning of commentators who profess to be uncontaminated by personal issues, bias or favour. We go further: we positively value the personal, and in starting from the personal we mirror the stance we adopt in this book. Learners are appreciated first as persons, with histories and real lives, before attempts are made to offer opportunities for acquiring knowledge, skills and experience, together with facilities for processing and reflection.

Our educational stories differ in a number of respects: gender, class, family background, chosen discipline and age. We believe that such factors have impeded many within the higher education system, and with mass entry to higher education, the prospect of minimizing them is at hand. It is true that our stories are 20 and 30 years old, and many things have changed, not least student numbers and levels of resourcing. Readers may be surprised to know that Anne studied mathematics in the 1970s, at a highly respected 'old' university, in a class of over 100 students. Ian experienced an irregular route to university via secondary modern and technical colleges.

Anne's story

I hold a vivid memory of being in the company of six or seven girls on a stage required to perform for the 'new' violin teacher, who would decide if we were good enough to be included in her class. I would be about 12 years old and a seasoned jumper-through-hoops, having passed the 11+ at 10 and the entrance exam to the local prestigious convent grammar school. I had had about enough educational force feeding, particularly in the music department, and I quite clearly remember scowling at the new teacher. She smiled warmly as I continued to scowl and she walked over to me, still smiling. 'Do you want to play for me?' she asked. I was dumbfounded. No-one had ever asked me what I wanted before (except as a threat). I nodded and gulped and realized I'd committed myself, but it was too late. I then *had* to do my best for her, somehow it mattered at last. My relationship with this particular teacher was to influence my life and the memory of that first meeting remains.

As the daughter of a graduate teacher I was destined for higher education whether I liked it or not. My mother was a living example of the power of education, having managed to attend university, in spite of her family background; she was the youngest of 17 children, brought up in slum conditions in Glasgow in the early years of the century. Her determination was undiluted by her status as a single parent, a particular social category which had no meaning for me then. After a magical childhood in the highlands of Scotland I was 'sent' (aged 6) to a small convent boarding school, in a suffocatingly small town, where a group of women did their best to suppress the most creative and imaginative parts of me. Fortunately they did not wholly succeed, but it was to take another 30 years to redeem those early regimentations. The education offered can only be described as boring and I remember (I must have been about 8 or 9) having read to the end of the prescribed reading book two weeks into term, and having to wallow with the others for the rest of the term.

I was afraid to voice my need for more stories as I felt ashamed of any pleasure, as pleasure of any kind was disapproved of in the convent.

I was quick at numbers so maths was no problem. Music, however, was a nightmare, delivered by a big woman, Sister W, who bullied us unmercifully. She achieved results, and her pupils and choir won festivals, but I found piano lessons a weekly purgatory, waiting for the inevitable swipe at my little fingers from her ivory paper knife.

The regimentation extended to eating and sleeping, with late marks for slow eaters, order marks for untidy socks, and conduct marks for any jumping about on beds. I have only just realized the nonsense of giving people 'marks' for what was deemed 'bad' behaviour. I was always in trouble, usually without realizing what I had done wrong, an experience which has left me fearful of unknown norms in any new group or community I may join.

When the family relocated in Liverpool, I was pleased and excited, only to find myself terrified of getting into trouble by not knowing the rules. As a privately educated child I had been well prepared for the 11+, and was considered such a 'sure thing' that I was admitted to the first year of the grammar school on the strength of the entrance exam only. This launched me, at the age of 10, into a class of girls most of whom were a year or a year and a half older than me. I remember that daily litany I would have with myself to be sure that I had all I needed for the day at school, which may include PE, housecraft and violin lessons. I loved housecraft and PE, especially ballet lessons, but was discouraged from pursuing them, as I was destined for higher education. Violin lessons were considered desirable as I was known to be musical in spite of the ministrations of Sister W. What transpired for me was an early falling-in-love. I must have been all of 12 when I met the violin teacher who would change my life. She was a lovely and loving woman, who took me in hand and did by kindness and care what Sister W could not achieve by bullying and cruelty. My violin became the only activity worth pursuing and I played out of love of her. (Note: my teacher behaved throughout with perfect propriety. My understanding of those early emotions is that of an experienced adult.)

Because of my premature entry to the grammar school, I took GCE O levels at just 15 and A levels at just 17, and my results were disappointing for my mother who clearly hoped I would follow her to become a science or mathematics graduate. By this time I didn't care as puberty had arrived, there were boys to be attended to and anyway I was determined to study music not science or maths. Encouraged by my violin teacher, herself a bit of a rebel, I found myself accepted, on the basis of my playing and an interview, at one of the prestigious Royal Colleges of Music, any one of which establishments would not even consider me today.

My three years at music college were a mixture of heady melody and difficult harmony! I found myself struggling with no grant, having to get a cleaning job to survive, and finding my fellow students to be far more talented than myself. With the support of my tutors I managed to finish the course, met my future husband, and started work as a teacher.

My teaching experience in the secondary sector was salutary and informative, beginning with that first year out, when I worked in one of the new comprehensives in Lancashire, educating 2000 children from 11 to 18, on a site laid out for a Mediterranean climate, including a swimming pool and bowling alley. The experience there would be material for another book, and served only to inform me about the adverse effects of imposing a largely class-led model of education (the school was based on a public school pattern) on a generation of adolescents many of whom were unable or unwilling to respond. The students excelled when experiential and activity-led methods were used, e.g. horticulture, housecraft, art and science/craft laboratory work. The finer points of French and musical appreciation were lost on the tiny 11-year-olds who looked tired and hungry at the start of the day, even before they began the pilgrimage of finding a new classroom for their 'set', which was different for every subject.

Marriage and motherhood intervened for a year or two, and my next interaction with the education system was night school at the local technical college, where I decided to redeem my abysmal A level performance, this time because I wanted to learn. The difference was dramatic, the class was of mixed ability, with many people coming straight from work to the college, the tutors were top-class, using interactive methods, and I achieved the highest grades possible.

Suddenly, with three small children, I became a mature student, reading mathematics at university, relying on the married woman's grant to pay for my au pair as the idea of men helping with children was still a new and unusual one, at least in my social milieu.

I found the traditional approach in a mathematics department of an 'old' university unhelpful for learning. Lectures were a passive experience, largely adding to my confusion and lack of understanding, and, with the staccato delivery of complicated mathematical concepts, mainly a show-case for lecturers to perform. Tutorials were useless, being another opportunity for men (tutor and students) to show off, while I struggled to understand and dare not ask for help. The most useful activity as far as learning was concerned was the *talking* with fellow students, helping each other to fathom the mysteries being presented to us. I became adept at finding the material in a textbook and making sense of it myself, rendering lectures a complete waste of time. Personal tutorials were difficult as my personal tutor, a man, was unnerved by women or anyone over 20, and it was not until my final year when I got the only female lecturer as my tutor, that I was able to talk about my learning needs. I was eventually able to find what I needed in the department and the kind of learning I wanted. For instance I was able to study statistics as a *practical* subject rather than some of the high-powered courses on offer which explored the deeper recesses of probability theory.

My experience, as a mature person, of what is now cited as a desirable higher education, revealed the uselessness of traditional lecturing, the failure of seminars/tutorials as opportunities for learning, and the need for some dialogue for learning to take place, dialogue with anybody, fellow student or tutor, it didn't matter, as long as I was able to 'process' my struggle with somebody. The one most valuable provision in that three-year period, was the students' work area in the department, where talking was allowed (quite separate from the library), and the precious learning-saving dialogue could take place.

As part of my degree I took options quaintly named 'liberal studies' and these provided a welcome relief from sigmas and omegas, offering real words for communication purposes. The serious learning from these 'liberal' options in the philosophy and history of science, was the beginning of an understanding about the power of the paradigm in which I had been brought up and educated. I realized some of what had happened to me and was encouraged to continue doing research and a higher degree.

However my earning power was needed and I returned to the classroom, albeit to teach music rather than mathematics, this time to 3-year-olds with tiny violins in an inner-city education authority. Here the music advisor initiated the historic Suzuki programme, through which hundreds of children, from schools anywhere in the city, were offered the chance to learn the violin. The children, with their parents, were taught through the internationally recognized Suzuki method, a highly structured and didactic system which relies on the quality of the relationship of teacher/parent/child for success. The system re-taught me the lessons of my adolescence when *my* violin teacher had loved me into learning. My tiny Suzuki pupils were 'in love' with learning through their relationship with mother/father/and, of course, me. The success of the programme was evident in the concerts with 300 children playing Bach, Handel and Vivaldi music they could barely read. The technicalities of reading music were painless when children had the confidence of playing successfully, another lesson in the power of success in learning.

Leaving my Suzuki children felt like losing family. Some had started with me at 4 and I left them at 14. What pulled me away was my own need to develop and an opportunity to pursue research in the field of emotional intelligence, an interest which I had found through counselling training. My Master's degree, taken part time, and full of opportunities for dialogue through group work, gave me a thorough grounding in applied social research, reinforcing much of my learning in 'liberal studies' and balancing out my rather scientific approach to research which, in my chosen field, was a non-starter. I learnt about supervision through a master in the field, engaging in reflective dialogue before I even knew what it meant!

Thus I became employed in higher education, first as a researcher, then as a lecturer and ultimately as a head of department. My mission was then, and is now, to enable those engaging in higher education as students or teachers to optimize opportunities for learning through group work, interactive methods, experiential projects, humane relationships and, the key to it all, reflective dialogue.

What have I learnt from my experience? That it triumphs over hope? My learning has valued experience certainly, but one thing shines out for me and that is the key role of emotion in learning. My will was driven by my self-image, my feelings about myself, which early treatment had rendered negative, and humane respectful treatment redeemed. My desire for learning, when it emerged, came from within me and was not imposed upon me. I found my desire from the dialogue I had with important others, through which I was able to identify my feelings about particular aspects of learning, establish what I wanted to learn, and gain support for the enterprise. I believe the equivalents of Sister W walk the corridors of universities, humiliating students and colleagues in adversarial gladiatorial interactions, suppressing the humanity of learners and denying them the dialogue they need.

Ian's story

I was 9 years old in a junior school in Kingsbury, North London, England in the afternoon in what felt like a Spring term. It was bright outside. I was in my class with a teacher and other children. He, the teacher, announced that at 3 o'clock an examination would take place. We would be given a test that was referred to as like the 11+.[1] But with a difference. We were not yet 11. More than this, we, the whole school, about 250 of us, were to be tested against one boy. When he finished we would all stop at whatever point we had reached. And yes, he did finish before anyone else in the whole school.

Significant for me at the time was that all the children in the school were to be tested in our own classrooms rather than go into the hall where I had seen children doing exams. Perhaps it was thought we would be more at ease. The boy we were to be tested against was in another classroom. I was perplexed that I could not see the person we were to be tested against. A bell went to start the exercise. A second would signify that the boy in the other room had finished and all of us would stop at that point.

The 'exam' paper was the general knowledge part of the 11+. I still recall the first question on the paper: 'What is known as the ship of the desert?' This question I found really difficult and yet pondered on it for some considerable time. I pondered on it and wondered why I did not know the answer and felt obviously that being question 1, I should know it as somehow I had a notion that the easy questions came first. They are there to 'warm you up'. This question did not warm me up. This question stopped me in my tracks. I was not versed in moving on; to think 'pass' and continue. Neither I nor the rest of my class were versed in the techniques of answering general knowledge tests, let alone, at speed. I was, nevertheless, aware of the need for speed as it was made fairly clear that this boy we were to be set against was very bright and the implicit message was that yes he would come first and score the highest points. I continued with a sense of panic. The second bell rang.

The papers were taken away and marked. I do not recall what I scored but I do remember coming 137th in the school. I did not share with anyone the feelings I had before, during and after the test and the results. When the results were announced we were all informed of the outstanding achievement of the boy in question and told that we could aspire towards him if we really put our individual efforts into studying like he did. We were not informed of how he studied. I did not know him well. I was aware of a difference between myself and him in terms of privilege and background. There was a class difference which as children we are highly sensitive to without being able to name.

He was my age. A message seared into me that afternoon. He was better than me. He was better than anyone else in the school older and younger. He represented what I could not be. Even then I was having the real meaning of 'objectivity' put upon me. Here was a measure that was to be given further legitimacy at critical points in later life. I use the language of later life to what went through my head then and at the actual 11+ and at secondary modern and at university.

Inevitably, I could not know what was in the minds and stance of the headteacher and teachers who conceived of the idea to undertake such an exercise. I had realized intuitively, even then, that this was unfair, bore no relation to myself but was the judgement of others about my potential that had everything and nothing to do with where I was coming from; what I thought, felt or did; what captured my wish to relate to my teachers and what was deep inside me to learn.

Despite this kind of start there were individuals (whom I would now call mentors) – but really people who saw a keenness, will, curiosity, love, interest – to want me to move on to do those things that had been previously blocked or were in danger of being blocked for ever more. Miss Stathers, Mr Broadhurst, Mr Cromby, Mr Price, Mrs Cox, Mr Thomas, Mr Corbishley, Mr Edinborough, Jack Greenleaf and John Saville. They span 12 years. They all have something in common in relation to me. They all – in exasperation, hope, love, sheer frustration, delight – had a belief that I could move, learn, make connections of which I was then only partially aware, or not conscious of at all. Somehow over these years I can recall their names and not those of other teachers because of their interest in my learning. What they have in common is the relationship they struck with me and the relationship I struck with them. At the formative years of my education, that took me eventually to university. What they did was not to intimidate, say I was stupid, set me tests that I was certain to fail. In their different ways I received affirmation of what was possible in me.

They were inevitably tied to examinations – RSAs, O and A level GCEs and degrees. I was not from a home familiar with the complexities of language to meet the hurdles of the academic route, but my father had an indefatigable faith in supporting my uncertain future in this vaguely known world. The fact that it was unknown to me happened one day towards the end of my period at the secondary modern after a day doing metalwork and technical drawing when Mr Cromby said: 'Do you know that you can go to a technical college [further education college] to take O level GCEs?' The local education authority, the defunct but relatively progressive Middlesex County Council had a pilot scheme that selected, without examination, young people in secondary moderns, near school leaving age, then 15, from across the County to enter Hendon Technical College. Twenty-three of us found our way there for two delightful years and the bane of life for the teachers, whom, even then, I realized (but without the language to name it), were genuine academics before the expansion of higher education. They loved their subjects and their sheer enthusiasm brought us in touch with ideas we had never experienced in the often jaundiced corners of the secondary modern school.

With the actual prospect of attaining some of these O levels, I was approached by Mr Thomas, the economic historian with another thought, 'Did you know that...' and I found myself travelling to Ealing Technical College (with a small grant from the County Council even) and began to find myself amid a group of more privileged young people from London, Iraq, Kenya, India and Pakistan who had wanted to get out of the stultification of their institutions, both public and private, for the informal, relaxed yet rigorous life in the College to complete A levels. I finally got the message. This was a route to those mysterious places – universities – where most of my new peers assumed they were to go. At this time, nationally, about one in four of those who had gone to grammar schools moved on to university, one in two from private schools, and one in 10,000 from secondary moderns. My wedge into higher education was, admittedly via these unusual opportunities, still something of a wonder and I entered what was known then as a redbrick university.

Temporary end of joy: I lost my voice. Not literally, just an unknown-at-the-time silence among a sea of words and language I had not experienced before. I did not connect with the distant, detached, apparently rarefied discourse that was around me. Moreover, I found a great dissonance between the espoused liberal values of the institution and the reality for those who breached the unwritten social rules of the time. Towards the end it was Jack Greenleaf, a sensitive, political philosopher and John Saville, a labour historian, who helped me connect. They both had a passion for their disciplines as well as ensuring that their students could tuck their own meanings into the meanings they were endeavouring to impart to us not at us. I gradually found a language, not quite mine yet, but when I spoke in the new discourse, I was beginning to know what I intended to say, say it and grapple with the response and still create meaning.

So I secured a degree, but left with the abiding belief that research was not something I would be able to engage in. The only problem was that I found myself employed in the world of higher education where research was a path expected to be trodden. In other respects I became a teacher who most of the time did connect with learners, combining an academic life with valuable journeys into local and central government.

The much later opportunity emerged to embark on a research-based MPhil. Commencing the research I still found myself putting a self limit on what I thought I could achieve. Then my supervisor said: 'Did you know that . . . ?' giving me key information about conversion to a PhD which I followed through to completion. Here I really found my voice. An old academic friend asked me when I was completing the last few chapters, why I was still enthusing about the write-up. Most PhDs in his experience had been bored out of their minds at that stage. I think my life was in the thesis.

What have I learned from this experience? The key for me, given my 'untidy' route to higher education was the significance of those people who related to me, in whatever circumstance prevailed, connected with me or anticipated what was possible. Some connected with me in my struggles to learn, others realizing opportunities outside my experience. The other key has been finding my voice as opposed to relaying the objective condition of a discourse. With that connected voice I was able eventually to relate to student learners and start the journey that has led to this book.

We continue with Chapters 2 and 3 where we unearth the embedded educational systems within our stories, and the implicit values and beliefs that both hindered and fostered our learning. We invite you, as reader, to engage in these and subsequent chapters by relating them to your own story. Engagement in some of our chapters may generate questions and possible feelings of dissonance. We recognize the challenge this offers to readers.

Note

1. For those unfamiliar with the system of secondary education in England and Wales prior to the introduction of comprehensive education, the 11+ refers to an examination that most children took at that age to determine whether they entered a grammar school or a secondary modern. In England and Wales approximately 25 per cent of children went to grammar school, the remainder to secondary modern. 'Parity of esteem' was to be the official term used to try to explain away the obvious inequity of the division. 11+ meant much more than an examination as can be imagined. But that is another story!

2
Learning: Philosophies and Models

In this chapter we explore how an understanding of learning as a human activity is influenced by the philosophies held about the human person. We believe that an understanding of learning relates to how the human person is perceived, and this is informed by the values and philosophies held. We maintain that such philosophies are present and influential in the stance of every teacher, *whether or not she is aware of it,* and may significantly affect her teaching approach.

We present alternatives based on a variety of philosophical approaches. In offering alternatives we seek to clarify the philosophy which informs a given approach or definition of learning, particularly the model of humanity implicit within it, as a powerful influence on a teacher's stance towards learning in higher education. We do privilege a particular philosophy and its implicit model of learning, and we declare this in Chapter 3. Suffice to say that we believe our approach will promote the learning appropriate to higher education as it now exists and may evolve.

We also aim to recognize that our approach carries its own embedded values and our survey of the history of learning is presented in a spirit of understanding and respect. We agree with Barnett in believing that some traditional models of higher education no longer command legitimacy (Barnett, 1992b), and we do maintain that the recent orientation towards adult learners as responsible for their own learning, while not the whole story, is a move in the right direction, and that the healthy development of higher education in the twenty-first century will include such orientations.

A philosophy of learning

Philosophy, in its original and widest sense is defined as the love, study or pursuit of wisdom. Other meanings include, moral philosophy (what we would now call ethics); natural philosophy (now called science); and metaphysical philosophy, the knowledge or study which deals with the most general causes and principles of things (this is now the most usual sense).

All meanings agree that philosophy attends to principles, be they scientific, ethical or educational, and attaches value to them. Therefore a philosophy of learning will seek wisdom through study of the principles of learning, and such principles will recognize axioms of value.

Our definition of learning is more difficult as this depends rather on the philosophy held. For example, the dictionary definition of learning, 'to get knowledge of (a subject) or skill in (an art, etc.) by study, experience or teaching', incorporates the duality we will find in almost all approaches to learning in the literature. We believe this to be insufficient for learning in higher education. Other definitions reveal the wide variety of approaches that exist about the concept of learning, for example:

* 'learning should be seen as a qualitative change in a person's way of seeing, experiencing, understanding, conceptualising something in the real world' (Ramsden, 1988:271).
* 'learning is a relatively permanent change in a behavioural potentiality that occurs as a result of reinforced practice' (*Encyclopaedia Britannica*).
* 'Existing cognitive structure is the principal factor influencing meaningful learning and retention . . . Thus it is largely by strengthening relevant aspects of cognitive structure that new learning and retention can be facilitated' (Ausubel, 1975:93).
* '[learning is] the grasping of what is signified (what the discourse is about) by the sign (the discourse itself), i.e. understanding what a written or spoken discourse is about' (Marton, 1975:125).
* 'If the teacher knows what he wants to do, there must be a scientific way of doing it' (Ward, 1975:13).
* 'the purposes of post-secondary education are the development of thought attitudes and motivation' (Bligh, 1978:249).
* 'Learning is a human process which has an effect on those undertaking it' (Barnett, 1992b:4).
* 'The learning that goes on in higher education justifies the label "higher" precisely because it refers to a state of mind over and above the conventional recipe or factual learning' (Barnett, 1990:149).

We shall be proposing adoption of a philosophy of learning which leads to reflective practice for teachers in higher education and ultimately the kind of reflective learning for students espoused in higher education, namely, holistic learning through reflective dialogue, which we describe in Chapters 7 and 8.

Taking a philosophy of learning, as above, to mean an activity which explores the principles of learning and knowledge and adopts some axiomatic stance towards them, we find three broad streams of thought to exist. A full treatment of the philosophy of education is beyond the scope of this book and our comments are intended to set the context for Part 2 where we seek to develop *how* practitioners may explore their own philosophies and reflect upon their practice.

Initially, two main streams of thought can be identified in the history of learning and education, from our Greek inheritance to the analytic philosophers of the twentieth century. First, the duality mentioned above has its roots in traditional concepts based on classical Greece, and the writings of Plato and Aristotle. Secondly, progressive ideas introduced revolutionary and innovatory developments, as exemplified by Rousseau and Dewey. Modern interpretations of traditional or progressive ideas provide a third stream, and attempts to combine both can be found in analytic and alternative philosophies of education.

Traditional

An important contribution to traditional learning theory ascribed to Plato is the early dualism betrayed in his Theory of Forms, privileging the intellectual and aesthetic activities of a 'guardian', i.e. ruling class of citizens over auxiliaries and traders who engage in manual but skilled work. For Plato, the class of persons likely to benefit from high level education are those who can 'see' reality, and therefore the Form of Good, in the full light of the sun. Such persons, i.e. the rulers, are said to have 'a capacity innate in their mind'. Other classes, i.e. the ruled, without the ability to 'see' forms, see only shadows, and the attempt to put knowledge into their minds is as hopeless as trying to 'put sight into blind eyes' (Jowett, 1953a:380) We can identify here the roots of twentieth-century selection processes and a justification for them, with its tendency to elitism with full education for the able and a minimum education for the 'less able'.

In addition Plato introduces value judgements about the 'rational' part of man, deemed to be 'of the soul', in harmony with the aesthetic 'spirit', in contradistinction to the 'irrational or appetitive' part, associated with bodily pleasures and satisfactions (Jowett, 1953a:293). We find here an early version of Descartes' soul versus body dualism, described as a 'category mistake' by Gilbert Ryle (1983) below.

The tradition of Socratic questioning stands apart from the Platonic theory of forms as it maintains that 'all inquiry and all learning is but recollection' and the Meno Dialogues prove that even a slave (albeit a male slave), may be brought from naïvety to an understanding of trigonometry through appropriate questioning (Jowett, 1953b:278). We identify in Plato's dialogues an early recognition of the importance of dialogue as the key to reflection, and therefore, critical thinking.

Plato and Aristotle championed the primacy of the intellect over practice, later enshrined in the dualism of Descartes and this model, dating to the fourth century BC has dominated education up to the eighteenth century and *is still influential today*.

Aristotle's development of Plato's thought includes an interesting contribution to which we will return: the idea that learning is achieved by doing, particularly in the learning of virtue. Aristotle, referring to the learning of virtue, suggests that most people, instead of doing virtuous acts, have recourse to discussing virtue, 'take refuge in theory . . . and in so doing they act like invalids who listen carefully to what the doctor says, but entirely neglect to carry out his prescriptions' (McKeon, 1941:956).

Gilbert Ryle, in his *Concept of Mind* (1983) provides a critique of the mind/body myth and suggests a rationale for its invention. Ryle seeks to undo the Cartesian myth about mind which he terms the official doctrine and names 'The Ghost in the Machine'. He identifies the basis of the doctrine in a category mistake about the mind domain of a person as private, internal and higher grade status than the bodily domain of the human person which is deemed public, external, situated in the physical and material world, and of lower-grade status.

The origins of the mistake are identified as the crisis in the established church with the scientific revolution of the sixteenth and seventeenth centuries, as well as the historical inheritance of Plato, Aristotle and the Scholastic tradition which incorporated their ideas from the twefth century onwards. The crisis for Descartes and others lay in the dilemma of human souls being divine and spiritual inhabiting a material body, trapped in the realm of the senses and possibly ruled by mechanical laws. The crisis was resolved by simply denying it, creating instead a separate 'mental' realm, within each human person, known only to the person and their god, and not accessible to other minds, uncontaminated by the material, sensual nature of the body. The implied value difference relates to the 'higher' faculties of the mind in contrast to the 'lower' or base faculties of the body, considered closer to animal nature.

This polarization and differentiation of mind and matter has remained intact and lives today in the persistence of dualism in academic life, with skills, 'knowing how', practice and affect being undervalued, while cognition, 'knowing that' and impersonal modes of communication are championed throughout the academy (Ryle, 1967). Quite simply, what Ryle describes as a 'typological error' has influenced education, the philosophy of education and the practice of education in the past, and continues to be influential in the present.

The privileging of the mind over other faculties was reinforced by rationalists who suggested that the mind has the power to create reality, the *esse is percipi* of Berkeley's philosophy of perception (Warnock, 1962) and the *das Ding an sich*, of Kantian philosophy, 'the thing in itself', being known only through acts of perception (Korner, 1955). The connection between the mind and external reality was an important step forward in recognizing the power of learners to influence, shape and determine their own reality. The dualism described above has survived in almost all aspects of learning and development, as can be seen in the pre-occupation with 'thinking skills' to the exclusion of material factors like affect (emotion) and action.

It is interesting to speculate on the reasons for the persistence of the dualist myth, and the payoff for Western rationalist systems in maintaining it in education and commerce, as, although a body of evidence has emerged which suggests that the myth is no longer beneficial (Michelson, 1995) our rationalist society tends to ignore evidence in a decidedly non-rationalist way (Easlea, 1981, quoted in Webster, 1995). In Chapter 3 we summarize some of the evidence and the recommendations for change which have largely been ignored in higher education.

Challenges to traditionalism

A notorious revolutionary in the learning field was Jean-Jacques Rousseau, who, with his account of Emile's ideal education (Foxley, 1969), offered an alternative approach to learning. The five books correspond to the stages of the fictional Emile, whose needs become the focus of the learning process, in contrast to the traditional focus of the subject being taught. In *Emile*, Rousseau presents seminal ideas of experiential learning, learning by doing, and the beneficial effects of travelling, as well as the more controversial (for its time) promotion of personal faith rather than institutionalized dogma.

John Dewey's book, *Democracy and Education* (1916) offered a new pragmatic approach to education, in a well-thought-out philosophy which challenged traditional philosophies. Dewey's idea of growth corresponded with the idea that immaturity was a positive, i.e. the power to grow, while maturity signalled the diminution of that power. Methods of teaching which created dependence in learners emphasized the power of teachers and the learner's weakness. Although Dewey spoke in his time, and addressed education in schools, we consider much of his thought as relevant to higher education today.

Dewey saw all humans as plastic, i.e. having the ability to learn from experience. Education is development and life is development therefore life is education and growing is living. Dewey believed that education does not need formal aims as it is its own end, and that education is lifelong, continuous to death. He clarified that the idea of growth having to be directed towards an aim or goal is a mistake. Correct growth is *being* and that is the goal, growth itself. Where goals are set in education, the adult environment is taken as a standard, while the child's natural powers are disregarded and suppressed, and this applies to students in higher education. The suitability of adult-defined goals remains unexamined, and in higher education lecturer-defined replaces adult-defined. There is an implicit norm in this mistake which tends to remain unarticulated and thus keeps the imposed aims of education as fixed and rigid. For Dewey, the true aims of education are a natural process made concious, i.e. making growth explicit, and this is sometimes referred to as *process* (as against content or task) or *procedures*.

Dewey's method identifies four essentials for learning: experience, data for reflection, ideas and fixing what has been learned, and, though he was speaking for education generally, we believe these apply to higher education.

First, Dewey challenged the traditional mind/body split with his insistence that experience should be the initiating phase of thought for the learner, on the grounds that, in ordinary life, we need an empirical situation (be it opportunity or problem) to engage our interest and generate action. The reference to experience has been dismissed by many as it deals with the body, appetites, the senses, the material world, while thinking proceeds from the (perceived) higher faculty of reason and spirit. Dewey recommends an unscholastic approach to learning, offering learners real situations/problems/projects as these are likely to include Dewey's second ingredient for success, i.e. *reflection* on the real world (Dewey, 1916:154).

Dewey comments on *reflection* as a required ingredient for success so that

> methods which are permanently successful in formal education . . . depend for their efficiency upon the fact that they go back to the type of situation which causes reflection.
>
> (Dewey, 1916:154)

and

> it is a matter of indifference by what psychological means the subject matter for reflection is provided, observation, memory, reading, communication are all avenues for supplying data.
>
> (Dewey, 1916:157)

Traditional arrangements for learning are criticized by Dewey as unlikely to develop reflective habits. The dearth of questions in formal situations contrasts sharply with endless questions in real life. Also Dewey comments that the learning environment needs more *stuff*, i.e. more opportunities for doing things so that learners can be engaged in 'doing things and in discussing what arises in the course of their doing' (Dewey, 1916:156) We will suggest that, for undergraduates, their *doing* must be their exploration of the discipline, their study and struggle to understand and this may be achieved for example through project work.

Additionally, Dewey emphasizes the disadvantages of setting problems which do not fit the learner's experience, but are actually the teacher's or textbook's problem. Learning is likely to follow investigation of a situation with personal significance rather than an 'aloof' thing, imposed from external requirements. This issue is particularly relevant for adult learners in higher education.

> the alternative to furnishing ready-made subject matter and listening to the accuracy with which it is reproduced is not quiescence, but participation, sharing in an activity. In such shared activity the teacher is the learner, and the learner is, without knowing it, the teacher.
>
> (Dewey, 1916:160)

For Dewey, when the starting point is personal experience and the context relevant, his third essential ingredient, ideas, will naturally follow. However,

> Thoughts are incomplete, they are suggestions and standpoints for dealing with situations of experience. Till they are applied and tested in these situations they lack full point and reality . . . only testing confers full point and reality.
>
> (Dewey, 1916:161)

Application and testing in real situations, has the effect of 'fixing' what has been learnt. This fourth ingredient is where Dewey's sources in pragmatism are revealed. Only when an idea has been tried out and applied in practice can the process of reflection begin.

Dewey articulated how the connection between mental and practical has been severed in traditional education, and emphasized that the essentials of learning are identical with the essentials of reflection:

1. a genuine situation of experience
2. a genuine problem in that situation
3. information and observation about the situation
4. suggested solutions for which the learner will be responsible
5. opportunity and occasion to test ideas by application, to make the meaning clear and discover for self their validity.

Rousseau's championing of learning as natural growth and development, followed by Dewey's careful philosophy which rejects dualism, values practice and emotion, and recommends learning in the real environment through scientific principles and reflective thinking have influenced educational ideas, with modest effect in higher education. This approach values the interests, rights and needs of the learner. Exams and tests are less important, with practice, learning by doing and the significance of emotion being emphasized. The teacher here is identified, not as expert, but as developer and facilitator of the natural process of growth.

Other reactions to the traditional approach have focused on methods which ensure behaviour modification while leaving the mental realm intact. Examples can be found in the work of Makarenko (1951) and Skinner (1954), who support coercion, control and behavioural methods of learning with the assumption that their assessment of what is worth learning must be correct. Progressive approaches to education are dismissed as utopian, and the results of behaviour modification are presented as evidence for its success, alongside perceived deficiencies of progressive approaches, e.g. independent thought and action. Some traditional and behaviourist approaches have been described by Rogers as 'deficiency models' (Rogers, 1983) as such models operate by identifying shortcomings and making good the deficiency.

New versions of progressive philosophies include Summerhill (Neill, 1967) and Risinghill (Berg, 1968), Steiner (Steiner, 1972), and so-called Free

Schools where children were permitted a freedom to learn previously un-heard of in Western Education. In such systems, the value of learning through doing is supported by learning through playing until the would be learner 'recovers from his education' (Neill, 1969:357) and teachers abandon their 'fatal wish to mould other people' (Neill, 1967). Such humanist approaches have been described as conforming to an 'abundance model' (Rogers, 1983). Such a model begins with an openness to abundance, an assumption that the learner already possesses in abundance what is needed for learning. In this model, given the opportunity, space and encouragement, then learning will happen.

A combination of traditional and progressive philosophies purport to be found in the work of R.S. Peters (1965), but his critique of traditional methods is lukewarm while his disapproval of progressive methods betrays a dualism, evident in more recent interpretations of this combined philo-sophy (Peters, 1977), where the primacy of intellect is maintained, while affect is devalued and the personal choice and freedom of a learner mis-trusted. Peters defines education as follows:

> education results in the learning of something of value that involves knowledge and understanding which is organised into some kind of cognitive perspective, and this learning has been acquired by methods involving awareness and some degree of voluntariness on the learner's part.
>
> (Bowen and Hobson, 1974:351)

Peters does agree that traditional approaches laid too much stress on con-tent or subject matter, but criticizes progressives for neglecting the impor-tance of passing on a body of knowledge which is worthwhile, with too much emphasis on procedures, identified as the means 'to be adopted in order to implement aims' (Peters, 1973:130), as ends in themselves. The platonist/dualist stance of Peters is betrayed in his privileging of 'some-thing of value' (Peters, 1973:87) and 'education implies the intentional bringing about of a desirable state of mind' (p. 85, op cit.) and his descrip-tion of the teacher being on the inside with 'a love of truth, a passion for justice and a hatred of what is tasteless' (p. 103, op cit.), while the learner remains 'the barbarian outside the gates' (p. 103, op cit.).

The measure of what is worthwhile appears to be no more than the inherited and Eurocentric account of the knowledge and skills developed by Western civilization from the time of the Greeks onwards with all its embedded dualism and implied exclusion of the less privileged. The pros-pect of giving the choice of what is worthwhile and valuable to the learner does not feature in Peters' otherwise laudable insistence on learner aware-ness and motivation to learn (Peters, 1973:106).

Although Peters had in mind the primary or secondary sector, his ideas are common currency in universities, where some academics believe that they 'know best' what is valuable and worthwhile for students to learn.

As experts in their field, and in what they believe to be the students' best interests, they impose a programme which may carry oppressive ideas embedded within it, through a course design which effectively denies any consultation or collaboration with learners. It is important to realize that teachers may not be aware of these inherited ideas, and many teachers in higher education have recently discovered the embedded values within their approach through developing reflective practice.

Peters reveals an understanding of Dewey which can only be described as incomplete. He uses the label 'progressive' to identify pedagogy which is laissez faire, lacking social control and offering an inadequate curriculum which neglects science and overemphasizes art and drama. Peters reveals his own difficulty here with affect and practice, as well as his declared abhorrence of 'procedures' which of course Dewey identifies as the key, i.e. 'the essentials of [learning] method', although Peters does admit that 'it is the manner in which any course is presented rather than its matter which is crucial in developing a liberal attitude of mind' (Peters, 1973:126).

The issue of procedures (we use the term process) is worth further discussion. The process used in teaching is often the only part which is learned (or at least remembered, albeit unconciously). If the procedures of traditional teaching implicitly communicate the power of those who teach over those who are taught, then what is remembered is the system of control and oppression, and that those in charge decide what is worthwhile. On the other hand, when 'progressive' teaching procedures communicate respect for the individual, the value of natural qualities and privilege autonomy and self-reliance, then it is just those values which are remembered. So the detail of procedures or process are dangerous activities to make explicit, because when traditional procedures are revealed in comparison with 'progressive' procedures, in the clear light of day they do not live up to the liberal and worthwhile aims that such practitioners often claim to pursue.

A development of this idea has emerged from the marxist interpretation of schooling given by Ivan Illich, where the school itself is seen as subversive of *real* learning, as society operates its 'hidden curriculum' (Illich, 1971:39) of class and power play, ensuring that learners become passive and docile, as they are 'processed' through the knowledge commodity for future employment and unemployment. Illich insists on the value of learning which does not take place in schools, and the importance of engagement in living and the real world for real learning. He was also one of the first to propose the provision of opportunities for life-long learning, now recognized as a 'good idea' in danger of being highjacked (Weil, 1992) by forces of technical rationality and instrumentalism. Illich made explicit the hidden reality in that learners in a school/college situation learn processes, referred to as procedures above, often more effectively than they learn the subject under discussion, albeit implicitly, in the powerful norms of classroom practice. The processes learnt in the classroom are carried intact into the lecture room at university, where students are ready programmed to expect 'more of the same'.

Learning in higher education

The particular history of higher education begins with the earliest university foundations in medieval Europe, professing to be open to all, though what that meant within the power structures of the Catholic Church, can only be imagined as no women or dissidents were likely to get degrees.

Vested interests reappear in Newman's defence of a liberal education, and although his *idea of a university* (Newman, 1976), recommends self-reflection as the means to higher forms of understanding, it turns out to be for the aristocracy. It is only from a distance of centuries that we can see how contextualized these learning values were in societies dominated by church, aristocracy or state. The intake of a modern university, which includes working men and women, and members of many faiths or none, would have been unheard of in a medieval university. Recent changes have opened up the possibility of a university education to those, described in earlier expansions, as having the 'ability to benefit' (Robbins, 1963).

In higher education, with little theory to draw on, learning has been understood in the context of the 'value background' of its time (Barnett, 1990:8). To be sure there are values which have stood the test of time such as institutional autonomy, the search for truth and objective knowledge, academic freedom and the emancipatory idea of a liberal education. It can come as no surprise to find that objective knowledge, truth and rationality have been undermined, when so-called 'givenness' (Barnett, 1990:48) turns out to be a product of powerful sponsors. So who are today's powerful sponsors and what 'objective' knowledge truth and rationality do they prescribe? Government and industry spring to mind, and, whatever the likely influences on higher education, the key to immunity from such influences lies in defining rationality on the basis of personal reason, and adopting a practice which enables students to challenge existing paradigms. The desired practice has been variously called criticism (Barnett, 1990), critical reflection (Mezirow, 1990), reflexivity (Beck *et al.*, 1994), or critical thinking (Brookfield, 1987).

Barnett clarifies the ideological nature of higher education but maintains that there exists a consistent 'value background' which persists throughout its history, and he maintains that the emancipatory essence of *higher* education can be achieved, not by replacing one ideology with another, not by persisting in believing that knowledge is objective and truth is absolute, but by developing the teaching and learning strategies which will enable participants in higher education, both staff and students, to engage in critical reflection (Barnett, 1990). The process of critical reflection, as described, reveals only the intellectual or knowledge part of the activity, perhaps another case of dualism? The process of becoming a critical being described more recently by Barnett reveals a more holistic stance, embracing knowledge, self and the world (Barnett, 1997). In this book we will show that to achieve true reflection, critical reflection, we must attend to process issues, including the learner's context in the world, just as Dewey averred, as well as maintaining the role of intellect within it.

Implicit theories

The philosophies described above suggest three approaches to theories of learning and education; first, the traditional, dualist approach, secondly, the progressive non-dualist approach, and thirdly, the attempt to combine them or depart from them completely. When educationists justify their practice they tend to refer to theoretical models based on their espoused philosophies, which may or may not coincide with their theory-in-use. We are using the terms 'espoused theory' and 'theory in use' in the way defined by Argyris and Schön (1974). They distinguished between what people say they will do in a given situation (their espoused theory), genuinely believe in, and their theory-in-use, i.e. what they *actually* do. Observation of behaviour allows re-construction of the pervading theory-in-use, which may be invisible to the actor, and may not be compatible with the declared 'espoused' theory.

Methods of unravelling the 'tacit' theory-in-use include a system of dialogue designed to unpack the hidden assumptions underlying overt behaviour by recognition of emotion and analysis (Argyris and Schön, 1974). We build on these methods and offer a holistic approach which we describe as reflective dialogue. A teacher who espouses the aim of learner autonomy and the development of critical reflection in students may be frustrated by results while being unaware of the dependency she engenders in students by passive teaching methods, mysterious assessment strategies and lack of feedback. When the teacher has the chance to engage in reflective dialogue about her teaching she is able to unearth her embedded theory-in-use, which is actually one of teacher control denying autonomy for the student.

Practitioners tend to operate with a model of learning (and an acccompanying model of the person) based on their implicit theory-in-use, and this may not always duplicate their espoused theory of learning. For instance, many practitioners espouse experiential learning, at least as part of a student's experience, and then offer their students an undiluted diet of 'tell', i.e. the passivity of continuous lecturing. We would identify such practice as based on an implicit theory-in-use, related to the dualism of 'expert' and 'banking' alluded to below. The practitioner, steeped in an education system which is based on the same implicit theory, may be unaware that she is carrying an implicit set of beliefs i.e. a model, and acting on them.

We take the view that a model is the cognitive map of a theoretical belief. For example, personality theory suggests that individuals can be variously categorized and a working model based on such a theory will, implicitly or explicitly, dominate perceptions as new information is incorporated into a cognitive map, leading to the categorization of persons in education which is all too familiar. The categorization 'map' is so powerful that it operates at admission (the 11+ or streaming) and at graduation (the honours classification system). Where learning is concerned, a working model which categorizes learners will result in new information about learning being absorbed in the context of such categorizations. Further, the presence of a working model leads to expectations of learners based on the assumptions of the model and these influence behaviour, in the teacher, the learner, and the researcher, e.g. Piaget's work (1932) on learning stages, replicated by Kohlberg over a period of 20 years (1958, 1981) pre-supposed that the behaviour of girl learners could be generalized from that of boy learners. Gilligan's battle (1982) to have this point revised has been only partially successful, indicating the power of such embedded theoretical models, especially when hugely unconscious factors like gendering are involved. Another obvious example is the racial bias revealed by early and more recent intelligence studies where the testing instrument is itself a product of a white eurocentric orientation, and ethnic minorities in an experimental group are automatically disadvantaged (Flynn, 1980).

As in these two examples, where one 'category' of learner is silenced by definition (here female or ethnic minority) the model persists unchallenged, rather like patriarchy has in almost every nation of the world. The job of undermining such powerful models can be assisted by a more egalitarian system of education, where such embedded 'gender' or 'race' models are open to be articulated and challenged.

Psychological testers have moved forward in this respect, but universities have hardly looked at the superior interpersonal skills of their women students, in relation to the competitiveness of their men, in assessing their 'core skills' for example, preferring instead to leave unexamined the competitive model which may favour men and penalize women. From personal experience of working in academia we are only too aware of the competitive model influencing staff behaviour, let alone student performance.

Theoretical models dominate the meaning we ascribe to our practice in every sphere, and in the field of learning we believe implicit models of power and knowledge have influenced our understanding of learning. In the social sciences of human behaviour emerging theories have tended to reflect the philosophies of the day, particularly in relation to the concept of a person. For example, behaviourist psychology influenced learning theory so that the learning person was not considered holistically, only their responses and environment were relevant.

The approaches to learning deployed in academic life are a product of the particular model of learning held by any given practitioner, dictated by an implicit theory. Where the model of learning calls for factual recall that is what will come through and be assessed. Where the model champions adversarial discussion that will be rewarded in assessment. Were the model to call for collaboration, joint endeavours would be rewarded and encouraged. Actual practice (the theory-in-use) suggests an underlying philosophy of learning and implies an implicit model of the human person as a learner, and this may or may not be in agreement with espoused theories of learning, either personally or institutionally.

The number of such models reflects the variety of philosophies in our educational history. The prevailing concept of learning and theory-in-use, in higher education, in the recent past, almost a hegemony it might be said, is a product of the rationalist outcome of that seventeenth-century dilemma mentioned above, i.e. the dualist solution. This philosophy emphasizes the primacy of reason over emotion, thinker over crafter, and the transmission downwards of knowledge and skills from 'expert' to lesser beings known as learners. The prevailing wisdom maintains the acquisition of facts and skills as *the* important outcome of learning, often to the exclusion of emotion and action.

The tenacity and persistence of this view of learning, variously called 'banking' (Freire, 1972), factory learning (Dwyer, 1995) is equalled only by the denial of it by practitioners themselves. Measures of learning persist in promoting 'average level of recall' and 'retention' as key outcomes of the learning process, while teachers complain that students 'swot for exams and then forget everything'. There is ample evidence that teaching and learning has suffered from the mismatch between teacher's declared objectives and what they require from learners. Teacher objectives in higher education as espoused theory do not always coincide with theories-in-use (Fleming and Rutherford, 1984). The university's purpose, mediated through its academic staff, may espouse the objective of inviting students to learn by engaging in scholarly discourse, designed to develop their critical faculties, and many teachers in higher education are passionate about their aim to develop their students as independent and autonomous learners, who are able to question paradigms and challenge received wisdom, as well as being able to creatively design scholarship for the next generation. On close examination, the university's systems, including course work/examination assessment actually values dependency, identification and representation, while the 'core skills/qualities' of creativity, for example, may be ignored. The actuality of assessment reveals the 'theory in use' while the university prospectus presents 'espoused theory'.

The discrepancy between espoused teaching objectives and what teachers actually do led to some educationists challenging the hegemony in higher education and attempts to dislodge it go back 30 years or more (Abercrombie, 1960; Beard *et al.*, 1968; Boud *et al.*, 1985; Collier, 1968; Freire, 1972). This has achieved some success, as the significance of 'experience' and 'doing' in learning has been slowly recognized in higher education, with industrial placements and projects increasingly featuring in course design (Gibbs, 1992).

We have summarized existing philosophical approaches to learning and considered their influence on higher education, as either espoused theory or theory-in-use. In particular, we have noted the persistence of dualism, the privileging of mind over body, and hence a pre-occupation with transmission of knowledge, while overlooking process. The social and political aspects of process reveal a teacher's model of human learning – her theory-in-use.

We believe that a commitment to reflective practice in pedagogy will enable practitioners to identify their own philosophies, and assess to what degree they are carrying the dualism of the mind/matter divide into their practice in higher education. Reflection offers the opportunity for teachers in higher education to examine their underlying philosophies, assess its usefulness in the context of higher education, and consider alternative approaches based on other philosophies or combinations of philosophies. The power of implicit theoretical models lies in their embedded nature. When they are brought into awareness then it is possible to address the theory which underpins them, and ultimately test it. In our attempt to 'unpack' the implicit models at work in models of university learning, we are offering teachers the opportunity, through reflective practice, to examine their embedded 'theoretical models', very much along the lines we recommend for students in higher education.

We now move to explore the outcomes of research using some of these models, and declare our own philosophy of learning with *its* implicit values which we aim to make explicit in Chapter 3.

3

What is Learning? – A Review of Learning Theories

In Chapter 2 we declared our intention of examining what is understood about learning in relation to the underlying philosophies which inform that understanding. We take the view, as explained in Chapter 2, that underlying philosophies influence theories and theoretical models, so that, while research methodologies may seem value free, almost every approach to learning so far examined reveals a (hidden) set of values and beliefs which cannot but affect practice and research outcomes.

In this chapter we explore a range of research approaches, identify the theoretical models behind them, and endeavour to appreciate the philosophies from which they come, with a view to uncovering some of the hidden (and not so hidden) influences on learning in today's higher education sector. We consider how researchers have addressed the question 'what is learning?' and evaluate their outcome measures against our philosophy and values. Student orientations, strategies and styles are variables investigated by educationists in attempts to improve student learning in higher education. Developmental stages, levels of learning, and double-loop learning, are also described and these form a basis for our approach to learning with which we complete the chapter.

There is no science or theory of learning which embraces all the activities involved in human learning. Most of what we do, think, feel and believe is learned so the field of activities is wide and varied. Researchers have addressed learning issues, often independently of each other and approaches have been strikingly different. There is little agreement among researchers about what learning is, e.g. the behavioural psychologist tends to identify learning in the changed behaviour of their subject, while cognitive psychologists seek for change *in* the learner as evidence that learning has taken place. A continuum has been suggested from behaviourism to humanism (Entwistle and Hounsell, 1975). For higher education, surprisingly, there is little attempt to theorize on the nature of its own activity.

Early research on learning, dominated by behaviourism and cognitive psychology, limited itself to measurable, observable behavioural outcomes.

Intellectual input was provided, passed through the student's brain and was reproduced for the researcher to 'measure'. These early 'testing' methodologies paved the way for categorization and inventories from which educationists could interpolate the intellectual capacity of the learner. The previous learning, past experience and expectations of learners were dismissed as confounding variables. The 'object' was the student, misleadingly called the 'subject' and the testing methods of these early researchers reveal their model of the human learner as passive receptacles, being at the mercy of their intellectual ability, known as their IQ.

Educational researchers have tried to redress the balance by exploring the impact on learning of individual differences, giving taxonomies of learning styles which recognize that individuals may vary in their response to learning opportunities (Honey and Mumford, 1992; Kolb, 1984). Such typologies have left the learning process as mysterious as ever, but emphasized the importance of teaching methods and techniques. For instance, when teaching an unknown group it is necessary to consider all possible styles and approaches to learning so that every individual's needs can be met. Hence the need for audio/visual/kinetic/practical learning aids as well as the traditional written or spoken word. The acknowledgement that individuals learn differently has alerted teachers to the danger of an approach which assumes homogeneity in a given group of learners, thus reinforcing the teacher's approach as the key to learning outcomes. We return to learning typologies below.

The research on individual differences shifted responsibility for learning outcomes from the learner to the teacher and, we assert, has mixed benefits. First, the student is again perceived as a passive receiver of intellectual material, with little or no responsibility, and secondly teachers are blamed for poor results by both institutions and students. Naturally enough this has not inspired cooperation from academic staff who do not see teaching as their main purpose, but the development of their subject knowledge as their raison d'etre. It is their subject, their discipline that commands their loyalty.

An early emphasis in the literature on the content of learning has been diluted by new research which has taken into account 'how' the student learns as well as what they learn, by using 'asking' methodologies known as phenomenography (Mann, 1987). Such studies provided dichotomies of orientations, approaches and strategies, and recommended that teachers should tailor their pedagogy to 'match' student orientations. However the move from 'testing' to 'asking' uncovered the importance of context in the learning process, revealing that students apprehend the system of learning and adopt their own coping strategies, often against their own instincts and best interests (Marton, 1981; Pines and West, 1986; Saljo, 1988).

The move towards 'phenomenography' builds on the ideas of personal construct psychology, allowing the learner to create their own constructs and meanings in describing their learning (Kelly, 1955), as well as recognizing that learning and knowledge is created within a social context. The socially constructed nature of knowledge has been explored at length else-where (Berger and Luckman, 1966), and we note the power of the social contexts in learning. The social systems in which a learner is embedded will dominate much of her learning, as 'no human thought is immune to the ideologizing influence of its social context' (p. 21, op cit.). The university, in the persons of its academic staff, has its own power here to replicate those systems and reinforce them, as well as imposing unconsciously the historically embedded philosophies of academia, outlined in Chapter 2. However, the power of the learning context can be used to enable develop-ment towards a more general concept of ideology, through recognition of other and self as sources of knowledge, and this book offers a method for doing this through reflection and reflective dialogue.

The use of 'asking' methodologies reveal models of learners as active responsible adults (in higher education) who are capable of sharing their meanings. Researchers have moved from 'objective' quantitative approaches to 'subjective' qualitative research designs, and recognition of the signifi-cance of context in the development of student approaches to learning (Ramsden, 1988).

The answer to the question 'What is learning?' provides the dependent variable for researchers exploring the influence on learning of teaching methods, motivation, ability and study skills. The categories, orientations, strategies and approaches revealed by a wide range of studies are described below.

Categories of learning

First, a survey of how adults respond to the question 'What is learning?', produced a typology of responses (Saljo, 1982) and five categories emerge:

1. a quantitative increase in knowledge
2. memorizing
3. acquisition of facts, methods, etc. which can be retained and used when necessary
4. the abstraction of meaning
5. an interpretation process aimed at understanding reality.

An additional category in recently published work gave a sixth category:

6. developing as a person (see Marton *et al.*, 1993).

Clearly 1, 2 and 3 imply cognitive learning which can be measured in terms of recall and retention. Items 4, 5 and 6 offer more holistic descriptions of learning and coincide with the learning outcomes most often espoused by teachers in higher education. Teachers publicly espouse theories which promote 4, 5 and 6 but their theories-in-use may tend to promote 1, 2 and 3. Theories-in-use, explained in Chapter 2, are revealed by practice rather than rhetoric and that practice is likely to be based on tradition and habit, and possibly imitation.

Orientations to learning

Intrinsic/extrinsic orientations to learning were identified as early as the 1950s by Abraham Maslow, exploring the developmental tendency of human beings to learn actively when their own interests and desires are driving them (Maslow, 1970). The neutralizing effect of extrinsic approaches to education is summed up in the term 'earning a degree' (Maslow, 1978) and the concept of 'wasting' an education (op cit.). The persistence of intrinsic orientations to learning in a society which promotes extrinsic methods in many of its institutions is a testament to the determination of those men and women who refuse to be herded and processed, preferring to take responsibility for themselves and their development. Many students find their intrinsic orientation only after leaving college/university and pursue their goals through independent or work-related development programmes. Recent confirmation of the extrinsic/intrinsic orientation in students established that orientations alter with time and are therefore learned (Taylor, 1983)! We discuss below the social construction of orientation/attitudes to learning and where the responsibility for them lies.

Learning strategies: serialist or holist?

John S. Daniel (1975) reports research results which suggest that learners divide unambiguously into two groups:

1. *Serialists*, who learn step by step, creating new hypotheses as they go, and who may be 'unable to see the wood for the trees' (Daniel, 1975:85).
2. *Holists*, who are global learners, with appreciation of complexity and 'the whole picture', and who may be tempted to 'overgeneralize' (p. 85).

The dichotomy of learners was statistically significant and persisted in further learning tasks. When asked to 'teach back' what they have learned, serialists reproduce the process exactly as they have learned it, whereas holists change the order and 'jump about', while retaining coherence and the sense of the material (ibid.).

The research emerged from an ongoing exploration of the theory of conversations, individuals and knowables with Pask *et al.* (1975) defining a conversation as an exchange between a set of 'procedures' (P), e.g. a role in society, and a 'processor' (M), e.g. the human brain or a computer. Researchers claim the universality of findings and potential application in a diversity of disciplines. Close scrutiny of the research design reveals that the initial task was a rote learning task, that subsequent categorization confirmed the serialist/holist dichotomy using more complex but predefined task material.

Around the same time researchers discovered another dichotomy of strategies, described as 'reproductive' and 'transformational' (Biggs, 1976). Those learners who reproduced material intact, in familiar examination regurgitation mode, were identified as reproductive while transformational learners make their own meanings from the material and survey the field holistically. The similarity with the serialist/holist is significant, suggesting that these are different descriptions of the same phenomenon.

Learning approaches: deep or surface?

Ference Marton (1975) carried out research using examples of written text, which social science students were given to study and their reactions to it analysed, both in terms of quantity and depth. The written text or discourse, known as the 'sign' provided the material from which students would learn what was 'signified' by the sign, that is, the meaning of the sign. For example, in an instruction manual, the words, phrases and sentences are the sign of the discourse, while the signified, what the discourse means is 'an understanding of how to work the washing machine'. When reporting their learning students were encouraged to speak in their own words, the form of words being unimportant in comparison to an understanding of what the discourse was about. Consequently, the learning was called 'non-verbatim learning'.

When results were analysed, processes of learning revealed 'deep' and 'surface' categories of learning behaviour:

1. *Deep* – concentrating on what the discourse is about and this was associated with an active approach to learning, and a desire to get a grasp of the main point, make connections and draw conclusions.
2. *Surface* – concentrating on the discourse itself, relying on memory and this was associated with a passive approach to learning, and a stance which minimized the task as 'just remembering'.

Deep learning is, described as follows:

> those who succeed best . . . seem to have an approach that aims beyond the written or spoken discourse itself towards the message the discourse is intended to communicate and these students *feel themselves to be the agents of learning.*
>
> (Marton, 1975:137)

Our italics highlight the fact that such learners say they internalize their learning, making it part of themselves, and relate it to their real life. A link has also been established between the quality of the learning environment and deep learning outcomes (Trigwell and Prosser, 1991). The role of the teacher in creating the particulars of the learning context cannot be overestimated and may be largely unconscious. We explore these issues in Chapter 9.

Strategies for learning

An additional class of learning behaviour was identified by researchers and named the 'strategic' approach to learning where students focused on what would increase the possibility of maximizing their grade. Strategies were often socio-emotional, having no connection whatever with the subject discipline under study, e.g. establishing a good relationship with the lecturer and imitating his/her style in submitted coursework (Entwistle, 1981; Entwistle and Wilson, 1977). One instance of a student choosing a surface strategy (in a series of repeated short-answer tests) and sacrificing a deep approach is disturbing when the same student respondent is reported as achieving a first class honours degree by virtue of his strategic approach, a clear example of assessment driving the quality of learning. Marton (1975) addresses the question of why deep learners do well in exams when exams rarely demand a 'deep' approach, and suggests that surface learners give up because this learning is boring and tedious, whereas deep learning is satisfying and so students persist. An assessment system designed to evaluate deep learning would recognize the value put upon it by course designers, and it seems likely that deep learning can be assessed imaginatively with a little care and thought.

The results presented by Svensson (1984) appear to replicate Pask's earlier findings, giving a holistic/atomistic dichotomy. The atomistic learning approach focuses on detail, in isolation, and in sequence, reminiscent of serialist behaviour (Pask and Scott, 1972). Holistic approaches emphasize overall meanings, attempt to contextualize new material within what is already known, and look for key/main arguments (Svensson, 1977). Programmes provided for atomistic learners revealed that learners can move their approach/conception of what learning is when a supportive learning environment is provided (Saljo, 1979b).

One interpretation common to all the above research outcomes was that students have particular, consistent, styles of learning, and that these remain constant over different contexts and in relation to different disciplines. Thus providing justification for the use of inventories, like Kolb's learning styles (Kolb, 1984) with the aim of categorizing students, albeit with the laudable aim of matching teaching strategies to maximize their learning opportunities. The outcome of Kolb's scholarly work, known as the Learning Styles Inventory (LSI) (Kolb, 1984) was essentially an identification of orientation to learning, based on self-report through responses to a questionnaire. Developments of Kolb's model (Honey and Mumford, 1992) focused on observable behaviour as more reliable guides to orientation. More recently the consistency of learning styles has been questioned and the importance of context and content has reappeared as factors influencing the learning process (Ramsden, 1988).

Critiques of both have found reliability and validity lacking while hoped-for improvements in teaching quality remain unrealized. In addition, self-report inventories focus on the learner as lone actor, neglecting the influence on learning of social and political factors, revealing an embedded assumption that learning takes place in a politically neutral context. Rather it seems likely that:

there is more point in attending to the social and institutional environment we create in education and development than in attempting to match specific teaching approaches to some dubious notion of a relatively stable learning style.

(Reynolds, 1997:121)

In addition, the maturity of the learner is known to influence favoured styles, as well as other issues around difference which learning styles may leave unchallenged (Reynolds, 1997). We recognize and endorse the developmental nature of learning suggested here as well as the significance for learning of differences in history and culture.

Stages and levels of learning

When researchers began to consider the idea of development in learning and the concept of stages or levels was introduced to research design, the student's experience as a learner, within her social and political context, was taken into account, and the findings have informed our philosophy in this book. We relate the 'higher' stages and levels of learning to the critical and reflective learning sought in higher education, and we introduce the conditions for such learning. A more detailed account of the conditions for reflection and reflective practice is given in Chapters 4 and 5.

In respect of stages and levels, researchers of learning in higher education can stand on the shoulders of the great by building on the findings of Jean Piaget (1932) Lawrence Kohlberg (1981) and Erik Erikson (1968) who explored the developmental stages of human learning. Carol Gilligan (1982) called attention to the gendered nature of perceptions of learning and development, as the children studied were boys, and the results generalized to girls. However, Gilligan proposed a psychodynamic explanation for the different stages and values in the learning development of females, drawing on ideas about separateness and connectedness in primary gender socialization (Chodorow, 1974). These concepts of separation and connection appear again in the work we report below.

William Perry (1970), holding the context constant, found that male college students moved through developmental stages, and his findings were partially confirmed by Belenky *et al.* (1986) for women. Perry (1970), interviewed students throughout their college years at Harvard and identified a developmental scheme incorporating nine epistemological 'positions'. Although women were interviewed the scheme is based only on the male interviews. The consistency of context (i.e. Harvard) and the relative homogeneity of the sample, enabled a clear linear sequence to appear. His research can be grouped in four 'stages' through which students gave meaning to their learning experience. Students progressed from *dualism*, through *multiplicity*, to *relativism subordinate* and ultimately *relativism* proper, where personal commitment is made. The movement from dualism to multiplicity took students from the basic, right/wrong absolutist position, through uncertainty/guessing the right answer to an acceptance of uncertainty or no answer yet available. In the multiplicity stage, students realized that everyone has a right to their own opinion, leading to a recognition that all knowledge is relative, and a crisis of personal commitment. The relativism/commitment stage implies commitment to a position, the implications of such a commitment and the development of mature approaches to it.

Belenky *et al.* (1986) replicated Perry's approach with a group of women only, using a phenomenological methodology, and identified further perspectives to supplement Perry's stages. Mary Belenky and her colleagues identified five categories of ways of knowing:

> *silence*, a position in which women experience themselves as mindless and voiceless and subject to the whims of external authority; *received knowledge*, a perspective from which women conceive of themselves as capable of receiving, even reproducing, knowledge from the all-knowing external authorities but not capable of creating knowledge on their own; *subjective knowledge*, a perspective from which truth and knowledge are conceived of as personal, private, and subjectively known or intuited; *procedural knowledge*, a position in which women are invested in learning and applying objective procedures for obtaining and communicating knowledge; and *constructed knowledge*, a position in which women view all knowledge as contextual, experience themselves as creators of knowledge, and value both subjective and objective strategies for knowing.
>
> (Belenky *et al.*, 1986:15)

Silence did not appear at all in Perry's scheme and the power of finding their voice is a particular characteristic of the women's group, and confirms the influence of gendered power relations on learning. For instance women respondents reported being unable to speak after an academic 'put down', as well as the silencing through culturally and socially determined difference with its implied disparities of power. As Perry's group were college men the likely silencing of less privileged men does not appear in results. It is possible to compare Perry's stages of learning and development with the categories given above (Belenky *et al.*, 1986) and two of his stages of development, dualism and multiplicity, exactly match the categories of received and subjective knowledge identified for the women's group. Although the Belenky model (op cit.) appears as stages, the research established that some learners may engage in the categories in a non-linear fashion. Nevertheless, we show the equivalence of the two schemes below:

Perry		*Belenky*
------		Silence
Dualism	⟵——————⟶	Received knowledge
Multiplicity	⟵——————⟶	Subjective knowledge
		Procedural knowledge
Relativism subordinate		• separated knowing
		• connected knowing
Relativism		Constructed knowledge

The stage described as procedural knowledge was realised in two forms: separated and connected. Researchers found the connected mode as more typical of female conditioning, while the separated mode was akin to the men's stage entitled relativism subordinate. When Perry's men move towards an understanding that all knowledge is relative, they are thought to adopt a strategy, also found among college women, entitled separated knowing. The separation strategy, known as 'the doubting game' or even 'critical thinking' is characterized by the objectification of the other (Elbow, 1973). A powerful account of relationships based on such objectification can be found in Buber (1965) where seeing the other as a thing-to-be-used is characteristic of an I–It orientation, while an aspiration to connect with the other as a person reveal an I–Thou orientation. Academics in universities tend to engage in separated knowledge, as they conduct adversarial interactions, putting concepts on trial in order to attack them, and 'its not personal' is something to be proud of. The adversarial jousting has been called 'ceremonial combat' and is a style peculiarly attractive to men, as to many women it seems silly. Indeed the feminist Adrienne Rich declares that: 'rhetoric is a masculine adversary style of discourse' (Rich, 1979:138). Connected knowing, builds on subjectivist knowledge, and, known as the 'believing game' (Elbow, 1973), it is learnt through empathy, without judgement, and coming from an attitude of trust, quite the opposite of separated knowing. Connected knowing differs from simple subjectivism as it is: 'the deliberate imaginative extension of one's understanding into positions that initially feel wrong or remote' (Belenky *et al.*, 1986:121).

Separated or connected knowing prepares learners for their next stage of development, the adoption of constructivist approaches to knowledge. For the constructivist, 'all knowledge is constructed, and the knower is an intimate part of the known' (p. 137, op cit.). In this category of learning, we are informed there is passion and participation in the act of knowing (Polanyi, 1958) and the stance is beyond the narrow objectivism of academia, which, as a philosopher Sara Ruddick knew only too well: 'instead of developing arguments that could bring my feelings to heel, I allowed my feelings to inform my most abstract thinking' (Ruddick, 1984:150). Such a stance alters one's orientation to experts, as: 'an expert becomes somebody whose answers reflect the complexity . . . the situation holds' (Belenky *et al.*, 1986:139), and constructivist learning is characterized by empathy and connectedness, so relationship is a key ingredient in what is a completely holistic stance towards knowledge and learning. We acknowledge the components of constructivist knowledge as those which lead to a recognition of relationship in learning, i.e. connectedness to others, empathy and awareness of feelings.

Levels of learning

Gregory Bateson (1973) offered a structure, adopted and developed by others, a typology of three levels in learning.:

- *Level I*: First order learning is confined learning, where facts or skills are defined by context, e.g. the classroom.
- *Level II*: Second order learning takes the learner outside a confining frame, enabling comparisons and connections to be made so that decisions are based on richer data, encompassing subjective factors as well as objective material. Learning by doing offers the opportunity for second order learning.
- *Level III*: Third order learning involves discovering the ability to doubt the validity of previously held perceptions, the learning being about learning itself.

Bateson's levels correspond to the stages of Perry and the categories of Belenky as follows:

Level I is learning which is factual, a consequence of the transmission of knowledge and information, known as 'banking' (Freire, 1974). The move from silence to voice and dualism, characterized by basic learning in a subject drawing on 'expert' sources and received wisdom/knowledge. Level II is learning which is aware of context, transferable from the classroom/laboratory to the real world. Learning by doing belongs here as it relates theory to practice and encourages multiplicity, subjective knowledge and the realization that knowledge is not so clear-cut as the experts suggest. Relativism subordinate and procedural knowledge are the academic manifestations of level II learning and would be expected from undergraduates at final level.

Level III is learning which is reflective, with an ability to take a meta-view, not only of content but also of process. Here the realization of the contextual nature of truth (relativism) and the power of the learner's framework (constructed knowledge) enables learning to be truly reflective. Personal engagement in research and supervisory support offer the opportunity to postgraduates of level III learning. This ability to contextualize the learning process and de-construct it in a dialogue with others is an important component of reflection and one that is regarded as important by those seeking transformative purposes on higher education.

Domains of learning

Three 'domains' of learning have been identified by educationists (Bloom, 1956, 1964) and they cover the three aspects: *cognitive* (knowing); *conative* (doing); *affective* (feeling). We recognize that these terms are abstractions and, as such will overlap in practice. However, they may be presented in terms which describe the outcome of learning in each domain, e.g. cognitive learning results in knowledge; conative learning results in action/ changes in the world; affective learning alters appreciation of the self in relation to self and others. The three domains of knowledge, self and world have been identified as necessary for the survival of higher level learning and the emancipatory endeavour of a university education (Barnett, 1997).

The importance accorded to each domain by a teacher in her practice is likely to reflect her theoretical model of a person as a learner. If the model is limited to one of these domains the others are affected and learning is limited. We maintain that the emphasis on cognition in higher education has neglected the development of conative intelligence and affective intelligence. While projects and practicals have redeemed the doing part of higher learning, the denial of emotion in learning remains in place for most academic endeavours. We will show that emotion holds the key to a higher level of learning, through reflective dialogue. We hold that emotional intelligence is an essential attribute of a teacher in higher education and that such qualities are needed to ensure the survival of higher education as a sector which offers genuine opportunities for level III, constructivist, reflective learning. Indeed, Barnett's (1997) call for 'critical being' instead of just critical thinking, is, in part, a recognition of the emotional and action dimensions in learning.

Our approach to learning values all three domains of learning. The need to achieve a balance of the three domains is more difficult than it may first appear. To simplify, if we consider a triangular model as in Figure 3.1a, with vertices as extremes which value respectively, only the cognitive and knowledge (K), only feeling and emotion (E), and finally, only action or interactions with the world (A).

Figure 3.1a The three domains of learning

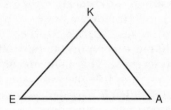

The middle line is not easy to hold, as those at extreme points of the model perceive any departure from their position as over-doing the other two vertices. The integrated model shown in Figure 3.1b suggests a valuing of all three domains and a recognition of the socio-political context.

Figure 3.1b The three domains of learning: an integrated model

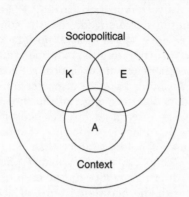

Some progress has been made in that projects and practicals which emphasize action are increasingly accepted as requirements for undergraduates. However, the perception of affective intelligence is thoroughly mistrusted as too 'touchy-feely' for many academics. So why is emotional intelligence needed in academic life? We have managed well enough without it up to now haven't we? Let us examine the rationale for extending the domains of learning in higher education to include emotion through an exploration of single- and double-loop learning.

Single- and double-loop learning

The terms single- and double-loop learning were first used by Argyris and Schön (1974) to distinguish between 'instrumental' learning, which leaves underlying values and theory unchanged, and learning where assumptions are challenged and underlying values are changed. Single-loop learning does change strategies and assumptions, sometimes on the basis of experience (Kolb, 1984), in ways that leave the values of a theory unchanged. However, double-loop learning, in challenging assumptions and 'givens' in systems, has the potential to threaten underlying values by cracking their paradigms. The process of challenging and changing paradigms has been described as revolutionary (Kuhn, 1970)! Argyris and Schön recognized the source of the idea in concepts of feedback in control engineering, and cited in Ashby's *Design for a Brain* (1952).

The concepts have been taken up by many and sometimes altered to fit a particular argument (Flood and Romm, 1996). A recent development of the double-loop model recognizes the significance of the socio-political context, where: 'Discontinuities and uncertainty are rife . . . generating needs for new forms of social learning' (Weil, 1997a:124).

In this book we retain the meanings originally given to the terms by the authors (Argyris and Schön, 1974) and we value both types of learning but within a social context. However, we do maintain that single-loop learning conforms to level II of Bateson's typology and is therefore characteristic of early undergraduate activity. Double-loop learning, where existing paradigms are questioned, assumptions challenged, etc., sits comfortably in level III learning, and as such is more typical of ideal postgraduate work or mature undergraduate activity, incorporating the external critique of the discipline itself, recommended as characteristic of critical reflection.

We do note that in valuing both we also recognize that paradigmatic activity cannot be sustained on the edge all the time by virtue of the fact that level III or double-loop learning involves 'shifting' a person's reality and involves change which may be disturbing. There is a need for some containing (in the sense of holding rather than controlling) in order to cope with a temporary 'chaos' in a transformative phase. Day-to-day learning, meeting goals and altering practice on the basis of experience, enables progress to be made, with the occasional burst of activity which leads to double-loop learning rather than pervading the life of the learner. For each learner any paradigmatic shift is necessarily a personal one, in that emergent knowing is the learner's and she must own it as her own. Being informed about paradigm contradictions may offer learners opportunities for double-loop learning, but the journey must be undertaken by the student herself, taking that energy leap into the unknown, to reach her own personal authority in learning. Reflective dialogue with others as described in later chapters, provides opportunities for: 'actively testing out alternative ways *with* others' (Weil, 1997a:130), and offers hope of generating: 'alternative models for learning and change to breathe new life into – to reanimate – our social processes and institutions' (p. 136).

The concept of effective single-loop learning has been described graphically in a well-known diagram by Kolb (1984), where goals are set on the basis of theory, action is taken, and, on the basis of this experience, a new action or plan is devised. For day-to-day learning the loop is productive and within the given variables and framework, the learner gains competence and confidence. The process is illustrated in Figure 3.2.

Figure 3.2   Single-loop learning

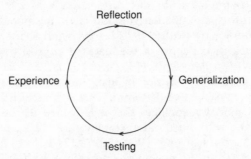

We refer now, with permission, to Peter Hawkins' original diagram to illustrate double-loop learning in Figure 3.3.

Figure 3.3   Double-loop learning

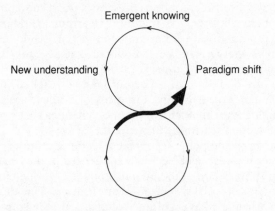

Source: Adapted from an original idea by P. Hawkins, 1997.

Day-to-day functioning in single-loop learning is indicated in Figure 3.3 by the lower circle. When the paradigm or context is questioned the learner swings out of lower circle orbit and begins to traverse the upper circle in double loop learning mode, returning to the single loop when appropriate, perhaps to test a new theory in the time-honoured way. The 'bold' arrow joining the circles in Figure 3.3 represents the point of reflection where the learner becomes aware of doubt or disturbance in relation to an existing paradigm. The single-loop orbit is contained and can be traversed within a standard programme of study, setting goals for learning within a given discipline, planning a learning route and achieving a level of understanding within the discipline concerned. The double loop orbit offers the potential for paradigm shift through reflective dialogue, in terms of knowledge, self and action in the world. Hence the return to single loop orbit is accompanied by a new understanding of the discipline, a potential development in conception of self and values, and an emergent intention to act.

What is needed to enable the learner to shoot out of the single orbit, and traverse the exciting and potentially disturbing orbit of double-loop learning? If we were to pursue our analogy of orbits and rocket science the answer suggests that what is required is *energy* to fuel the 'burn' of a changed trajectory. When double-loop learning occurs it is often serendipitous and requires the 'energy' for engaging in critical debate (Barnett, 1997:171–2) as 'critical energy has to have a head of steam behind it' (p. 172). Where is the source of this energy to come from?

Emotion

The evidence suggests that emotion is the source of human energy (Hillman, 1997). Emotion fuels our passions, our battles and our behaviour, notwithstanding our espoused rationality. The combination of a thinking neo-cortex fuelled by powerful emotion represents a good source of the energy required for many endeavours, including learning. Giddens avers that 'emotion and motivation are inherently connected' (Giddens, 1992:201). The learner fuels energy from her emotional being, giving rise to expressions like 'passion to learn'; 'hunger for truth'; 'thirst for knowledge', which recognize that the double loop trajectory may be reached in a projectile path fuelled by emotional energy. Instances of adults developing critical thinking through triggering incidents support the idea that strong emotion stimulates double-loop learning (Brookfield, 1987).

However, the social and political context of learning cannot be neglected as this will influence the degree of 'agency' experienced by the learner. The idea of agency as an appreciation of the potential power of strong emotion, recognizes the constraints of social systems for many learners. The idea we propose, of reflection in learning takes cognizance of this, acknowledging that learners are not lone actors, dependent only on themselves, but that learning is a socially constructed event lived out in a social and political context, which may not always be conducive to bursts of productive energy and emotion (Salmon, 1989).

It is in the field of emotion that we find academia sadly missing – emotion is not and rarely has been valued in academic life, built as it was on the premise that intellect was superior to body and that only the mind could be rational, the emotions being untrustworthy. The dualist roots of the academy has led to devaluing the body, emotions and feelings, privileging only the mind and the intellect. Academics have been trained to ignore, mistrust and devalue emotion. So how can it be used for learning?

We shall need those who are comfortable, and who are willing to take the risk of being sometimes uncomfortable with emotion, to handle the volatile fuel and ensure that the energy is contained for the benefit of learning. An understanding of human emotion and the emotional interactions of people will be needed to support this kind of learning. Also a structure which will harness the emotional energy productively is required to support the learner who chooses to go into the double loop 'orbit' (see Figure 3.3) The qualities needed for teachers in higher education to support potential double-loop learning, including emotional intelligence, are those of a facilitator. We have said that academia has not valued such qualities, but many academics have acquired them and use them in their practice, often as a result of the influence of Carl Rogers.

Carl Rogers, in his book, *Freedom to Learn for the 80s* (1983) expressed the goal of education: 'if we are to survive in a continually changing environment . . . [the goal of education] . . . is the facilitation of change and learning' (Rogers, 1983:120). What are the necessary and sufficient conditions for learning? For Rogers, learning is: self-initiated, significant, experiential, 'gut-level' learning by the whole person, a process described as person-centred: 'the facilitation of significant learning rests upon . . . qualities that exist in the personal *relationship* between the facilitator and learner' (p. 121), and:

> the person-centred way . . . is something that one grows into. It is a set
> of values, not easy to achieve, placing emphasis on the dignity of the

individual, the importance of personal choice, the significance of responsibility, the joy of creativity. It is a philosophy, built on the foundation of the democratic way, empowering each individual.

(p. 95)

What are these qualities?

1. *Realness or genuineness*: some disclosure, a willingness to be a person, to
   be and live the feelings and thoughts of the moment.
2. *Prizing acceptance and trust of the learner*: a belief that the other person is
   fundamentally trustworthy . . . this means living with uncertainty.
3. *Empathic understanding*: this must be communicated (silent or invisible
   empathy is not much use).

We discuss these qualities in detail in Chapters 10 and 11.

All three qualities call for a high degree of emotional intelligence, in that
to be genuine implies a willingness to express feelings, acceptance relies on
managing competing emotions, and empathy is the key skill for handling
emotional material. When a facilitator holds such attitudes students are
given 'freedom and life and the opportunity to learn' (Rogers, 1983:133)
and, we are told that, as outcomes of the process, 'students learn more and
behave better when they receive high levels of understanding, caring, genuineness, than when they are given low levels of them' (p. 199), 'for students
identified as having learning difficulties, the teacher's level of interpersonal
facilitation was the single most important contributor to the amount of gain
on all outcome measures' (p. 207).

While we are not recommending a leap towards another corner of the
learning triangle, we *are* favouring a move towards balance in the domains
of learning. The history of higher education has emphasized cognition,
knowledge and content. The person-centred approach to learning emphasizes emotion and seeks to tap the energy available there. We are proposing
an adjustment to include elements of all three domains in the practice of
teaching in higher education in order to generate the conditions for reflection, critical thinking and critical reflection.

Critical theorists in education have challenged what has been called
the 'new romanticism' of Rogers, for failing to consider the significance of
power relations, difference and the socio-political context of learning.
The decontextualization of learning which results, it is claimed, from self-
direction or learner-centredness, leads to a denial of the patterns of social
inequality in the wider society (Reynolds, 1997).

The material argument presented by critics, that the learner is offered a
theory of personal growth which denies the significance of external social
and political factors, betrays an incomplete understanding of Rogers' seminal thought. Rogerian practice is based on *The Necessary and Sufficient Conditions for Psychotherapeutic Personality Change* (1957) which includes *empathy*,
operationally defined by Egan as the ability to discriminate and communicate in the field of emotion (Egan, 1976). The discriminating ability means
that to be empathic one can 'get inside the other person, look at the world

from his perspective, or frame of reference, and get a feeling for what his world is like. This includes the external social and political world. The ability to communicate to the other means that one can offer understanding of his feelings, and the experiences and/or behaviours underlying these feelings, (Egan, 1976:108). Accurate empathy demands an appreciation of the other's world, the social systems in which she is embedded, and the impact on the self as a consequence. We believe that a true recognition of the oppressive nature of social systems is enabled by empathy, and without the capacity for real empathy, difficult for those who are not affected to appreciate. The operational definition given above has been replicated by Mearns and Thorne (1988), giving empathy at four levels, including the social and political context.

We are only too aware that so-called learner-centred approaches often rely on such incomplete understandings of Rogers and that person-centred teaching may fall far short of that outlined above. Hence we would include, as an adjunct to a person-centred approach to learning, an existentialist orientation, recognizing and *articulating* the realities of oppression and social inequalities in the learner's context (Yalom, 1980), explored further in Weil and McGill (1989).

Recent aspirations for learning in higher education

Recent aspirations for learning in universities cannot be separated from the debate about the purpose of universities (Barnett, 1992a, 1997; Dearing, 1997; Harvey and Knight, 1996; Knapper and Cropley, 1991). Our task here is to briefly review some of the recent writers in respect of what they have to say about learning in higher education. Barnett and Harvey and Knight place learning explicitly at the pinnacle of purpose for universities. In describing their views of learning we take a stance about how we think our work on the practice of learning relates to their ideas. We will first consider Harvey and Knight's notion that the primary purpose of a university is to encourage the conditions for learning that is transformative for the learner.

For Harvey and Knight, if higher education is to play an effective role:

> then it must focus its attention on the transformative process of learning . . . To be an effective transformative process, higher education must itself be transformed . . . so that it produces transformative agents: critical reflective learners able to cope with a rapidly changing world.
>
> (Harvey and Knight, 1996:viii)

Higher education is therefore seen as engaged in the transformation of the participant, in two senses, one that effects changes in the participants and thereby enhances them, the other, which empowers them. In relation to the latter, they consider four main ways in which the student may be empowered: students being involved in the evaluation process; the guarantee to students of minimum standards of provision; giving students greater control over their own learning; *developing students' critical ability*. It is the latter in which they emphasize the real potential for empowerment in students. In terms of encouraging the transformation of the participant, critical ability means:

> their ability to think and act in a way that transcends taken-for-granted preconceptions, prejudices and frames of reference. Critical thinking is not to be confused with 'criticism', especially the common-sense notion of negative criticism. Developing critical thinking involves getting students to question the established orthodoxy and learn to justify their opinions. Students are encouraged to think about knowledge as a process in which they are *engaged,* not some 'thing' they tentatively approach and selectively appropriate . . . an approach that encourages critical ability treats students as intellectual *performers* rather than as compliant audience. It transforms teaching and learning into an *active* process of coming to understand.
>
> (Harvey and Knight, 1996:9–10, our italics)

We note here the use of words such as 'engaged', 'performers' and 'active' alongside knowledge and coming to understand as processes. Harvey and Knight are clearly saying that transformative learning is created through developing a student's critical ability where the student is really a participant with others, including teachers, in a process that brings about critical transformation. For Harvey and Knight education at this level is more than the development of domain expertise – bringing about changes in the knowledge and abilities of students. Higher education is more than 'producing skilled acolytes' in a particular discipline, though they recognize that this is important. Critical transformation is about people who can produce new knowledge and

> go beyond the present and to be able to respond to a future that cannot now be imagined . . . Just as metacognition involves being aware of our thinking processes, of their limitations and possibilities, so too critical transformation depends upon understanding the limits of our frameworks of understanding, an appreciation of when and where they might be profitably used, as well as an insight into ways in which they constrain thought, value feeling and action.
>
> (pp. 10–11)

Students thus work and study in an educational system that enables them to transform their conceptual ability and their self-awareness. Engaging in critical transformative action involves getting to the heart of things as well as being able to stand outside, to be able to: 'shuttle backwards and forwards . . . between practice and reflection' (p. 11).

Critically transformative learning involves not only deconstructing meanings and the taken-for-granted attitudes and myths and ways of seeing things, but also reconstructing by reconceptualizing and rebuilding – a continuous process that becomes the subject of further transformative learning. It is a restless, ever-changing process of evolution for the learner where the basis is laid in the experience of higher education for life.

Harvey and Knight do place emphasis upon domain expertise and the generic skills that enable them to deal with knowledge obsolescence and the recognition that students will probably move beyond their original domains of study. However, while these are necessary conditions of higher education experience they are not sufficient. The outline above of becoming a critical transformative learner will be the goal that is most significant.

Harvey and Knight have taken the idea of learning beyond the deep/ surface debate with their notion of learning that is critically transformational. We endorse their aspirations about the primary purpose of higher education and their ideas on learning. We comment in Chapter 6 on the 'hard questions about how this transformation is to be promoted' (op cit.: p. 134). At this point we emphasize those attributes that have a fit with our ideas on the promotion of such learning, that: it involves the person's thinking and being as well as action; process is integral; the learner is an active, engaged, performing participant; there is continuous interaction between practice and reflection.

Another writer in the field who has reviewed the purposes of the university in Western democratic societies is Barnett. His latest work (1997) continues his earlier work (1990, 1992a, 1994) but also offers a more explicit vision for the future of higher education. Concentrating on his 1997 work, in essence, Barnett critiques the idea that the defining concept of the Western university is that of critical thinking. He broadens this concept to the idea of critical being so that the students continue to reflect critically on knowledge but they also develop their powers of critical self-reflection and critical action. Students thus take into account their sense of self and their potentiality for action – a more holistic concept than critical thinking. The ideas are not dissimilar to those of Harvey and Knight (1996) though Barnett (1997) pays more attention to the idea of critical being. Both texts recommend empowerment or emancipation. These writers have in common the idea of learning being critically transformatory. Again we review Barnett to help answer the central question of this chapter: what is learning as it relates to higher education?

For Barnett, critical thinking cannot be adequately construed in isolation where knowledge can be considered only as a form of individual action or mental state. Knowledge cannot be separated from society. Society places differing value on different kinds of knowledge:

> Accordingly knowledge is not given: it is socially sustained and invested with interests and backed by power . . . A critical higher education has, therefore, to take on knowledge itself. We cannot leave our students sensing that there is a givenness to the knowledge structures that they are encountering or that those structures are socially neutral. However, a social epistemology of this kind has a deeply personal character to it. If the full promise of critical thinking is to be achieved, then it will have to be achieved *not only through students but also by them*.
>
> (Barnett, 1997:5, our italics)

Thus students must continue to aspire to be critical thinkers, but this social epistemology has a personal component for the individual student which can be constraining as well as emancipatory: 'Through higher education students can come not just to inhabit a different universe, but also to be changed as *persons*' (op cit., p. 5, original italics).

Barnett's route, through critical theory, yields this potential emancipation through a cognitive awareness that cuts through the 'misapprehensions to which they have been in thrall' (op cit.).

But that is not all. For our purposes a definition of society has to include the inherent change that is an inevitable characteristic of modern society. But for that change not to be wayward, unwieldy or in the hock of those with some power, there has to be some agency within society to seek enlightened change. That requires a reflexive capacity not only at personal and societal levels, but higher education has the crucial task of supplying, significantly, that capacity:

> Reflection and critical evaluation, therefore, have to contain moments of the creation of imaginary alternatives. Reflexivity has to offer resources for continuing development. [In addition] reflexivity, critique and imagination have to be accompanied by *personal capacities for change and for critical but constructive action.*
>
> (op cit., pp. 6–7, our italics)

Thus higher education has the responsibility for providing the engine of criticality.[1] But for this to have relevance to the kind of society that has 'careful and informed direction' (op cit., p. 7), higher education has to move beyond the narrow interpretation of critical thinking, 'being confined largely to its place in relation to formal knowledge' (op cit.) and to include and embrace critical self-reflection (the self) and critical action (the world). Hence our emphases in italics in the above extracts. Three forms of criticality are possible expressed through: critical reason, critical self-reflection, and critical action. In other words, it is no longer sufficient to rest with the realm of knowledge and critical reason as the raison d'etre of higher education. What is required is the recognition of and capacity for higher education to work with students' enhancing capacity for critical self-reflection and critical action.

Moreover reflexivity is not only a condition of modern society and a means of enabling people to cope with uncertainty or as a resource for effectively responding to change. For us the capacity to be reflexive requires the *means* to critically engage in self-monitoring (Barnett, 1997) and self-confrontation (Beck *et al.*, 1994). The means to be reflexive necessitates engaging in a way of learning that realizes that reflexive capacity is – through reflective dialogue – one of the central purposes of our book. With such reflexive capacity, learners can transform their relationship to their disciplines (both within and across), to themselves, and to their world. By being self-aware we extend and further our understanding of situations and our potentiality for action.

Barnett is concerned that the criticality required in the three domains are being confined to instrumental levels of operation. The emancipatory potential of critical being across the domains is in danger of being vitiated. Only by integrating the three domains of knowledge, self and world, lived out at the highest levels of critique in each domain will the full potential be realized.

Again we can ask what is the fit with our own view of learning? Barnett has provided a rigorous explanation of the potential purpose of higher education as well as a profound statement of the potentiality of learning for the individual and collectively for Western societies. We have experience and privilege, as students and academics, of living and working across and within the domains. Indeed, breaking beyond the constraints of the knowledge domain and working in all three domains including self and action in the world has been our struggle, imperative, excitement in recent years, often at the margins of orthodoxy.

We will return to Barnett in Chapter 6 with the statement of Harvey and Knight as to the 'hard questions about how this transformation is to be promoted'. But in concluding this chapter we wish to bring together some of the themes emerging from the review of theories of learning in order to explain and underpin our approaches to learning.

Our purpose

In working with the theme of learning in higher education three inter-related questions are raised:

- What is the purpose of higher education?
- What is the nature of the learning that teachers and learners are and should be engaged in?
- How can learners and teachers engage in learning so that what may be advocated can be realized?

The response to the last question is the primary purpose of this book. We will start with this question, working in the issues that relate to the other questions as we proceed.

The purpose of our writing is to explore and explain *how* learning of a critical transformatory kind might more effectively be encouraged and promoted in higher education. We find that there is a gap between the learning that is prescribed for higher education and how learning is currently realized. There is a disparity between the declared purpose of transformatory learning in higher education, described, for example, by Harvey and Knight (1996) and much of the prevailing practice of higher education, which is, in the main, transmittive. By transmittive we mean that form of teaching which is primarily didactic, one way transmission of knowledge from the expert teacher to the dependent student learner. We seek to enable learners to become transformative by the focus we place on how this can be achieved, by aiming to make the declared aspirations potentially possible. Current discussions of technology-based learning recognize the limitations of such methods in supporting critical transformatory learning (Laurillard, 1993).

We are also suggesting that for transformatory learning to occur a congruity is required between what is espoused and what is practised. If we ground this in the learner, this means that she is more likely to become a transformatory learner by engaging in activities and processes that enable such learning to occur.

By transformatory we mean that the learner is encouraged to become a critical thinker according to the standards and requirements of her discipline. In addition she is in a position to engage in critical thought with her peers and colleagues within the discipline, as well as recognizing the relativity of knowledge, that it is, and continues to be, socially constructed. In addition, by recognizing the domains of self and the place of self in the world as well as knowledge the learner can, by engaging in dialogue with others, reconstitute her way of seeing herself, knowledge, and the world and in the manner in which she acts in the world. In terms of the description of Belenky *et al.* (1986) she (and we would also include he) comes to a connected constructed knowing that enables her to recognize and utilize her autonomy. The capacity emanating from critical thought can 'open up the possibility of entirely different and even contrasting modes of understanding' (Barnett, 1997). The learner in realizing this stance in the realms of knowledge, her self and her potential actions can be transformative in the emancipatory sense of self and in the world of action. However, we are not here suggesting that a linear or smooth process to emancipation, as:

> We discover over and over again (and despite our experiential learning, with recurring dismay) that there is no linear world that we can neatly order or predict from the sidelines. Defying our attempts at rational scrutiny and reductionist analysis; one world dances out of sight as another one comes into view.
>
> (Weil, 1997b:14)

More specifically our purpose, in supporting the transformational endeavour, is to enable persons to become critically reflective learners. Here we focus on the means by which dialogue, referred to above, yields processes by which a person can become a critically reflective learner through reflective dialogue with others. In order for learners to be critical both from within and beyond their discipline, to recognize and work with the relativity of knowledge, to become aware of diversity and power issues, learners require a form of discourse, reflective dialogue, that enables them to breach the 'settled' paradigms of their world.

How is the understanding and practice of reflective dialogue, and through it, critically reflective learning to be realized for the learner? Such understanding and practice is, in our view, the emergent responsibility of teachers in higher education and their institutions. Teachers who seek to enable critically reflective learning are faced with the task of communicating, not only their understanding of the reflective dialogue process, but also to model the discourse in their practice. Hence the attention we give to enabling teachers to engage in reflective dialogue themselves.

The nature and the form of the discourse that occurs in reflective dialogue has profound implications for the way in which teachers in universities relate to the learner. Teaching that is primarily about the transmission of knowledge will not engender the concept of a critically reflective learner, because the one-way process of transmission is antithetical to the means by which a person can become a critically reflective learner. A different relationship is required between teachers and learners where two-way interaction occurs. Here we recall, the idea of students being engaged actively in a process as 'intellectual performers' (Harvey and Knight, 1996:10). The learner, by engaging in an active process with the teacher through reflective dialogue, begins the journey to greater agency, autonomy and independence rather than remaining dependent and passive.

The journey to autonomy and independence needs to be qualified. We are not positing an individualistic journey for we are asserting that while the learner may be experiencing a journey towards that autonomy and independence of learning, it is one undertaken with others. Learning is a social process. Here we are using that term to convey the interdependence between teachers and learners, and between learners and learners. Reflective dialogue to be effective for the learner requires a relationship between these parties. By relationship we are implying a mutuality. In the words of Buber (1994) 'thou affects me' in contrast with an object relation where thou is an it or object. (We explore this notion more extensively in Chapter 9.)

Such a different way of relating with the learner can be achieved through facilitation, where the focus is on the learner, as learner (not as object), rather than the transmission, primarily, of content. While the teacher works in transmission mode, although he may seek transformatory learning, there will be an incongruity between his intention and outcome. Therefore, we are putting forward the idea that teachers, if they seek to be facilitators of learning, will move into a different way of seeing their role. Further, teachers will move into a different way of being and relating with the student, as well as working in ways different from traditional teaching. The journey can be emotional, inspirational and exciting, and may be characterized by the enduring passion of committed academics (not always shared).

In the facilitator's role is embodied, knowledge, self and world, the three domains of expression, whereas, in traditional teaching, the practice emphasizes primarily one domain, that of knowledge. If critically reflective learning incorporates all three domains, then it is incumbent on the teacher in higher education to embrace those three domains in her practice.

Thus facilitation, as described in this book, is dramatically different from traditional teaching, and may imply, for some, a paradigm shift. The laudable purposes of higher education as presented in our recent sources above, to be realized, require this kind of paradigm shift in the teacher, potentially an outcome of reflective practice. A teacher working and being in the three domains will be an important model for student learners. Such paradigm shifts are likely where teachers are supported by opportunities to engage in reflective dialogue themselves, as well as by departmental, faculty and institutional support.

Because three domains of expression are brought into the picture we are giving greater emphasis to self. Not only is the approach designed to enable the learner to become and embody knowledge in herself as connected constructed knowing; self recognizes the significance of that part which is represented as affect or emotion and feelings. We draw attention to the lever of emotion referred to earlier. Emotion is often the lever or source of energy that can yield the shifts in ways of seeing the world, impacting on knowledge, self, and (recognizing social context) agency in action. Therefore reflective dialogue for us is not an arid discourse where emotion is absent but one where it is acknowledged as an important contributor to the learner's development.

A further underpinning necessary for reflective dialogue to be effective is the notion of transparency. Because the relationship between teacher and learner and between learners is a much more complex interaction and process than the traditional form of teaching, it is important to surface what is going on in the process. We refer to this in more detail in Chapters 4 and 5. Part of the means by which a learner becomes critically reflective is by reflecting on the process of learning and the relationship as it is happening. An example of the implicit relationship between teacher and student learner is the power the teacher unconsciously exercises in relation to content and the process (say a lecture). In addition, there will exist other power differentials possibly around, such as, race, class and gender, which affect relationships between learners and between teacher and learner.

In this chapter we have reviewed a range of learning theories that underpin reflection, reflective practice and critically reflective learning. We now consider the nature of reflection and reflective practice in Chapters 4 and 5.

Note

1. Barnett defines criticality as: a human disposition of engagement where it is recognized that the object of attention could be other than it is. Criticality takes place along two axes. The first, a number of *levels* from critical thinking skills where standards of reasoning are applied within specific disciplines by the individual, through critical thought to critique which opens the possibility for entirely different and even contrasting modes of understanding. The second axis is that of *domains* of expression: knowledge, self and the world. There are three forms of criticality in relation to its three domains of expression: critical reason, critical self-reflection and critical action.

4

The Requirements for Reflection

In this chapter we examine key requirements for reflection or reflective practice to prevail. We name these as dialogue, intention, process, modelling and the notion of personal stance. In achieving this we will need to examine these terms. Each of these key terms and actions contribute to the effectiveness of reflection by the learner and therefore the quality of their learning.

We examine the term reflection more closely in this chapter. We are using the term reflection in two senses. First, the *process* or means by which an experience, in the form of thought, feeling or action, is brought into consideration, while it is happening or subsequently. Secondly, deriving from the first, the creation of meaning and conceptualization from experience and the potentiality to look at things as other than they are. The latter part of the second definition can embody the idea of critical reflection.

Before examining these conditions we will refer to the idea of learning as embodying relationship.

Relationship

Underlying the capacity for teachers to engage in reflection with learners is the explicit recognition of the interaction as a relationship with learners. Without explicit recognition of the interaction as embodying a relationship, then in working with these conditions we may be less effective. We have already referred in Chapter 1 to the tendency in higher education for knowledge to be treated as static, disembodied, as a product rather than process where students may be detached from the knowledge being imparted.

In recognizing the interaction for dialogue as constituting a relationship between teacher and learner and between learners we are saying that knowledge that is the material of the interaction comes through communication. As one writer has expressed it: 'and what is implicit in communication is the sense that the other person can understand and make sense of what is being said. Where this sense is absent, what is ostensibly being offered is unlikely to be assimilated' (Salmon, 1990:14).

Dialogue

Our purpose in this chapter is to describe what we mean by dialogue and set the conditions for promoting reflective dialogue. It is through reflective dialogue that critical learning can be encouraged. The skills required for reflective dialogue in the teacher and ultimately in the students are detailed in Part 2 chapters and in our chapter on facilitation.

The notion of dialogue has a long history in the West from the Greeks onwards (see Chapter 2). The body of knowledge held as valuable in the medieval university was subject to continual revision, by 'disputation', a form of dialogue where the existing body of knowledge was tested against the standard rationality of the time. We noted earlier, that the participants in such a university were a select group of males who could be relied upon to maintain the religious status quo, and that rationality was defined by its time. Dialogue was limited by the embedded intellectual and social paradigms of the time just as the modern equivalent, the seminar, may be. The student is in a game of guessing the disciplinary paradigm to satisfy the requirements of the curriculum without being 'moved' in his own paradigm. A parody, yes, but near to many a student's experience! In Barnett's (1990) terms the seminar is limited to the internal critique of the discipline rather than the external critique which challenges the assumptions within which the discipline resorts. The traditional seminar necessarily invites the student to be deferential to but internally critical of the discipline.

As teachers it could be said that we engage in dialogue all the time. But is this synonymous with critical reflective learning? Not necessarily. For us dialogue that is reflective, and enables critically reflective learning, engages the person at the edge of their knowledge, their sense of self and the world as experienced by them. Thus their assumptions about knowledge, themselves and their world is challenged. By this we mean that the individual is at the edge of their current understanding and the sense of meaning they give to and with the world. Existing assumptions about understandings, self and the world are challenged. That learning becomes reflectively critical when the emergent ideas are related to existing senses of knowledge, self and the world and a new understanding emerges.

For the individual learner there will be points at which the prevailing view of the world becomes dislodged, certainty may be eroded with uncertainty, chaos becomes apparent rather than stability. There may be loss and mourning. There may be exhilaration and release or euphoria. That these circumstances prevail in life is plainly evident for all of us, often triggered by an event that may have been unanticipated such as the death of a loved one; the reality of having a child as opposed to thinking what it will be like in advance; the recognition, through feedback, of a positive quality in oneself not previously personally acknowledged, such as a capacity to really listen to others.

We can be informed about the potential impact of these ways of seeing the world (or ways in which we do not see the world!) but each person has to make their own journey. For some the reality say, of sexism and racism is something which they experience every day personally and with consequent oppressions of varying degrees. We may understand the idea of sexism and racism yet not personally experience the effects, and we may unconsciously exhibit sexist and racist behaviour. Only with the challenge of others may I be able to really understand what it is like to be sexist or racist. I have a choice. I am faced with a new way of seeing the world – that I can be sexist and racist in my behaviour. The choice I have is to change my behaviour or not. With that recognition comes further choices about how I relate to the world as a white male in future. Understanding sexist and racist behaviour intellectually may not have made the slightest difference to my behaviour. Someone calling attention to my behaviour is similarly futile unless the challenge is constructive and enables me to make the move. We discuss constructive challenge in Chapter 11.

Dialogue as social engagement

We distinguish internal dialogue, within individuals, from dialogue between individuals and with others. For, without dialogue, reflection is limited to the insights of the individual (which are not to be underestimated). Personal reflection demands detachment on the part of self, to look at another part of self, and in this there is a danger of self-deception (Habermas, 1974). On the other hand, dialogue that takes place with others reflects our view that learning is not merely an individualistic process. Jarvis (1987:15) stresses that:

> learning always takes place within a social context and . . . the learner is also to some extent a social construct, so that learning should be re-garded as a social phenomenon as well as an individualistic one.

In the requirements for reflection we have set out one of the preconditions as being aware of the personal stance of the learner and educator. Learners and educators do not operate in a social vacuum and hence learning does not take place in a vacuum. We are all imbued with the influences of our personal biography and the social and economic forces that mediate the way we 'see' the world and ourselves in it: 'The interaction of these give rise to assumptions, beliefs, perceptions and ways of construing and acting upon experience' (Weil and McGill, 1989:247).

Different forms of dialogue

Dialogue does occur quite naturally between people. However, this does not necessarily equate with the intentional reflective dialogue which is conducive to the potentiality of critically reflective learning. Dialogue, where the speakers intentions are to hold forth didactically at one another in order to convey their position or knowledge on or about a subject is a form of dialogue that is unlikely to lead to some new understanding. This didactic form of dialogue is often characterized by one party claiming to be expert in interaction with other(s) who may not be. Indeed, the *Shorter Oxford Dictionary* in its primary meaning defines didactic as 'having the character or manner of a teacher; characterized by giving instruction' of which the lecture, where the transmission of knowledge and ideas is the purpose, is a good example. For the receiver what is received may be significant, but the mode is primarily one way.

Dialogue can be among any number of people, not two as may be implied from the first syllable, which means 'through' and the second syllable, which means 'the word'. As Bohm conveys: 'this derivation suggests . . . a *stream of meaning* flowing among and through us and between us . . . out of which may emerge some new understanding' (1996:6, original italics).

Dialogue that is reflective and enables shifts in assumptions about a person's sense of reality will be grounded in their experience and interactive. It will be a dialogue engaging the participants' realities as opposed to that which is simply didactic. Belenky *et al.* (1986) suggest that women come to know and to learn from a position of constructed knowledge, that is, one that takes knowledge as contextual (see our commentary in Chapter 3 on their epistemological categories). Women create knowledge by valuing their subjective experience as well as the objective features. We believe that dialogue which does not take into account the subjective experience as well as the objective will be less effective in promoting reflective learning. It will be what Belenky *et al.* refer to as 'didactic talk' rather than 'real talk'. For us the talk or dialogue will be 'out there' detached from the learner and we suggest from the talker too!

While Belenky *et al.* referred to the position of women in higher education we would maintain that this stance is not restricted to women:

> In didactic talk, each participant may report experience, but there is no attempt among participants to join together to arrive at some new understanding. 'Really talking' requires careful listening; it implies a mutually shared agreement that together you are creating the optimum setting so that half-baked ideas can grow. 'Real talk' reaches deep into the experience of each participant; it also draws on the analytical abilities of each.
>
> (Belenky *et al.*, 1986:144)

Thus holding forth didactically, may have its purpose in the occasional lecture, where the speaker is transmitting information, ideas, and concepts, but to achieve real learning the approach may be found to be wanting. We would exception from this the lecture that does reveal the presence and inspirational qualities of the speaker that actually relates to and moves the listener.

Another form of dialogue is that which may be described as adversarial. Here the, often implicit, intention is a win–lose engagement where each contributor sets out to defeat the other in argument: 'in which the "other" becomes an opponent to be annihilated' (Weil, 1996:10).

Such a style can be underpinned by:

> Appeals to abstract polemic and grand theory [which] can be experienced as completely disconnected from experience, and resistant to contradictions between rhetoric and lived experience ... [and] how prevailing modes of academic discourse have rendered so many voices as insignificant.
>
> (p. 10)

Here the latter reference is to the dominance of some modes of discourse such as the adversarial and didactic, at the expense of other voices who become silenced or find that the only way to have a voice (albeit somewhat disconnected) is to engage in the form of dialogue that prevails. The form of the discourse (not necessarily the content) thus deeply affects the social interaction and may be reflected in seeing students as objects rather than independent subjects (Belenky *et al.*, 1986).

Thus dialogue as social engagement has another implication in respect of the power relations that exist between parties to a dialogue. To be reflective the dialogue should make explicit the social power relations between the parties. In the context of higher education the teacher is afforded a power in relation to the learner through her position of authority and her expertise in the subject or discipline area as well for the process by which the learners engage with the teacher. How the teacher uses her authority to create a ' "learning climate" that creates a process of dialogue that enables, rather than disables' (adapted from Weil and McGill, 1989:2) will influence the quality of the dialogue and model conditions appropriate for reflective dialogue. This is not to deny the expertise of the teacher. There is virtue in making that power explicit because it enables the learner to recognize the teacher's authority bounded by qualities that can enhance learning or inhibit learning, in the exercise of her power.

Intentional reflective dialogue

It is clear that in some of the situations described so far, dialogue that affects our way of seeing the world, happens through the sheer experience of life. The specific condition we are addressing for facilitating learning in higher education, is reflective dialogue that has as its *intention* the provision of a context and support for reflective learning.

We describe the notion of intentionality in relation to teaching and learning interactions that takes place between the teacher and the learner. We are using this term to emphasize the quality or fact of being intentional, as an explicit act with purpose or volition. This contrasts with what happens without intention. The explicit intention to engage in reflective dialogue is suggested as a requirement for such dialogue.

Our reason for making intention explicit is that if we are to engage in reflective dialogue we need to be clear what the purpose of that kind of interaction is intended. By understanding my purpose I can more consciously attend to the means by which I achieve that purpose. If my intention is to transmit knowledge then engaging in reflective dialogue will be probably inappropriate. If my purpose is to engage in transformatory learning (Harvey and Knight, 1996) where the focus on the learner is as a whole potentially critical being (Barnett, 1997), then engaging in reflective dialogue is likely to be appropriate. It is only by explicitly examining my intentions, and behind those, my values, that I can begin to aim for my intentions to be congruent with my practice. We will assume that the teacher is endeavouring, through reflection on and in her actions, to ensure that her espoused practice (that which she believes in) is as close as possible to her practice in-use. An example of espoused practice being incongruent with in-use practice would be an articulated belief in transformatory learning while using transmittive methods! (Harvey and Knight, 1996).

Naming that which is unnamed

If I am going to undertake, say, a traditional lecture with a group of students, I may have articulated to myself what is my purpose and what the content will be to fulfil that purpose. Also, I may have decided how I am going to undertake the session. I may have done similar sessions like this one before and I will, perhaps, from habit and experience, adopt the same approach again because it appeared to 'work'.

As teachers we would expect there to be some explicit intention for the session and that an intention is also identified by the student learners whom I expect to come to the session. Such intentions may not be explicit or apparent. Ask students why they are going to the lecture and the answer may be because like Everest it's there! The teacher may be giving a lecture because it is part of the course and she has always done it. Given explicit intentions, in addition, there may be a whole range of unintended happenings on my part (let alone the students) of which I am not entirely aware. Assume that I am aware of the content, intention and the purpose of the lecture. Let us look at *how* I intend to organize the session. Here we are referring to the *process* by which I engage with the learners to enable them to understand, appreciate, and learn about the content and its relation to the rest of the curriculum and the course.

Given explicit intentions, say, of task and purpose, what is happening at levels where there is an absence of intention or where intention is not evident? There is certainly not a vacuum. There could be inadvertent consequences arising out of the intended. More fundamentally and beyond the latter, we can ask: what may be inadvertently happening that has not been intended and yet is implicitly happening in the session? With this last category there may be no articulation of what is happening. There may be 'silence' in the sense that what is happening is not overtly apparent but is nevertheless influencing the situation (and potential learning). To borrow a phrase, what is happening may be unknown and therefore not be named. However, because it is not named, is unknown, yet is happening, 'it' may be influencing what is going on. In our experience we have all been in (and can still be in) situations like this. Unless we can name it, we cannot work with or assess the significance of that which has not been named. This can happen for the teacher as well as the learner. We will examine one significant example of that which is often unnamed, – *process* – and consider the effects this can have on learning. We will then relate the term process more closely to intentionality.

Process

By process we refer to *how* a task is undertaken as opposed to the task itself. When we make explicit the process in which we are working as opposed to the task we are undertaking, we begin to explain the way in which we are working. What is the distinction between task and process? The task is what I do, the process is how I do it. This may appear obvious but we do find a barrier in the identification of task and process in teaching as opposed to other professional contexts. For example, an engineer will be able clearly to explain the distinction between constructing a road and an optimum process by which that road gets built. The teacher lecturing on that topic about task and process in relation to road building may be totally unaware and/or give little emphasis to how the session can best be undertaken (process) to achieve effective student learning (purpose) on the construction of a road (task).

Each lecture or session with learners will have a purpose(s) which may or not be explicit. The task derives from the purpose. For example, in Economics the purpose for students may be to acquire an understanding of the theory of perfect competition. The task will be, inter alia, to explain the operation and effects of supply and demand in conditions of perfect competition. We have, then, purpose and task. What we do not have as yet is the process, *how* this is undertaken between the teacher and students. That process may be intentional, articulated to the students and performed. The word performed is used in order to convey an aspect of the teacher's role that is crucial. In order to carry out my part of the task as teacher, I perform, act, do a set of activities in relation to and with the learners who are in the same room. That performance, activity, and doing, with the learners is one where I relate in a particular way with the learners. Whatever I am doing to carry out my part in the session I am 'modelling' a process with particular sets of behaviours, qualities, values and skills in relation to and in the presence of the learners. We now need to examine the term modelling which is intrinsic to process in situations of teaching and learning.

Modelling

Let us take an example from the experience of one of us in the early years of our teaching.

In the early years of teaching in higher education, I adopted a model of teaching of which I was not really conscious. I could name it as a lecture but not much else. Yet, if I could have 'stood outside it' I may have been able to explain the characteristics of that model. However, at the time I did not and could not recognize process, let alone understand that what I modelled as the process was the process – I just did and was it. Now when I look back with some hindsight and embarrassment, I realize that I adopted that which prevailed around me. I adopted that which I had myself experienced at university and what I had seen was the norm in the institution in which I now worked. I did not question the lecture as a model appropriate to what I wished to achieve. Of course, I knew that I was preparing a lecture and that was what I intended but I was not aware of some of the implicit features that I was modelling within the category of interaction called a lecture. I had some notions about an optimum lecture like enthusing about the content and bringing in my personal experience. I realized, even then, that being a good entertainer and involving students in the session at least made the session less boring for all of us. I am not sure what the effect on their learning was. Our point here is that even though I did not realize it, I was 'modelling' a process that was inadvertent and unintentional in the sense that I was not aware that it was a model complete with a whole range of values and behaviours implicit in the model. It is likely that the students may well have adopted, emulated or imitated 'my' model albeit one I was not consciously modelling.

Another example of the unintentional being modelled by me was my explanation of the theory of perfect competition to students as if the theory was, by simply explaining it, obvious or apparently obvious. I thus modelled implicitly the absence of struggle on my part when I learned about the theory. This behaviour and stance can convey a myriad of meanings and feelings to the student learner!

Thus whatever we do in relation to the teaching/learning situation we are modelling the process we use by doing it. There is not only the complexity of the content of what we are saying but a whole wealth of 'things' that are happening that are 'concealed', inadvertent and, in the sense above unintentional. If we can begin to explain what and how we are working, with learners, then in giving voice and 'explanation' to how we are doing it, we can then begin to explain aspects of the relationship between the teacher and learners. When we can do this for ourselves as teachers, with our colleagues and with learners particularly, we can then begin to understand and therefore influence, that relationship for the purpose, inter alia, of asking the question: how is the process I am using and the relationship I am creating (having) with the students enabling their learning? Moreover, once I have insight into what it is I am modelling in the process, I begin to have choice in how I model process. I have revealed what is happening (or at least partially) and can more consciously influence how I model my process and therefore my practice toward teaching and learning.

More important, in being explicit as teacher with the learners about the process going on between us, we begin *enabling the learners* to be explicit about that process. Once we engage in this dialogue about the process something else happens. In making explicit the process that is occurring (i.e. saying what we think is going on over and above the interaction itself) we are also describing the process that can be adduced 'above' the inter-action between teacher and student. Once we have described the process, we can then engage in discussion and analysis of process, that is meta-process. This is one aspect of what we mean by reflection on our practice – reflective practice. This reflection derives from the desire to 'know' what is going on 'above' the content (task) and purpose of the session. At this point it is necessary to refer to that aspect of process that is significant to the relationship and interaction between teacher and learner – modelling.

Modelling as imitation

We have already alluded to the notion that in modelling we are conveying to the learners a way of being and doing. It is important, too, that the teacher is conscious and intentional in relation to the modelling of her process. Another aspect of modelling that is useful, particularly for the learner, is that of imitating the teacher in her practice. This is most obvious in those teaching situations where the learning is explicitly around a skill, say in music, where the playing of an instrument is the skill under attention. Here the learner will, among other things, imitate and emulate the teacher. Schön (1987) attached significance to modelling that yields effective imita-tion and is part of the process of engaging in action that enables the learner to begin to understand what he is doing and to reflect upon it.

Thus, the teacher by intentionally modelling her process, and for our purposes, reflective practice, by explicitly drawing attention to the process by which reflective practice can be undertaken, enhances the possibility of the learner engaging in reflective practice. The modelling of the process of reflective practice becomes a necessary condition for this to occur (but not as we shall see a sufficient condition). The conscious imitation (by drawing attention to the modelling) can enable the learner to acquire the skills to do it herself. In addition, by considering and reflecting upon the process, the learner can acquire a conceptual understanding that is grounded in practice.

We will return to the notion of modelling as creating effective imitation not just in terms of the content or knowledge and skills the learner acquires but also in the teacher engaging in modelling by enabling initially, imita-tion in the learner to engage in reflective practice.

The 'black box' within process

Barnett (1992a:99), referred to his work as opening up the black box of higher education. Barnett's 'black box' is the: 'institutional space (between entry and exit) . . . a collection of intentional and unintentional, happenings oriented toward changing the student in various ways' where entry refers to entry into and exit refers leaving higher education.

Playing on the metaphor, we explore an inner more elusive black box. We seek to open up the black box of process hidden in teaching and learning that, we believe, can, if opened up and made much more explicit, promote learning more effectively. Within *process* lies a 'black box' of significance, a repository of the often unexplained, unnamed and invisible.

This is another way of explaining one of the purposes of our writing this book – to make explicit and to explain the significance of the content of the black box of process by sharing our knowledge and practice. We recognize that there may be aspects of the black box which we as authors may not be aware. Public knowledge on process may still be limited, with aspects still to be unravelled and added to the pool of public consciousness.

We distinguish public knowledge from the personal subjective knowledge of the individual as teacher. Another way of explaining this is that each teacher lives their own journey about their teaching. Our purpose is to endeavour to make some of that journey explicit by (wherever possible) relating to that journey and offering meaning to the reader who is also a teacher or who is an actor in the higher education arena. By explicating some of that journey the teacher can become more conscious of her practice in enabling others' learning.

Another way of saying the above is that there will be (and has been) an area of 'innocence' about aspects of my teaching. That innocence is partly a result of my own background and influences and partly an innocence on the part of all of us – until that which has been unnamed is named. For example, it is only in the last decade that teachers, academics and writers have articulated the notion of reflection and its implications for learning. Now that reflection has been named, and shown to be a more complex idea than previously existing notions of reflection, the concept has been given more meaning. We can now use it consciously to attend to the quality and effectiveness of learning more rigorously. (This despite the fact that as thinking, feeling and acting individuals and colleagues we had done this in the past but not consciously.) Another example is the recognition of the innocent but nevertheless powerful impact of gender bias in, inter alia, education. Once the bias has been named we can begin to work on countering it and learning from it.

Once I am aware of my process practice I have insight. That insight destroys my innocence, my ignorance and, possibly, my collusion. Until my process 'practice' is brought to my consciousness I do not know about it. Until my process practice is brought to my attention I do not know. My lack of knowledge and awareness of my process will influence my ability to reflect upon my practice. As soon as I am aware of process and aspects of process then and only then do I have choice and can then influence that practice. Once I am aware of process, I can incorporate process into my intentions for the sessions I am undertaking with learners. While I remain unaware of my practice then I cannot reflect upon it and therefore cannot act on the reflections. It is possible to imagine the teacher who does engage in reflective practice herself and with students but is unaware of it in the sense that it is not named. Naming 'it' is important in order to have power in using it (Griffin, 1987). If I am aware of reflective practice but do not do it or am unwilling to do it then I am letting the learners down. I am potentially limiting learners in their opportunity to engage in their reflective practice. However, this paragraph has stepped into reflection and we have yet to place meaning on the term as we intend in Chapter 5.

There is an array of 'invisibles' in the black box of process. Among some of the invisibles we are aware of that we can call attention to in process are:

- the values a person holds – in use as opposed to espoused
- the extent to which we are aware of the modelling of our values, processes, and how we use our power
- the feelings we as teachers may have at any one time
- the extent of our own levels of learning in our domain, discipline or subject
- the impact the above have on the learners
- the feelings learners may bring to the situation
- the implicit power relations that exist in the situation between teacher and learners, between learners and in the wider context, the discourse that maintains these
- the stance we as teachers convey to students and the stance they are each and collectively having towards us
- the impact all the above have on the teaching/learning situation.

An example of the values that a teacher may display of which she may not be aware, is the teacher's mental stance (exhibited in her behaviour to the learners) about the learners' resources. She may believe learners to have an abundance of experience upon which to draw in a learning situation. Alternatively, she may believe learners to be empty repositories to be filled!

We aim to work with some of the above invisibles above across the book. However, there is one significant 'invisible' that we consider is necessary to bring into this chapter as it is such an important condition for learning – personal stance.

Personal stance

One aspect of the 'black box' within process and therefore one of the conditions that influences learning is personal stance. Here we draw upon

Salmon (1989) for highlighting the significance of personal stance as one part of the process by which we all learn. For Salmon:

> because personal stance refers to the positions which each of us takes up in life, this metaphor emphasises aspects of experience which goes deeper than the merely cognitive, and which reflect its essentially relational, social and agentic character.
>
> (p. 231)

For Salmon, human learning is highly particular; there is fundamentally no distinction between what is personally understood and what is personally, intimately experienced through living. Salmon continues:

> But, as yet, I do not think we have gone very far in understanding how it is that individual learners actually come to construct their own unique material. This because the *material* of learning has been traditionally viewed in different terms from those that define the learner.
>
> (p. 231, original italics)

There are two dimensions to personal stance. The first relates to the content of what we learn. The second relates to the context that teachers and learners bring to the process of learning.

Taking the first dimension, that relating to the content of learning, Salmon (1989) states:

> In the conventional understanding of learning or teaching, *content* is viewed as essentially 'out there', independent of the persons of both learner and teacher. Because of this, there is typically quite a massive disregard of the inescapably personal meaning of every curriculum.
>
> (p. 235, original italics)

Thus part of the problem has been exactly that the material of learning has been treated as if it could be detached from the learner's context.

The second dimension attends to the learner's context. We are taking as a given that learners will bring their social contexts as necessary influences with them to any teaching and learning situation in order to make the following statements. Within that situation there is then the context in which the teaching and learning takes place. Salmon captures this well: 'How we *place ourselves,* within any given learning context, whether formal or informal, is fundamental' (p. 231, original italics).

The learning context is a relational one. Let us take the learner. The learner may come to the session with their own attitude to the potential material. How then will the personal stance of the learner towards the material be affected by the teacher? Salmon shows that even before the teacher teaches the material the learner will have formed, usually unconsciously, some personal stance towards the teacher. That stance may be about the teacher's class, race, age and apparent disposition towards the learners in the eye of the learner. The learner will necessarily be engaged in the 'delicate act of "reading" someone' (Salmon, 1989:232) which is a way of the learner implicitly placing themselves towards that person. The learner's interpretations of how she 'sees' the teacher and what the latter says will inevitably frame the learners' understanding of the curriculum as interpreted by the teacher.

What of the teacher's personal stance towards the teaching/learning situation? When we teach we set out to convey what we know, understand and have experienced, that is, we set out to communicate our knowledge and understanding. We:

> convey our own position, our own stance toward it. This means that, as teachers, we do not just pass on the curriculum; we actually represent, even embody it. Knowledge – understanding – is no more separate from teachers than from learners.
>
> (Salmon, 1989:233)

For example, in the earlier discussion about process we referred to the lecture where the teacher conveys no sense of the struggle he may have had in acquiring the knowledge himself when trying to come to understand and learn the material. The teacher, in teaching and relating the subject as lucidly and fully as possible by means of the lecture, may convey unconsciously that the material was, and therefore is, easy to acquire, understand and learn. This may be perceived by some learners to mean that the material should be 'easily' acquired, absorbed and learned.

Again, when we teach we may not intend to but we vary in our enthusiasm towards particular parts of a subject or discipline. We may be teaching a part of the curriculum that we are personally at odds with or find boring and possibly repugnant yet try to teach it in a dispassionate way. The true feelings the teacher may be trying to hide will no doubt spill over. The inauthenticity of the way in which the material is taught will come over. Contrast the situation where the teacher is deeply inspired by their enthusiasm for the subject where there is a strong relation between the content and how they feel about and 'deliver' it.

In terms of our endeavour to invite teachers to engage in reflective dialogue with learners we would add that, in addition to the personal stance towards the content of any course programme or discipline, the same authenticity applies to the processes we use that are intended to be conducive towards learning. If I feel resentment towards a particular approach to learning, for example, leading groups, then that will affect the learning situation.

We are conscious that for learners and teachers we are advocating potential changes in the way in which both parties relate to each other in learning through using and adapting process that may be at odds with previous experience. By articulating the context we are making it possible for process to be explicitly acknowledged, spoken of, and shared so that teacher and learner can make their own meanings. It is not enough to convey to learners that personal stance affects our learning. That would be insufficient and another example of 'out there'. The key is for both teachers and learners to engage with the realities of the struggle to understand and learn as it happens by constructing their own knowledge with each other.

Transparency about process implies openness in terms of personal interaction as a teacher or learner and this is a deeply personal matter with a degree of personal risk. However, only through a healthy dialogue between teachers and learners with openness, trust, respect and mutuality can the dependence model inherent in transmission be superseded by collaboration.

Summary

We can now set out the conditions for reflection as a contribution to transformative learning of students. We have noted the different forms that dialogue can take. Prior conditions for reflection require the teacher to be aware of process and intentionality about that process as well as the form of the dialogue. The teacher also needs to be aware that she is modelling the process she uses. In the next chapter we explore reflection in more detail. For the teacher to create the conditions for critically reflective learning she needs to attend to modelling the processes that are conducive to the encouragement of that learning. In particular, if part of the process is to engage in reflective practice, she will be more likely to enable the learners to achieve that if she models it herself.

In the next chapter we will also develop the meanings of reflection and reflective practice and show how they contribute to transformative learning in the learner. In Chapters 7 and 8 we show how teachers and student learners can become engaged in reflective dialogue. In Chapter 9 we show how reflection by learners requires to be effectively modelled by teachers and that modelling reflection requires effective facilitation by teachers.

5

Reflection and Reflective Practice

In this chapter our purpose is to set out our meanings of reflection and reflective practice and convey their importance to learning in higher education in promoting the potential for deep and significant learning. What does it mean to engage in reflection? What do we mean when we engage in reflective practice? When can we refer to ourselves as 'reflective practitioners'? How can reflective practice encourage the deeper levels of learning to which universities and colleges aspire?

We will make the journey through development of the notion of reflective practice as a means to convey our meanings. Before embarking on this journey we make a note about the chapter for readers. We wish to explain the ideas on reflective practice as clearly as possible. In doing so, we realize that we are using a cognitive, analytical and fairly rational means in order to make the explanation as accessible as possible to readers. In the description we may inadvertently convey the idea that once cognitively understood as a concept, then reflective practice is a straightforward and rational process. A cognitive understanding of reflective practice is a step towards what is in practice a complex and more holistic endeavour.

Barnett (1992a) uses the phrase, 'We're all reflective practitioners now'. There is a continuous search for knowledge; there is no end point. Moreover, this applies to how we practice in that the criteria by which we practice require constant evaluation. We need to be aware, therefore, of our actions in order that we may evaluate them. The capacity to engage in reflective practice becomes one of the means of enhancing the quality of the educational process and of promoting learning appropriate to higher education. We endorse that view as an aspiration which is as yet generally unrealized.

Engaging in reflective practice for Barnett is a means by which the student learner can be:

enabled to develop the capacity to keep an eye on themselves, and to engage in critical dialogue with themselves in *all* they think and do . . . it is a reflexive process in which the student interrogates her/his thoughts or actions. The learning outcome to be desired, from *every* student, is that of the reflective practitioner.

(Barnett, 1992a:198, original italics)

We will comment and qualify his meaning later but first we will go to the origin of the contemporary meaning of reflective practice. Barnett relied upon Schön's (1983, 1987) contribution to the idea of reflective practice as a means of enhancing a learner's critical and reflective abilities. We offer and adapt our reading of Schön as a basis for our use of reflective practice in the context of critically reflective learning in higher education.

Schön's reflective practitioner

Schön, in developing the notion of 'reflective practice', drew largely upon applied areas of university programmes where students were receiving an education designed to equip them directly into professional occupations such as architectural design, music and medicine. Schön set out the limitations of those teaching disciplines in universities that were in the business of creating and promulgating largely propositional knowledge (learning that, about things, concepts, ideas) in a technically rational value framework. Propositional knowledge is even more evident in courses where there is no vocational element where there is likely to be no action on which to apply the knowledge, e.g. philosophy.

Schön suggested that propositional knowledge, on its own, is of limited value for the emerging professional, e.g. lawyer, social worker, physician. Propositional knowledge is limited because it does not take into account the realities of professional life and practice.

Yet the emergent professional does go into practice and many of them are effective 'despite' their professional training. They develop *practice experience* and professional knowledge and excellence. This practice experience includes the propositional knowledge they acquired in order to qualify but is also more than that. So what is it that is more than propositional knowledge that nevertheless enables professionals to engage in their practice effectively?

Schön unpacked the means by which professionals enhance their practice while they engage in it. He referred to this as professional artistry, where professionals deal with the unique, the unanticipated, the uncertain, the value conflicts and indeterminate conditions of everyday practice for which there was no 'textbook' response. Reference to such enhancement as 'artistry' is not much help. It is like asking a person how he does something who replies, 'Oh, y'know'. Schön, not satisfied with this apparently intuitive means of learning, set out to describe tacit knowledge (Polanyi, 1967). He looked to those relatively unusual institutions where reflecting in and on professional practice was an intrinsic part of the professional's training. He went to the 'margins' of academia and to 'deviant' parts (Schön, 1987) of those marginal institutions to find examples of the reflection on practice that he was beginning to articulate. For example, within medical schools ('marginal' institutions, in terms of mainstream traditional universities) attached to mainstream universities he found 'deviant' practice among clinicians working with medical students dealing with questions that had not come up in the lecture theatres but were essential to professional understanding, knowledge and real practice.

Schön found the teachers and students engaged in *reflection on* emergent practice that was to underpin their learning and therefore enhance their practice. Putting it more simply, students learned by listening, watching, doing and by being coached in their doing. Not only did they apply what they had heard and learned from lectures, books and demonstrations but when they did an action that was part of their future profession, e.g. using a scalpel, they also learned by reflecting themselves and with their tutors, how the action went. They *reflected on* their practice. In addition, they would 'take with them' that reflection on their previous action as a piece of 'knowledge' or learning when they went into the action the next time. Thus in the next action they would be bringing all their previously acquired understanding and practice and be able to *reflect in* the action as they did it, particularly if a new circumstance came up.

Thus for the moment we have built up a meaning for reflective practice as reflection-on-action and reflection-in-action. We also adopt Schön's use of the hyphen to suggest two things. One is to convey interaction between action, thinking and being. The second is to suggest an immediacy inherent in reflection and action. This is particularly apposite in relation to reflection-in-action where the professional may well be 'thinking on her feet' as we say.

Reflective practice in higher education

Transferring these ideas to higher education, we would assert that whether trained as a teacher or not, the teacher (and student) engages in reflective practice at some level. But we wish to go beyond what is perhaps an 'unaware' use of reflective practice to that which is explicit and intentional. Our purpose is to articulate the components of reflective practice in the context of learning in higher education for three main reasons.

First, consciously engaging in reflective practice enables the teacher to learn from and therefore potentially enhance their practice and learning about their practice. Practice here can include teaching, encouraging learning, research, scholarship, course design and management. Indeed, it can include any of the myriad activities of the professional teacher. For example, by reflecting on my approaches to how I teach and to what purposes I teach, I can potentially learn more about the efficacy of my approaches, the underlying models of teaching and learning that I am using, and how my practice may contribute to student learning.

Secondly, by engaging in reflective practice, I as teacher can uncover, unravel and articulate my practice with a view to learning from that reflection.

Through that engagement, I may then come to an understanding of the process of reflective practice (as opposed to what I learned about my practice). In understanding and knowing the process I may be able to convey that understanding, model it and in doing so, make it accessible as an idea and a practice to students. Because I have engaged in reflective practice myself I may be able to speak about it from a standpoint of really knowing. In addition because I have experienced reflective practice as a corpus of knowledge, action and real practice, I will be able to model how reflective practice is done.

Thirdly, making reflective practice accessible to student learners, enables the latter to become more conscious of their own approaches to their learning and thereby promote critically reflective learning (see Chapter 3) via reflection on their practice and learning about their learning. For the student learner practice could include doing laboratory experiments, projects, for example. As a teacher, through reflective practice, I can not only engage with students about their learning in relation to the discipline or subject/course they are experiencing but relate with them about how they are learning about their learning. As a student learner, by engaging in reflective practice, I can ask myself (and with others) key questions about my learning in my discipline as well as asking (again with others) about how I go about my learning.

The key for us is that reflective practice is a core attribute of critically reflective learning (Chapter 3) which we have been using in our own work with students at undergraduate and postgraduate levels. Barnett (1992a) has underpinned Schön as far as learning in universities is concerned by submitting the idea that *all* students can engage in reflective practice. If all students whatever the discipline can engage in reflective practice then we have a means by which learners can potentially achieve critically reflective learning. We agree with Barnett's proposition. Returning to our main purpose in writing this book we would assert and wish to show that a key condition for such learning to happen is for teachers to engage in reflective practice themselves, to be able to articulate and model that practice for learners in order that learners can engage in reflective practice too. Hence the significance we conveyed in the last chapter to the teacher being explicit about intention, recognizing the importance of process and modelling a process that yields reflective practice in the learner.

Reflective practice: further exploration

We will now extend and deepen the meaning of the terms we are using in order to convey the significance for engaging in reflective practice.

What then do we mean by reflective practice? Here we define our terms and in doing so also set out some of Schön's category of terms to construct a vocabulary and typology of reflection that together, enables a professional teacher to be a reflective practitioner. The terms will also be useful for our purposes in the rest of the book.

1. *'Knowing that'*. This is another way of defining propositional knowledge and is that which the professional student acquires in the mainstream part of their professional study at university. This can also be referred to as *textbook knowledge* or *'knowing about'*.
2. *'Knowing-in-action'* and *'knowledge-in-use'*. That which comes from professional practice. Schön refers to this kind of knowledge as *knowledge-in-action*, a description or construction of that *knowing-in-action* that is tacit, spontaneous and dynamic. Knowing-in-action is hyphenated by Schön probably to emphasize that 'the knowing is *in* the action' (Schön, 1987). Knowing-in-action becomes knowledge-in-action when we describe it! Until we describe it we just do it – intelligent knowing-in-actions that we perform in all manner of situations from sawing a piece of wood in a straight line, to riding a bicycle, to a surgeon making an incision. Once we know how to do these actions we do them spontaneously without putting words to them.

> The knowing-in-action is tacit . . . yielding outcomes so long as the situation falls within the boundaries of what we have learned to treat as normal.
>
> (Schön, 1987:28)

3. *Reflection-in-action* happens when we are in the midst of an action and in doing and being reflective-in-action we are, for example, saying:

   • something is happening that surprises me – it is not usual
   • is what I am doing appropriate at this moment?
   • do I need to alter, amend, change what I am doing and being in order to adjust to changing circumstances, to get back into balance, to attend accurately, etc?
   • I must check with myself that I am on the right track
   • if I am not on the right track, is there a better way?

For Schön what distinguishes reflection-in-action from other forms of reflection 'is its immediate significance for action . . . the rethinking of some part of our knowing-in-action leads to on-the-spot experiment and further thinking that affects what we do – in the situation in hand and perhaps also in others we shall see as similar to it' (Schön, 1987:29). To the outsider, and even for the skilled individual engaged in the act, it will appear a smooth act without apparent hesitation or thought. This meaning signifies reflecting while the action *is* happening – a kind of checking function and if there is to be any modification arising from the reflection-in-action, adjustment will take place to resume normal service!

However for Schön, reflection-in-action has an additional meaning:

> a critical function, questioning the assumptional structure of knowing-in-action. We think critically about the thinking that got us into this fix or this opportunity; and we may, in the process, restructure strategies of action, understandings of phenomena, or ways of framing problems.
>
> (Schön, 1987:28)

This latter meaning of reflection-in-action is very different. As Eraut (1994) has suggested, this is more difficult to 'fit' into the more intuitive reflection-in-action posited by Schön. In Eraut's view this is because Schön tends to be less clear about the time scale in which reflection-in-action may occur. For Eraut it all depends upon how the action is defined in terms of time and what is determined as the action: 'is the action a scene, an act or a whole play? Or is it reflection-in-action while the actors are on stage and reflection-on-action when they are not' (Eraut, 1994:147). This raises definitional problems of when our practitioner is reflecting-in-action or reflecting-on-action? But the contribution of Schön is nevertheless important in emphasizing that knowing and knowledge are constructed in and out of practice not only derived from propositional or technical knowledge that is resident on the page or from the lecture hall.

To summarize to this point, knowing-in-action and reflection-in-action are integral parts of the task or event. They happen during and in the event, not after it. Each supports the other. The distinction between the two is that the former follows accustomed practice, the latter enters when there is a surprise occasioned by the unaccustomed, a change in the usual circumstances or an emergent critique of the way of doing something that gives rise to a modification in the way the action will be undertaken.

Reality and reflection-in-action

It is useful at this point to refer to how Schön fits reflection-in-action into ways of seeing reality:

> Underlying this view of the practitioner's reflection-in-action is a *constructionist* view of the reality with which the practitioner deals – a view that leads us to see the practitioner as constructing situations in practice, not only in the exercise of professional artistry but also in all other modes of professional competence . . . In the constructionist view, our perceptions, appreciations, and beliefs are rooted in worlds of our own making that we come to *accept* as reality.
>
> (Schön, 1987:36, original italics)

Here Schön is recognizing the subjective construction of reality. This is close to Belenky *et al.* (1986) in relation to women's experience of higher education, where they note that the individual learner comes into her own when she is able to be in a position of constructed knowledge where knowledge is seen as contextual and created by the person valuing both the subjective and objective.

As we have seen in Chapter 3, Belenky *et al.* (1986) recognize that there is an earlier stage of coming to know in higher education contexts, that is, a stage of procedural knowledge where some women apply objective procedures for obtaining and communicating knowledge (separated knowledge). This stage is akin to Schön's position about technical rationality which rests:

on an *objectivist* view of the relation of the knowing practitioner to the reality he knows. On this view, facts are what they are, and the truth of beliefs is strictly testable by reference to them. All meaningful disagreements are resolvable, at least in principle, by reference to the facts. And professional knowledge rests on a foundation of facts.

(Schön, 1987:36, original italics)

An additional category (connected knowing) was more characteristic of the women's group, leading naturally to constructed knowledge as above. There are implications here for teachers and students as learners. Belenky *et al.* (1986) undertook their research in relation to women's experience of higher education in the USA and identified constructive learners in their sample. However, our experience suggests, and we have no reason to doubt, that it can apply to men as well. The implication we are making is that propositional knowledge (knowing about) really only comes to have internalized and real meaning as knowledge when the receiving learner begins to apply that propositional knowledge to themselves by relating in some way to their experience, as part of developing a constructivist orientation to learning, where the learner as actor creates knowledge, in collaboration with others.

By consciously engaging in reflective practice, the learner has created and in turn creates the conditions for the type of learning that is the essence of higher education. More specifically, if I as a learner am to bring the propositional knowledge into a reality for me, then by immersing myself in a task that employs that knowledge, I will internalize it and make it have meaning when I bring it to bear with my existing knowing-in-action and emerging reflection-in-action.

Having investigated some of the components of reflection-in-action we now need to complement this with reflection-on-action in order to encourage reflective learning that contributes to making learning critical through critical reflection.

Reflection-on-action

Reflection-on-action is significant in the process of engaging in critical reflection. What meaning is within the term reflection-on-action? How can the conditions be created to enable reflection-on-action to happen?

Working with knowledge, in whatever form, is an important part of the work of a university in relation to student learning. We will therefore refer to situations or events where teachers and learners together work with knowledge for the purposes of learning, as actions, albeit of a particular kind. An example is appropriate here. A philosophy seminar working with objectivity/subjectivity can be seen as an event or action with the potential for reflection-in-action and reflection-on-action that promotes the learning of the students. Reflection here can include, inter alia, content, process and the practice of the teacher and students.

We will take initially Schön's reference to reflection-on-action. It is critical to his main thesis of developing the professional practitioner. Schön

(1987) refers to the frequent tendency for improvisers (in music) having difficulty conveying a verbal account of their reflections-in-action.

Clearly, it is one thing to be able to reflect-in-action and quite another to be able to reflect *on* our reflection-in-action so as to produce a good description of it; and it is still another thing to be able to reflect on the resulting description.

(p. 31, original italics)

In this extract is the recognition that there will always be some aspects of action where explanation after the event in words will not be possible. Given this, there is much that can be unravelled and described in words that can then be used for reflection. We will take the situation of a learner. In our view the capacity of a learner to reflect-on-action is significant in developing critically reflective learning. But we need to unpack Schön's statement by treating this as thinking, feeling and doing at a number of levels and incorporating propositional knowledge and that which occurs in the action as considered earlier.

Drawing upon Schön we can refer to a hierarchy of levels illustrated in Figure 5.1, starting at the bottom with the action, at level 1.

Figure 5.1 Hierarchy of reflection

4	reflection on the description of the reflection-in-action
3	description of the reflection-in-action
2	reflection-in-action
1	action

We wish to show the levels as dimensions as in Figure 5.2. Levels imply a hierarchy and implicitly that which is at the 'lower' level is less important. Further levels can imply a separateness between levels. As dimensions they are related and overlapping. Experience in action is just as important as reflection on reflection. Each and all interrelate just as thinking, feeling and doing fuse and intermingle.

Figure 5.2 Dimensions of reflection

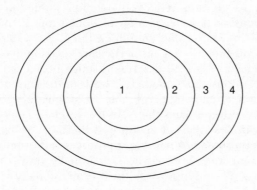

Strictly speaking dimension 2 happens within dimension 1 but because it is action that is somehow different from that taken in the past and therefore modifies the action, we will delineate it as dimension 2. We have here, following Schön's description, dimensions of thought based in and on an action (including thinking and feelings about past and current doings). Within dimension 1, action, we would include any propositional knowledge brought to the action but now probably embedded; knowledge-in-use brought from previous experience; and current knowing-in-action as well. These are all in harness, working together. So Figure 5.1 can now be revised as in Figure 5.3.

Figure 5.3   Four dimensions of reflection

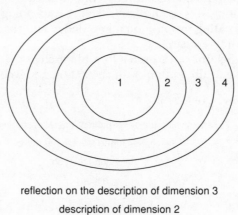

4	reflection on the description of dimension 3
3	description of dimension 2
2	r-in-a
1	action: prop k; k-in-u; k-in-a

Note: (Abbreviations: prop k = propositional knowledge; k-in-u = knowledge-in-use; k-in-a = knowledge-in-action; r-in-a = reflection-in-action)

For the learner to go into reflection-*on*-action mode on dimension 4, requires on dimension 3, a description of dimension 2: the reflection-in-action and the action, as recalled on dimension 1. We would also add that describing some of dimension 1, in particular, knowing-in-action, will also be novel at dimension 3, for to describe is sometimes to name that which may have been previously unnamed. This leads to the common difficulty of a skilled practitioner, namely, being able to articulate what she does in action. This ability differentiates the reflective teacher, facilitator, coach or mentor, as she can describe her action and therefore reflect upon it. We emphasize the importance of naming the process and the importance, in dialogue, with someone who has the skill initially (and therefore to be modelled for the learner), to identify these dimensions of reflection.

We do not wish to skip this point in the last paragraph about the significance of engaging in critical dialogue. We do have more to say about the
value of dialogue elsewhere for encouraging critical learning (Chapters 4, 6
and 9). Obviously, reflection-in-action is within the action of the person
engaged in the action and therefore part and parcel of the action. Reflection-
on-action can be undertaken by the person on their own after the action.
This personal reflection-on-action is important in the continuing internal
dialogue about their practice and may influence their future action and
reflections-in-action. However, while this form of reflection is necessary and
desirable it is not necessarily sufficient.

Reflection-on-action with another(s) in dialogue which encourages critical reflection about the actions a person has undertaken will be more likely
to be effective in promoting critical reflective learning. In Chapters 7 and 8
we outline in more detail the levels of reflection that, for our purposes, a
teacher and student learner can engage in. Critically reflective learning is
that which enables the learner to engage in deep and transformatory learning (see Chapter 3). Without the interaction brought about by dialogue
critically reflective learning may not happen. Hence our emphasis on conditions we recommend to enhance the quality of that dialogue.

The learner brings to any action all her accumulated propositional knowledge (and we include that which has become tacit), knowledge-in-use as a
result of her prior experience (again now likely to be tacit), knowing-in-
action and reflection-in-action. At the point of reflection-on-action all the
aforementioned come into potential play.

Thus returning to our question, about reflection-on-action, we have a
reflection, above, say at a meta level on which the learner is able, initially to
describe or name what has happened and then reflect on, that is, work with
that material that is before her. Schön describes the 'levels of action and
reflection on action as the rungs of a ladder. Climbing up the ladder, one
(the learner, teacher or both) makes what has happened at the rung below an
object of reflection' (Schön, 1987:114, italics added). We refer to the notion
of dimensions in order to mirror the idea of permeability across dimensions and to prevent the demotion of experience against reflection.

We will take an example to illustrate reflection-on-action through dialogue. A student may have engaged in a project which is in draft report
stage (current action completed, or levels/dimensions 1 and 2). With the
tutor and/or other student colleagues the student is reporting upon her
progress to date following a reading by all parties of the project. The student, in reporting upon her progress, describes her journey to date (level/
dimension 3) and the difficulty that she had in writing an early section. She
nevertheless pursued working on that section before moving on with the
next section sequentially. The whole group then go into discussion, that
is, dialogue with her about her experience in writing up the project. (We
distinguish dialogue from discussion in Chapter 4.) At one point another
student asks what was the reason for writing the sections in sequence. She is
surprised by the question and at first replies 'but that is how I have always

done it'. Questions follow that pose why such a procedure is necessary. Gradually, the student in question realizes this is a habit (knowledge-in-use) she has applied up to now without questioning it. Recognition becomes apparent to her that she could have adopted alternatives to writing up the project. She could work on a section where she is not 'blocked' and there is energy and will, or, she may undertake a section that appears at the moment 'easier'. Here we have reflection at dimension 4 for her but also for the group among whom this notion appears novel and potentially useful.

Thus through the dialogue about the reflection-on-action of one student she has learning about her process, as well as, potentially, for some of the others in the group. Moreover, we have the possibility that had she reflected on her action (after the writing) on her own she may not have realized that potentiality. Therefore the dialogue, necessarily with others, *enabled* her to reflect upon her actions and hence her learning.

If we briefly stand outside the above, the student learner is engaging in some aspects of reflective practice *and* is also becoming aware of her practice of reflective practice. That is, she is also learning about some aspects of the way she is learning – meta learning, described below as dimensions.

Another way of describing the above approach is that of Boud *et al.* (1985) who describe the relationship between learning experiences and reflection which we outline below. Given an experience there are three elements which are important in the reflective process:

- returning to the experience by replaying it by description of some kind, e.g. describing it to others. This is dimension 3 that we described above.

This description provides data and possible clarification for the learner and others and may provide insights not recognized during the experience, e.g. particular feelings of which the person was not conscious.

- attending to the feelings associated with the experience

The learner's feelings may have, at the time of the action, affected how she responded to the events. Negative feeling from getting stuck in the project may have disabled the response to the event resulting in a less effective or inflexible response. Returning to the event enables the learner to engage in reflection on her actions as well as obtaining an 'outside' view of what happened if she is in dialogue with others.

- re-evaluating the experience following attention to description and feelings

This is equivalent to dimension 4 above. Boud *et al.* (1985) elaborate the stages through which this re-evaluation is undertaken via four aspects which are not necessarily stages but elements of a whole:

first, *association*, that is, relating of new data to that which is already known; *integration*, which is seeking relationships among the data; *validation* to determine the authenticity of the ideas and feelings which have resulted; and *appropriation*, that is, making knowledge one's own . . . While reflection is itself an experience it is not, of course, an end in itself. It has the objective of making us ready for new experience . . . a new way of doing something, the clarification of an issue, the development of a skill or the resolution of a problem. A new cognitive map may emerge, or a new set of ideas may be identified.

　　　　　　　　　　　　　　(Boud *et al.*, 1985:30, 34, original italics)

In addition to cognitive outcomes, there may also be outcomes that are affective as well as a new stance towards action and a sense of agency. Thus Boud *et al.* provide a methodology for reflection-on-action to take place in the context of our four dimensions.

Dimension 5

Returning to the dimensions we can refer to the another, inherent here, dimension 5 – where the group reflects on the reflection-on-action. On this dimension, learners are working on the significance of reflection itself, that is, learning about how they learn! Thus in reflective dialogue on this dimension there may be learning for the individual that derives from the interaction in the group. In Figure 5.4 below we will refer to dimension 4 as reflection on action and dimension 5 as reflection on reflection.

Figure 5.4　Five dimensions of reflection

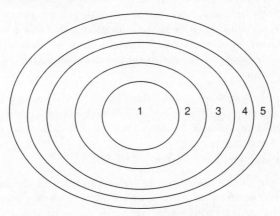

5	reflection on the reflection on action
4	reflection on the description of the reflection-in-action (reflection on action)
3	description of the reflection-in-action
2	reflection-in-action
1	action

In summary we would suggest that reflection of a learner's practice may take place *within* actions and *following* actions. The reflection can be a conversation with oneself during it and/or with others engaged in it through, but not necessarily via dialogue. It is possible to communicate by non-verbal means. It is also possible to engage after the action by oneself and/or with others. Indeed, the ability to reflect after an action is critical to the potentiality of future actions and events. We are also arguing that reflection-on-action after the action is important with other(s) in dialogue for the actor may not be able to *see* herself without some self-deception, thereby limiting her range for potential reflection (here reflection is an act as well as the past action being reflected upon).

The key for us is how best to engage in reflection-on-action, in dialogue with others, in order to attain critical reflection. This is taken up elsewhere in the book (Chapters 7 and 8).

Paradigm shift?

It is useful to draw a further potential effect of reflection across the five dimensions referred to above. We have already referred to the effect of dimension 5 in learning about learning. We can also consider the idea of reflection-on-action that takes place within a paradigm and reflection that enables a move(s) out of an existing paradigm. This is another potentiality and links with what we have referred to as single- and double-loop learning. In single-loop learning I am endeavouring through reflection at level 4 to understand and take 'corrective' action from the reflection in order to make future action more effective. My reflection-on-action becomes my potential knowledge-in-use. So, for a student learning about a discipline or domain, it is about enhancing the way I understand and or do something in relation to my domain and within a particular paradigm. With double-loop learning through reflection, particularly with others in dialogue I may:

- recognize a paradigm that I have been in without realizing it
- recognize/realize that there is another paradigmatic framework other than the one I am in
- shift my paradigm
- understand and work across paradigms.

An example of the above would be recognition of the idea of relativity in relation to the mass of a body, in contrast to earlier ideas of mass as constant. Another example would be recognition of the discrepancy between my espoused as opposed to my in-use notions of sexism – what I espouse perhaps being very different from my actions and my being made aware of the incongruity.

Refining the meaning of reflection

This point brings us to the ambiguity in Schön that Eraut (1994) has endeavoured to untangle. To help us in our work we, like Eraut went to the *Shorter Oxford Dictionary* to find meanings for reflection. There were two definitions:

1. The action of turning (back) or fixing the thoughts on some subject; meditation, deep or serious consideration. Linked to this meaning was an apposite phrase from Paley: 'Mankind act more from habit than reflection' which seemed a very useful justification for all this effort!
2. The mode, operation, or faculty by which the mind has knowledge of itself and its operations, or by which it deals with the ideas received from sensation and perception.

For us, the first definition refers to the process or means by which we reflect. And for Eraut it additionally treats reflection as a form of deliberation, where the focus is on 'interpreting and understanding cases or situations by reflecting on what one knows about them' (op cit.:156). This reflective process or deliberation may bring previous knowledge to bear as well as that which is currently unformulated in the person engaged in the action.

In terms of our writing we are aiming to convey through reflective dialogue, and a range of applications, a process by which reflection can occur. Our aim is to create the conditions for reflection that promote and encourage critical learning. This incorporates thinking, emotion, and in-the-world action that a person undertakes, while recognizing the social and political context and values within which the person lives.

The second definition is distinct from the first in that the latter may lead to a reframing or reconceptualizing about actions or situations, the potential result of which is to be able to move into a different paradigm from that previously; to engage in metacognition (Eraut, 1994); to engage in transformatory learning (Harvey and Knight, 1996); to engage in critical dialogue (Barnett, 1992a). Schön's contribution is that this meaning of reflection can happen in action as well as after action.

That the second definition fits the raison d'etre of higher education is probably (with a great deal of profound disputation) accepted. However, it is on the first definition, the process, the means, the deliberation by which the second meaning can emerge that we rest our justification for this book. It is the process of reflective dialogue, significantly with others, for the second meaning to be realized. We are not asserting this is the only way, just that it is time for the process of facilitating reflective learning to be practised.

Finally in this subsection we wish to draw attention again (see Chapter 2) to the dualism of the Western tradition and the rationalist roots of educational theory. Reflection as a concept has emerged from this rationalist tradition in the dualism of the mind/body divide. Definitions of reflection therefore are prone to privilege the rational and cognitive over the physical, that is, in such definitions reflection is an activity of the detached mind, using reason as its tool. Alternative approaches to reflection which avoid the mind/body split have been described as a reintegration of 'cerebral ways of knowing with thinking through the body' (Michelson, 1995:22). We assert a more holistic definition which values the senses, recognizes emotion and draws in personal experience through dialogue.

We define reflection in two senses, first as a process by which experience is brought into consideration and secondly, deriving from the first, the creation of meaning and conceptualization from experience and the capacity to look at things as potentially other than they appear, the latter part embodying the idea of critical reflection. When experience is brought into consideration it will include, thought, feeling and action. Moreover some treatments suggest a static, separated quality, as if reflection on action can be, after the event, totally separated from the previous experience. The reality is that the learner will, where the reflection is intentional for promoting learning, bring that action into the dialogue. This point further explains our circles as dimensions of the totality of experience.

In terms of reflection as part of reflective practice and within this reflective dialogue the integration of mind and body (affect and action) means that in the act of reflection we bring to that act our cognitive and affective experience. For example, a learner grappling with a new concept that may well disturb existing patterns or mindsets of seeing reality. In mathematics, the concept of many dimensions in geometry can only be appreciated algebraically rather than imagined as three dimensions are, and the struggle to accept and work with hyperspace may lead to learner frustration. The affect, a feeling of frustration may, in dialogue, generate the energy to grasp the concept. Similarly, in the laboratory, the researcher may be excited about the potential outcomes of experimentation. Dialogue with others, may, in releasing ideas and creative imaginings, lead to a breakthrough in the researcher's understanding about the experiment for future action.

Critiques of reflective practice

We now address the recent scepticism about engaging in reflective practice in higher education. Harvey and Knight (1996), in relation to the potentiality of academic staff engaging in their professional development, convey a view of the reflective practitioner as a 'fashionable solution' to some of the problems of professional development. Harvey and Knight refer to the reflective practitioner as one:

> who consciously engages in a dialogue between the thinking that attaches to actions and the thinking that deals in more abstracted propositional knowledge . . . This practitioner is regularly thoughtful and continually learning from the interplay between procedural and propositional knowledge.
>
> (p. 160)

They continue:

> However, being a reflective practitioner – hence helping staff to become such practitioners – is more than a matter of copious injunctions to reflect on teaching and learning. For example, reflection can easily be self-confirming.
>
> (p. 160)

They further state:

> that 'reflection' is a good intention frequently found to be fallen on hard times. There is nothing to distinguish it from 'thinking', which is a quintessential human activity. What is important is the quality of thought.
>
> (p. 161)

We agree with Harvey and Knight that there can be a difference in terms of quality that makes reflective practice more or less useful. Thus reflective practice that uses experience to change ideas as opposed to adding information to existing ideas is of significant value.

However, we do note that, the reflective practitioner, as described by Harvey and Knight, appears to be reflecting *alone* only. Thus in the first extract above the reflective practitioner appears to be having an *internal dialogue* between thinking attaching to actions and the thinking that deals in more abstracted propositional knowledge. We have identified this as application 1: personal reflection in Chapter 7 and we would endorse the danger of such reflection being self-confirming. The exhortation to improve the 'quality of thought' in the third extract above, can do little to protect against self-confirmation. Clearly, if Harvey and Knight are meaning an internal dialogue then their fear of the notion of the reflective practitioner being 'an illusionist's charter' would be well founded.

We emphasize that the idea of a reflective practitioner reflecting in the transformational sense used by Harvey and Knight is one we recognize and endorse and that it can be taught or be made explicit as a tool for development. However, the key notion we are making in our writing is that reflective practice undertaken through reflective dialogue with an other, or others, may promote transformational learning.

Where there is reflective dialogue between colleagues or learners there may also be collusion and this can inhibit them from opening up to experience changes in ideas and action. However, part of the skill in facilitating reflective learning through reflective dialogue is to grapple with that tendency for inter-personal collusion. Moreover, facilitation includes the capacity to give feedback to another person about that which they may be unaware of themselves. If I do receive feedback about that which I am unaware, I now have, at least, a choice. I may resist the one I am not familiar with but I am no longer ignorant of it. We discuss the importance of giving feedback in Chapter 11.

Let us take an example. Harvey and Knight (1996) refer to the need to enable teachers to be able to move from transmittive to transformational conceptions of teaching. If I as a teacher have no notion conceptually that I am transmittive as opposed to being transformative then I will have difficulty moving to the latter. I could be informed of these two conceptions and assert that I fall into the latter category, but in fact, in practice, I am teaching in the former mode. Yet how will I move if I have a belief that it is invalidated in my behaviour? Reflecting on my own may simply endorse my position. Feedback from dialogue with another may at least reveal that what

I am espousing is not happening in practice. I have a choice even though the recognition of the disparity may be painful, and my choice may be transforming my practice.

In encouraging reflective dialogue with others is the issue of the sense of power and powerlessness that can be found and felt in any group (or organizational) setting. The sense of power or powerlessness can be innocent (Baddeley and James, 1991) in that the person or persons may not be aware of how they are being but nevertheless live it. Examples would be: where a group in dialogue is dominated by one person to the exclusion of others; where a man only addresses the other men in a mixed group; or where a group attempt to learn about diversity from the person who is 'different' instead of recognizing that the issue of difference resides with them. Dialogue with others is not neutral. Recognition and making explicit what is happening is important in ensuring that learning is encouraged rather than discouraged and this is primarily the responsibility of the facilitator.

Harvey and Knight cite the teacher engaged in reflective practice for the purposes of professional development, but of course our discussion will equally apply to student learners. Indeed, we noted earlier that the idea of students being reflective practitioners was taken up by Barnett (1992a) when he refers to 'We're all Reflective Practitioners Now' as the title to one of the chapters. Barnett recommends reflective practice to all student learners not just those students engaged in courses leading directly to professional practice. Barnett, in common with Harvey and Knight, takes a similar solitary conception of reflective practice.

The idea of the learner for Barnett (1992a), as reflective practitioner involves four concepts:

1. '*the action*': to be able to make knowledge claims and form their own which can also be stated as being engaged in forms of reasoning
2. '*interpersonal engagement*': being engaged in forms of reasoning is a kind of interpersonal engagement which presupposes a listener, an audience and a critical one at that. The engagement could be in the form of an essay, film, computer programme or tape: 'the student has to understand that her views only have substance provided they can withstand the critical scrutiny by others' (p. 195)
3. '*reflection-in-action*': 'some kind of internal dialogue' of which an essay may be the outcome. 'What is presented on paper is simply the outcome of current stage of the student's reflection-in-action, the reflection occurring during the action of conducting the internal dialogue' (p. 195)
4. '*Knowledge-in-use*': for a student this is essentially all the existing propositional knowledge that she brings to or is exhibiting in a new situation with all that is going on around her, for example the differing voices, that contained in books, journals and other media in contributing to the problem in hand to work through the solution to a satisfactory conclusion be it an essay, project or studio presentation.

The last concept is less easy to adapt from Schön who applied knowledge-in-use in professional practice. Barnett neatly applies it to learners in universities who are engaged in practice in even 'the purest of subjects'. The importance for Barnett is that these notions or concepts used by the reflective practitioner: 'are or should be found in the day-to-day experience of every undergraduate' (p. 196).

Barnett asks what are the implications for engaging in critically reflective practice for the development of the student's critical and reflective abilities. He recognizes that he is only hinting at them in his text (1992a) but argues that there are implications for the content and organization of the curriculum, its design, implementation and the student experience.

Barnett includes the space to enable self-reflection which implies 'significant levels of student autonomy and independence in thought and action'. This in turn implies student responsibility for their own learning. Didactic teaching should be minimized in favour of real interaction between teacher and students and between students themselves (on group exercises).

He concludes by stating:

> Higher learning calls for higher order thinking on the part of the student. Whether engaged in propositional thought or in professional action, students should be enabled to develop the capacity to keep an eye on themselves, and to engage in a critical dialogue with themselves in *all* they think and do . . . it is a reflexive process in which the student interrogates her/his thoughts or actions. The learning outcome to be desired, from *every* student, is that of the reflective practitioner.
>
> (Barnett, 1992a:198, original italics)

Again, although there is a hint of interaction with teachers and other students, the primacy for engaging as a reflective practitioner is the student reflecting alone, albeit critically, and armed with the conceptual understanding of reflective practice. Thus the student 'engages in a critical dialogue with themselves', 'interrogates her/his thoughts or actions'. It is an important but restricted level of reflective practice comparable to Application 1: personal reflection, in Chapter 7.

Barnett's (1997) recent thinking moves on to a more fundamental criticism of reflection and the reflective practitioner. He is now critical of Schön's ideas on reflective practice, as a socially driven concept which may not stimulate real critical reflection. Barnett writes of reflection as a code word masking the hidden agenda of instrumentalism because: 'the student's inner self is constructed more by external agendas . . . than by the student's own personal aspirations, values and hold on the world'. (1997:100)

Reflection as defined above is unlikely to meet the objectives of higher education. However, we are offered a new idea, the concept of a critical being, which we have outlined in Chapter 3, integrating domains of knowledge, self and the world.

The task of higher education is to enable student learners not only to become critical learners in all three domains but:

> calls for nothing less than taking seriously students as persons, as critical persons in the making . . . the student is challenged continually to

make connections between her knowledge, self-understanding and actions at the highest levels of criticality.

(Barnett, 1997:114)

On the basis of Barnett's recent critique of reflection, high levels of criticality in the three domains cannot be achieved by reflection as *he defines it,* and he is right. For the reconstruction of self, the reconstruction of world and the transformatory critique of knowledge he recommends, we need a system of reflection which enables these forms of criticality.

The question for us is what Barnett writes about, namely, *how* a student is to gain high levels of criticality in all three domains, i.e. become a critical being? He recommends a curriculum which: 'has to be one that exposes students to criticality in the three domains and at the highest level in each' (p. 102).

Such a curriculum differs from the current academic model which over-emphasizes critical thinking, the competence model which is focused on performance and also from the solitary version of the reflective practitioner as outlined above. We are proposing an approach which accommodates such a curriculum with one important difference – reflection, which enables the potential for critical transformation.

Self-reflection as described by Barnett, we believe to be a necessary but on its own an insufficient form of reflection for high levels of critical thought, activity and self-transformation. These require dialogue in reflection – what we have termed reflective dialogue in Chapters 4 and 5. The prospect of refashioning traditions and engaging in a transformatory critique (critical levels in the three domains) *without the benefit of interaction with others* is indeed a faint hope. When we bring dialogue into our definition of reflection we can see how possible it is to reach high levels of criticality. We note that the conditions for the balanced curriculum recommended by Barnett, requiring 'quite different pedagogic relationships' (p. 108) are expressed through a discourse of dialogue, that is: 'self, being, becoming, action, *inter*action, knowing, understanding, risk, exploration, emotion, interpretation, judging, insight, courage, exposure, daring, authenticity, collaboration and dialogue' (p. 108, original italics).

Hence our emphasis on dialogue, but more specifically, dialogue that encourages reflection not only about learning in the domains of knowledge, action and self, but reflection on that learning. In this way students begin to embrace the notions of transformatory learning, critically reflective learning, deep learning, that are prescribed in the literature yet which omit the means to achieve such levels of learning.

In this chapter we have sought to explain reflection and reflective practice and how the concept of reflective practice can contribute to critically reflective learning. In Part 2 we relate the requirements for reflection and the concept of reflective practice to current academic practice, as well as to the future of teaching and learning in higher education. We will follow these with the practical means by which reflective dialogue can be engendered for critically reflective learning.

Part 2

Facilitating Learning and Reflective Practice

In Part 2 we convey how reflective practice can be developed, facilitated and utilized by students and staff in enhancing student learning.

In Chapter 6 we address some of the major issues that are the subject of some considerable difference in higher education circles, both in terms of prescriptions about what should be the approach towards teaching and learning and some of the realities of current practice. We move on in Chapters 7 and 8 to offer a detailed approach to reflective practice through reflective dialogue for both teachers and learners. Five structured applications provide a basis for incorporating reflective dialogue into practice, either with colleagues or learners. Teachers may wish to embark directly on reflective dialogue with student learners and therefore use at the outset the framework suggested in Chapter 8. Obviously, the frameworks suggested in these chapters can be modified.

We consider the rationale for facilitation in higher education in Chapter 9, exploring how and why facilitative methods foster learning relationships through intentional dialogue. We discuss the difficulties and benefits of adopting facilitative methods while maintaining subject expertise. In Chapters 10 and 11 we set out the detailed process of facilitation, what a facilitator actually does, and how to enable critically reflective learning.

To achieve clarity of exposition within the confines of a book, we have, particularly in Chapters 7 and 8, endeavoured to be clear in describing the unfolding possibilities for reflective dialogue that can create the conditions for critically reflective learning. An important proviso is necessary which we do allude to in the text. Learning is often a messy process. Teachers and learners may come to this approach to learning with a deal of scepticism and anxiety as well as optimism. Critically reflective learning is necessarily disturbing as well as potentially exciting and exacting. These chapters aim to provide a relatively coherent structure within which to embark on the journey where the relationship between teachers and learners is different from that which may prevail for transmission.

In relation to student learning it is important at an early stage, including the induction process, to lay the bases for creating the more interdependent relationships that are conducive for such learning. There are inevitably, preparatory implications at course design and/or review stage of a course programme in terms of course aims, rationale and implementation flowing from the approaches we are advocating.

In Chapter 6 we highlight the need for preparation for the above, at the course design and review stage of programme development, in terms of professional development, the potential institutional response, and student expectations.

6

Academic Practice and Learning

Our purpose in this chapter is to place our approach to facilitating learning in the institutional context. To this end we examine existing and espoused academic practices in respect of teaching and learning and underline the relevance of our approaches to the purposes of higher education in respect of learning. Following from this is the question of how academic staff can utilize these approaches to maintain their own professional development. For student learners how the approaches towards such learning are assessed is critical to their effectiveness. Finally, we examine the potential response of the institutions themselves.

While it is a comment of its time we could not resist recalling a phrase we came upon in our explorations, by Dewey (Boydston, 1969:301). Although he was mainly concerned with primary and secondary education in the USA, Dewey wrote: 'The higher institutions are freighted with a definite body of tradition.' Here we take 'freighted' to mean laden with a substantial cargo. Higher education represents an extraordinary capacity to extend understanding, knowledge and innovation. However, in respect of the practice relating to teaching and learning the institutions do tend to be freighted with methods that have an unerring continuity and resistance to change. We examine more closely some of the possible reasons for the continuity of the freighted traditions in respect of teaching processes.

Existing practice

We have referred in Chapter 4 to endeavouring to open up the 'black box' of process. Initially, we examine that part of the box which is about academic practice in relation to teaching and learning. We examine aspects of existing practice and prescriptions about recommended future practice.

We have shown in Part 1 that in any teaching and learning situation the teacher will be modelling a process that will affect the relationship between the teacher and the learner. We have claimed that how the teacher engages with students in enabling their learning may affect the latter. We cannot say that teaching causes learning: it may or it may not (Harvey and Knight, 1996). The student could learn despite the interaction. This is true whether there is explicit attention to process by the teacher or not.

We have also noted the tendency for teaching to be dominated by a mode that places emphasis on transmission of knowledge and ideas which is not conducive to critical reflective learning. We examine this aspect later in the chapter.

Nevertheless, process is important in influencing intentional learning. What prevents an apparent resistance to investigating the impact of the very process that is supposed to promote learning? Why is there a tendency to hold back from the exploration of process?

First, there is somehow the idea that teaching and learning is above technique and skill. This is the level of disparagement. We smell elements here of old but still living discriminations. There is the discrimination between those who think and those who do; between the higher realms of the non-vocational against the vocational; the traditional split between theory and practice; between higher order of thought and lower order of doing; amateur and professional; gentlemen versus players. Over the top? Maybe, but technique and skill does tend to get attached to the latter of the couplings.

Secondly, we recognize that part of the reason for the relative inattention to technique and skill is that teaching and the promotion of learning has not rated the significance that is attached to research and recognition in the discipline upon which academic career advance depends. This stance has been questioned by Dearing (1997). It is part of our justification for writing this book that the relationship to learning that is inherent in real scholarship actually promotes the teacher's development in their discipline. It is not a question of either teaching or research. Further, we endorse Boyer's (1990) view that teaching at its best means:

> not only transmitting knowledge but *transforming* and *extending* it as well . . . In the end, inspired teaching keeps the flame of scholarship alive. Almost all successful academics give credit to creative teachers – those mentors who defined their work so compellingly that it became for them, a lifetime challenge. Without the teaching function, the continuity of knowledge will be broken and the store of human knowledge dangerously diminished.
>
> (p. 24, original italics)

Thirdly, we can look to the resistance to teaching as professional practice in higher education compared with any other professions where qualification is a prerequisite. Universities are often the fundamental arbiters of whether someone shall be able to pursue practice as in the health professions, accountancy, law and social work. Yet being professional as a teacher in higher education has somehow not been necessary and with it the attendant skills, techniques that would be a part of the wider issues about the nature of teaching and learning just as skill and technique is part of being a surgeon and advocate in medicine and law.

Fourthly, there is the teacher who is unaware of process or the potential relationship between teaching and learning and the requirements for learning that may be reflective. Being unaware of process does not mean that the teacher is not using technique or skill in her interaction with student learners. The teacher may be unaware, or even partially aware of process, but in her teaching will, perforce, be using some *form* of interaction that will use technique and skill. That the 'technique and skill' is not defined or articulated is not the point here. The fact is that technique and skill is being used.

Let us make explicit that which has remained or can remain implicit. In any interaction in a teaching and learning context, technique and skill will be evident. Technique and skill is part of the practice of teaching in higher education. If we wish to create the conditions for critical and reflective learning then we cannot avoid investigating what processes are conducive or less conducive to the encouragement of that level of learning. Making what happens in the interaction transparent is part of the reflective process.

Fifthly, if there is an articulation and examination of techniques or skills, they tend to be taken to mean 'low' level attributes such as how to use an overhead projector or a flip chart and denote again some disparagement that prevents deeper examination. A version of this is highlighted by Harvey and Knight (1996) who report that the teacher preferred by students is one who, when appropriate, is:

audible, writes legibly and uses technology; who is knowledgeable, well prepared and who alerts learners to the structure of the teaching session; who uses varied techniques; who is up to date in the field; who provides support material when necessary, and who does likewise with bibliographic advice; who is punctual and reliable; and who is clear.

(p. 151)

These are basic techniques which we take as givens. If that was all teaching was about at this level it would be an indictment. But as Harvey and Knight also point out, these techniques could be utilized yet do little to promote even a surface understanding let alone deep approaches to learning. Such techniques may be necessary, they are hardly sufficient.

Sixthly, teachers do often use higher level techniques and skills that promote reflective dialogue such as, questioning, summarizing or giving feedback. However, they may remain unarticulated or ignored as processes and form part the unexamined and unreflected practice of teachers in higher education (see Chapters 10 and 11).

In summary, examination of process, technique and skill may not surface but are still present and having unknown and unknowable effects on learning. We could adopt the stance which says that students learn anyway or despite their interactions with their teachers. We suggest that route is a cul-de-sac for the cynical.

Espoused practice

In considering espoused forms of teaching and learning, we encounter the terms, lifelong learning, critically reflective learning and transformational learning. In much of the writing about learning in higher education there is clear attention to the nature of learning and what learning should be for in contemporary societies. However, there is often a holding back, which may not be intentional, about how such learning should be attained. It is as if the learning will be achieved by exhortation to the best in academic life and the qualities inherent in the 'good' tutorial or lecture (though the latter does appear to be increasingly pressed to the margin in usefulness in contributing to learning). Failure to unpack what may be involved in the process of facilitating learning is more likely to mean that we are thus stuck with laudable and prescriptive statements about what is good learning without being able to address how such learning can be engendered.

The holding back is typified by Knapper and Cropley (1991) who in recognizing the need for universities to respond to changing needs of lifelong learners offer numerous examples of changes that could be made to teaching methods. They assert:

> Transforming universities and colleges to a system that will promote lifelong education, however, will require the adoption of a common goal that focuses on the *process* of learning instead of just the content.
>
> (p. 160)

Their examples of changes in teaching methods are helpful in pointing to new directions and ways of relating with students, but little attention is paid to unravelling the processes by which teachers and learners relate, in order to promote lifelong learning.

Barnett's latest writing (1997) places the student learning experience at the forefront of a university's purpose in the emphasis he gives to the idea of the student embodying critical thought, critical being and critical action. Attending to the process of how teachers and students can facilitate such learning is crucial to fulfilling this wider definition of a university's role.

When we come to some of the conditions that should reside in the teacher and in the learner, which Barnett advocates for critically reflective learning, sophisticated qualities, techniques and skills are implicit in the text. A recent example is to be found in Barnett (1997).

> The educator's task, for a critical consciousness, is to set up an educational framework in which students can make their *own* structured explorations, testing their ideas in the critical company of each other. This is a highly structured process, in which the students are subject not only to the local rules of the particular discipline but also to the general rules of rational discourse as such. Turn-taking, acute listening, respect for the other's point of view, expression of one's ideas in ways that are appropriate to the context, and even the injection of humour:

the critical consciousness can be too serious for its own good. More than that, there would have to be elements of genuine openness such that students can feel that their own voice and their own existential claims matter. This means that the lecturer's own position can and will be challenged.

(Barnett, 1997:110, original italics)

This strongly felt statement does reflect reality on occasion when the conditions are there. We will not assert that such a scenario does not happen now. It does and is often more intuitive than orchestrated. As Barnett is suggesting it is rare but will be necessary if universities are to serve their students well in future. But let's examine the statement more closely.

Our purpose here is to go behind the detailed phrases and ask what is necessary for the conditions Barnett advocates, to prevail. We are suggesting that more than exhortation is required. We break down the paragraph.

'set up an educational framework for students to make their *own* structured explorations'

The teacher creates the framework that enables students to test their ideas with each other, critically, whether with the educator or not. What are the appropriate conditions for this framework to happen so that the students *feel* safe to take risks and receive feedback on their work in a way that does not leave them personally attacked yet for a time, perhaps, be dissembled about their way of seeing the world?

'subject not only to the rules of the particular discipline but also to the general rules of rational discourse'

This is the arena in which the teacher is more likely to be imbued and be able to inculcate the format appropriate to the discipline but the wider general rules are not necessarily explicit and may not be part of the academic's discipline. Examination of the term, 'rational discourse' could also imply 'holding forth' rather than endeavouring to achieve 'connected knowing' (Chapter 3).

'turn-taking'

Obvious, yes, but in reality we know that differences between students may not be recognized by the educator or students, and that perceptions exist which prevent this recognition so that some voices may be heard more than others.

'acute listening'

What does it mean to acutely listen and how do we as educators and learners know when it is happening and how do we create the conditions collectively for it to happen?

'respect for the other's point of view'

Agreed, but how many readers have been in situations as student learners where to speak is to be subject to verbal annihilation?

'there would have to be elements of genuine openness . . .'

Openness requires a willingness to disclose. How are conditions of genuine openness to be created and maintained?

'. . . such that students can feel that their own voice and their own existential claims matter.'

We take this to mean that students can feel heard and enabled to struggle with their own meanings and emergent constructed meanings. Again the question is how to create the conditions for this to happen.

Thus by taking the phrases from a significant paragraph, we are demonstrating that there is more to the phrases than is immediately apparent. We are not suggesting that Barnett is not aware of these underlying matters. What is apparent is that Barnett does not attend to the requirements to make the outcomes desired for the student to happen.

In parenthesis, we could add a further task that the educator could engage in which incidentally makes our point about the significance of process and how best to facilitate process so that in turn it promotes critically reflective learning. In addition to creating the framework for students' own structured explorations, the educator should enable them to reflect on the framework after some activity within the framework. The students thus reflect upon their process and action. When students return to a 'revised' framework they will be able during the subsequent action, to reflect-in-action. To give an example, students may have been using closed questions when open questions would have been more appropriate and this was drawn out and reflected on after the event. Returning to the framework or event, the students can then apply this understanding while they and others proceed in the action. They are able to reflect-in-action.

Barnett (1997) acknowledges that for academics 'to live out their own identities fully and utterly', that they 'reveal themselves as the hard-pressed inquirers that they are'. We have alluded to this in that academics as teachers tend to hide the struggle they are engaged in, in relation to their chosen discipline and its attendant dilemmas. Barnett wishes that academics would give of themselves as persons and engage in critical action and place themselves in a situation not unlike that for the student. This process calls both for: 'courage, integrity, and authenticity on the one hand, and the qualities of intersubjective patience, sensitivity, respect and reciprocity on the other' (p. 110).

Moreover, the educational process has to become uncertain for there is risk; relationships are less fixed between teachers and learners if the latter are: 'to have the space genuinely to form their own critical evaluations and to engage in critical acts' (p. 110).

But with this commendable uncertainty comes further difficulty for academics in that Barnett exhorts them to enable the student to use their educational experience to acquire dispositions of critical thinking to sustain them beyond the immediate framework of their course programmes. In doing that the student will in return be able to interrogate the very framework that they have lodged themselves in for their period in higher education. What place then the framework in which the academic has lodged her and himself?

Lastly, the educator's role will be to ensure that the curriculum requires real space for students to develop as critical persons. It is a curriculum that asks students:

> to take on their own responsibilities for their own continuing explorations ... an existential space in which students can, interactively, form their own critical evaluations from this perspective or that without any sense of intimidation or of being ruled offside.

> (p. 112)

Barnett's commentary, suggests that getting students embarked on the road to a critical consciousness, 'lies in academics avoiding concepts of teaching and learning as such', setting aside the conventional roles of teacher and student and 'abandoning teaching as such'. We agree that new relationships will emerge between academics and learners when the interactions take different forms, struggles in learning become shared, uncertainty becomes more likely to prevail and roles become less rigidly adhered to. The relationships will change, but this is not to deny some structure and process in which the emergent relationships can form. Intuitive as academics are, enabling students to develop their own critical stances in a 'non-threatening' environment, that sustain them beyond in the future careers will not just happen by exhortation.

We endorse Barnett's prescriptions, but by attending explicitly to the process for critically reflective learning, we wish to make that learning more likely to happen.

Harvey and Knight (1996) set out techniques that can encourage the 'esteemed deep approaches to learning' within individual courses and distinguish these from those required for a good lecture. They highlight and we paraphrase:

- depth over breadth – rather than coverage which results in coping strategies on the part of students
- keep questions, concepts, procedures and principles to the fore: information is valuable only in relation to them
- emphasize mental activity and involvement on the part of the student
- use a variety of teaching-and-learning techniques and tasks
- maximize student choice as far as is consistent with the development of principles, procedures, concepts and questions in the content area
- feedback from the tutor to students, particularly that associated with assessment, and from students to tutor.

While we can endorse these techniques as necessary for encouraging deep rather than surface learning we could say that a teacher employing them may not be effective if she is not aware of how to use them. For example, questioning and feedback skills are crucial in the repertoire of the teacher, particularly at this level, and are a fundamental part of effective facilitation. However, they can be used ineffectually in a way that would not, for example encourage the creation of the framework that Barnett would wish to have for critically reflective learning.

Harvey and Knight link these techniques for good teaching that support deep approaches to learning with the notion of 'teaching skill'. The term is not to be associated with the personal qualities of the teacher that are sometimes loosely identified in such phrases as 'respecting students' and 'sharing enthusiasm and making laboratory work enjoyable for students'. Such terms are bland and meaningless and less than useful for identifying effectiveness in teaching. We use the term skill in relation to a specific technique that a teacher employs to encourage reflective learning. Skill relates to the ability to use the technique. However, technique and skill are only useful in the context of a real understanding of process and relationships appropriate to creating the encouragement of learning. Teachers will utilize process as part of their reflection-in-action and reflection on action to enhance the opportunities for learners and to reflect upon their own practice.

In reviewing existing and espoused academic practice we have endeavoured to highlight the need for attention to process and the detail within process, considered in other parts of the book necessary for the lifelong, transformational or critically reflective learning that is espoused.

Academic beliefs

Finally, within espoused practice for such learning will reside academics' beliefs about their role as teachers. A mode of teaching that places emphasis on transmission of knowledge and ideas is not conducive to critical reflective learning.

Harvey and Knight (1996) suggest that good teaching is that which: 'depends upon academic staff seeing their role as facilitators of transformational learning, not as merely purveyors of data' (op cit.:155).

They cite Trigwell (1995) in stating that if a teacher sees their role primarily in terms of the latter, as transmitters of knowledge, then they may well dwell on activities that lack transformative power (for the student). We agree with this. We would add that a teacher may espouse transformational learning, but their practice may not reflect the intent.

Indeed, Dearing (1997) endorses this view based on recent research:

Despite the changes in the learning environment, teaching methods do not appear to have changed considerably . . . Initial findings from research suggest that many staff still see teaching primarily in terms of transmission of information, mainly through lectures. There are many teachers who are ready to adopt different methods of teaching as circumstances change, but others find change hard to accept and *do not reflect much on their teaching* or consider the basis of good teaching practice.

(para 8.14, pp. 116–17, italics added)

As we advocate in this book, developing the experience of reflective practice in staff will enable teachers to reflect on their teaching and raise the possibility of alternative purposes of using teaching for transformative learning as well as being the basis for promoting critical reflective learning in student learners.

Professional development

Here we address the contribution our approach to learning may have in supporting the professional development of academic staff. To recapitulate briefly , we have put forward the idea that by engaging learners in reflective dialogue on their practice (whatever form that practice may take in the journey through higher education) we encourage critically reflective learning. In order to be able to promote the idea, practice and process of reflective learning, staff will necessarily engage in and model those ideas, practices and processes that are conducive to such learning.

Academic staff, by facilitating reflective practice have one of the key tools for their own learning and development. As teachers adopt an approach that promotes the kind of learning that is envisaged as appropriate to learners in higher education they will have within that approach a basis for their own continuing professional development. Thus, intrinsic to their role as teachers, lies the means for their own development. This is not a 'bolt-on' staff development activity that may have some potential relevance to a teacher's practice. Reflecting directly on professional practice is a core element of a teacher's work.

Professional development as we envisage it can happen in a number of ways.

First, when adopted by teachers, the facilitative approach to reflective practice places them in a more open stance towards the learning context. When in expert transmitting stance the teacher is in potentially a one-way relationship *to* the learners. When in tranformational stance using reflective dialogue the teacher is potentially in a two-way relationship *with* the learners. Thus teachers are more open to the situation having a potentiality for learning for themselves as well as the student.

Secondly, in adopting the facilitative approach to reflective practice we are recommending that teachers may initially wish to engage in reflective practice with colleagues in order to familiarize themselves with the approach. We are suggesting that teachers take examples of *their* practice to the reflective dialogue. Their practice could be about their teaching, research, scholarly activity and course design. Within this second approach to development we have the basis for colleague-to-colleague support and challenge.

Our point here is that developmental activity is a continuing one that is an integral part of their work as professional academics.

Thirdly, for development to be more formalized, particularly with the advent and requirement for staff development reviews, teachers will have longer term aims they may wish to achieve. By facilitating reflective dialogue between teachers each have a vehicle for working on and through their developmental aims using pair work with a colleague. Teachers may choose to pursue their development through supervision, mentoring (Chapters 13 and 14) or group based work using action learning (Chapter 12).

Thus in addition to development being continuous, integral and dovetailed to the teacher's needs it is undertaken with others and not all in isolation. The potentiality for self-collusion is less though the danger of mutual collusion should not be ignored.

As we suggest in Chapters 5 and 7, such dialogue whether in pairs or in groups involves not only reflection on the improvement of practice but also potentially reframing practice to overcome the tendency to become professionally rigid and habit struck. A number of writers attest to the fact that experience does not necessarily equal learning (Boyatzis *et al.*, 1995; McGill and Beaty, 1995). The tendency to get into habits that we come to live by is inevitable. We can tend to be collusive with ourselves. The opportunity to engage with others in reflecting on our practice can limit the tendency to take too much for granted and at worst to avoid atrophy.

There is a double edge here. We cannot simply recommend critically reflective learning and transformational learning to student learners without aiming to be such learners ourselves. Thus in reflecting on our own practice we do this in the recognition that it is about, not only our meanings we give to knowledge, but also about our selves and our actions, not merely instrumentally, but also critically in being able to envisage possibilities of other understandings, self and action that are not yet extant.

Assessing critically reflective learning

We start from the Latin root of the word assessment: 'to sit beside'. This classical meaning reflects the values being promoted in critically reflective learning as collaborative rather than inspectorial. In the spirit of sitting beside a learner we begin with their account of their learning.

If critically reflective learning has occurred then the first person to know about this is the learner. When his learning is communicated to others in writing or verbally, this is known as 'self-report'. When others, possibly fellow students or tutors, report on their observations or experience of the learner to a third party, this is known as 'other-report'. Clearly, the presence of other-report supports self-report, and, if added to by a presumed independent other, e.g. the tutor, then the well-known reliability of 'triangulation' is achieved.

Whether criterion or norm-based methods are used, the assessment of reflection, either formative or summative, will include a judgement about the outcome, i.e. the quality of learning which emerges, and this will be very much embedded in the traditions of a given discipline. For instance, evidence of critically reflective learning in philosophy will require students to have not only understood and critiqued key aspects of philosophy, but also will reveal that students have begun to question the paradigmatic basis of the discipline itself, as well as some record of their reflective journey to that point.

The existing allocation of a distinction grade, or first class, to a student's piece of work, is likely to indicate that some of the above is present, that is, there is some evidence of critically reflective learning, and we acknowledge that teachers have, consciously or unconsciously, registered this in their grading of students.

While a written assignment may provide the vehicle for such questioning, it is not possible to record in an essay, presented once, the process of dialogue whereby a student may grapple with an issue, share it with others, and come to some joint understanding of a concept or difficulty. What cannot be recorded in such an assignment is the *relationship* which evolves between learners, teachers and the material with which they are involved.

To provide evidence of the learning relationship and the learning journey, 'other-reports' are essential, therefore evidence from fellow-students is needed. This is not peer-assessment, because students do not judge each other, but they are a source of information about process, the learning process revealed in reflective dialogue. Opportunities for dialogue may be limited to the reviewer of a learning contract and tutor, and this provides evidence from two sources. However if students are encouraged to dialogue with several colleagues as part of the developmental process, then there is potential evidence from a number of sources.

Clearly if reflection is part of the overall assessment strategy it is part of a whole, which must also address the body of knowledge related to the discipline concerned. Theoretical understanding has traditionally been assessed through an academic essay, report or examination, and this will continue to be necessary. The assessment of *the process* of reflection, reflective dialogue and critically reflective learning will need to be addressed differently. Where personal reflection is concerned, self-report is the only evidence, and if assessment of reflection on learning is required, the assessment strategy may need to be revised to value self-reports of reflection on learning. Thus the spectre of unreliability re-emerges, as self-report is assumed to contain implicit bias in favour, usually, of the reporter. When reflective dialogue is present other reports are possible, e.g. the records of those involved in triad reflective dialogues (see Chapter 8 for details). For some teachers in higher education such reports may be biased in favour of the student being assessed. Additionally, tutor accounts of process reviews may incorporate the group's reflection on its learning (see Application 5, Chapter 8).

How can assessment address both the evidence of critically reflective learning, in terms of outcome within the subject discipline, as well as the process of the student's reflection, the reflective learning process? The assessment strategy seeks to ascertain that critically reflective learning has occurred in terms of both outcome and process, and will therefore include:

1. A way of identifying critically reflective learning in terms of outcomes within the subject discipline.
2. A way to ascertain that reflective dialogue has taken place (at least personal, but ideally with others).
3. A way to establish that there is evidence of the learner's participation in that dialogue.
4. A way to identify evidence of a developmental process over time, regardless of the start or end point.
5. A way to ascertain that there is evidence that a process review has taken place, enabling the student to take away an understanding of the learning process.

Assessment of the reflective process can draw on two sources:

1. self-report, that is, the learner's own account, in the form of a reflective document which may recount either, internal (personal dialogue) or dialogue-with-others
2. other-report, that is, accounts by others of the learner's reflective activity, in the form of written excerpts of dialogue-with-others.

The issue of confidentiality in self-report has been addressed in recent programmes with which we have been involved. An account of a reflective and critical learning journey is likely to be sensitive and may include material which is highly personal, which individual learners may prefer to keep entirely private, or at least control who reads the material. We offer a brief excerpt in Box 6.1 from guidance offered to masters students in compiling a learning portfolio where private learning journals are used as a basis for self report material, designed for assessment:

Box 6.1   Learning log, diary or journal: a private document (not for assessment)

A learning log, diary or journal is a continuous record, compiled privately, *which will not be assessed*, of your experience as a learner throughout a module or programme. You will be able to draw on this private record for written assignments in particular modules (e.g. the personal learning portfolio) which are likely to incorporate extracts from this *private* record.

Your learning diary is therefore:

(a) private and confidential
(b) about you rather than others (except where interaction with others forms part of the learning process, e.g. group dynamics)
(c) a place for reflective reporting
(d) a vehicle for learning.

Personal learning portfolio: a public document (intended for assessment)

This is a compilation of learning intentions, accounts of learning activities, learning outcomes, records of reflective dialogues. It includes evidence from a variety of sources including your *private learning journal/diary/log*, and, most important of all, a reflective document detailing your learning process. The personal learning portfolio, while confidential to you, is intended for assessment, and therefore you will need to consider what to include/exclude and adopt a style which is appropriate for others to read who may not have witnessed the event or process.

A typical assessment strategy for a course or module which incorporates elements of reflection might include:

1. An account of the theoretical basis of the field of study concerned, through the usual medium of essay, report or examination. Such an assignment would demand an intellectual critique of the material, e.g. analysis of the social and political context for a given historical orientation, a critique which would be likely to appear as the material element in reflective dialogues. The outcomes of reflective dialogues could be expected to appear in traditional modes of assessment, and a criterion to this effect would be articulated, very much in the way teachers demand some evidence in written work that students have, not only reproduced and transformed the subject material, but that the student's orientation towards it has also been transformed.
2. Evidence of developmental learning through reviewer reports, based on learning contracts, at two or more assessment points indicating the learner's journey in relation to 1. For information on learning contracts and learning contract reviews we refer readers to Anderson *et al.* (1996). Reviewer reports may incorporate records of meetings for reflective dialogue, accounts of the learner's reflective journey, seen through the eyes of her reviewer, as well as formal evidence of the review process relating to learning contracts.
3. Evidence of reflective learning through the contents of a learning portfolio, which may contain one or more of the following items:

   • learning contract
   • learning review
   • review records

- reflective document
- reviewer reports (including accounts of reflective dialogue)
- tutor accounts of reflective dialogue
- peer accounts of reflective dialogue

with the reflective document and reviewer reports as a minimum for evidence of reflective dialogue. Accounts of reflective dialogues should relate to the reflective process for the learner concerned, i.e. an account of the learner's reflective activity, where the learner engaged in reflection on their learning, ideally through dialogue with others.

In summary, then, an assessment system which addresses critically reflective learning should do so in terms of both outcome and process. Assessment strategies are likely to include traditional mediums to assess the outcome of reflection, and also mediums which provide evidence of reflective activity as well as some detail of the reflective journey. Learning outcomes in criterion-referenced assessment schemes should relate to the evidence for critically reflective learning in both theoretical or 'content' evidence and 'reflective' evidence, some of which we have described above.

The response of the institution

How can institutions of higher education respond to a radical departure from much prevailing practice, even though, there are moves in this direction?

We are aware of the danger of providing universalist suggestions and blueprints as to how an institution should respond to the ideas, values and approaches to facilitating learning represented here. Universities and colleges of higher education are rightly, not susceptible to such centralized impositions, particularly in relation to learning. Secondly, even if there were an attempt to impose such ideas they would fail. Thirdly, top-down instrumental approaches are out of kilter with the values held by academic staff and by ourselves. Such approaches are associated with outdated notions of controlling and imposition.

We are also aware of the risk to the lone enthusiast who endeavours to bring about change amidst a sea of sceptical resistance. Tacking reflective dialogue on to one module or subject of an interrelated programme or course that may be primarily transmissional in nature will no doubt meet resistance by learners and appear tangential and incongruent.

Our approach is to advocate that any innovation that takes place is underpinned by a change in the approach to learning that is adopted in the design of courses and programmes. Therefore we are asserting that to practice what is espoused here is to adopt a stance of seeking support in association with others who will be potentially involved in developing reflective practice for staff. For example, if the ideas for facilitating reflective practice are being considered for a particular course – as, say, a pilot for other courses – then those who are to be involved in the outcomes of the process of design and implementation of the change in approach should be involved in that process. Such an approach will recognize a variety of starting points, so that meaning and understandings about transformational learning are appreciated conceptually alongside beliefs and potential action. As other writers have demonstrated this is not an easy journey.

There are many entry points to moving along the transformational journey that we can highlight:

- Course design and implementation. In reviewing or initiating a new programme, course teams can aim to promote transformational learning at the design stage and follow through the development of the programme attending to the values, processes and methods advocated, so that significance is given to how such learning can be achieved.
- Professional development that is supported by reflective practice can be initiated by staff themselves grouping together to support each person's continuing development. More formally, this process can be initiated at department, faculty (here defined in structural terms) levels or by staff/educational development units.
- Accreditation programmes for new and existing staff where the programme promotes values and practice appropriate to encouraging critical reflective learning in the teacher and later for students.

Space and the learning environment

Critical to bringing about change in higher education institutions, apart from some of the value issues we have reviewed in Chapters 3 and above, are two fundamental issues about space: time space and physical space both of which can enhance or be to the detriment of learning.

Physical space

The first, physical space may seem a banal issue to raise. However, we cannot underrate the rigidity with which staff and students frequently regard the use of space.

Most institutions of higher education are equipped to utilize large spaces to support mass lectures in tiered theatres or large rooms. Space is designed for transmission of content mainly by monologue to listeners who attempt to make a record that is meaningful for them. Space for dialogue requires different space needs. The focus for dialogue moves from plenary to small groups and back to plenary. The emphasis is on manoeuvrability and flexibility – moveable chairs. Use of rooms should enable teachers to ask themselves what is the appropriate arrangement for facilitating reflective dialogue for the number of students and to be able to make the changes necessary quickly. There is also a tendency for teachers and students, on entry to a teaching space, to take the existing arrangement of furniture as a given.

With small groups of students a circle of chairs is appropriate for plenary reflective dialogue. In the forms of dialogue we are suggesting in subsequent chapters where participants are working in small groups of three, the facilitator can make maximum use of a space and ensure maximum space between small groups. Flexible and easy movement of chairs is a premium. Because the emphasis moves from transmission of information to dialogue, the need for desks is unnecessary. Time will be allocated for students to make a personal record of the outcomes of their dialogues but this will not require the design necessary for prolonged transmission.

Time space

Many organizations in which people work have a culture in which time is rarely available for reflection, particularly with others. By this we mean that there are imperatives to do, act, rush. To take time out for reflection, particularly with others is overtly, or more likely, covertly frowned upon. Universities, formally at least, are supposed to be organized to provide that time space to reflect. Yet even with that 'space' in universities, time for reflection may not be taken up because the imperative is the pressure to transmit knowledge rather than reflection on knowledge, self and practice and the related conditions for encouraging transformational learning. This position may well be endorsed by student conceptions of what properly constitutes teaching and learning for students may well endorse transmission as the legitimate format.

Engaging in reflective dialogue creates a different learning climate with those involved. It is unlike ordinary meetings where there may be detachment and varying degrees of involvement. If reflective dialogue is happening effectively all are really engaged. There will be an intensity of listening and contributions, where the endeavour is to create and challenge meanings and understanding, where each person is attending to the issue of the moment. Concentration is high and prolonged. The pace of the dialogue may be quite slow, there will be silence to await response or consideration. In contrast, where the emphasis is upon transmission the speed of delivery tends to be greater and, of course, one sided and more potentially surface in impact. In reflective dialogue, this slower pace and the shared time space becomes a means, potentially to reach meaning and understanding that goes beyond the surface to where those in dialogue really are and who are searching and truly struggling. Once connection is made, then movement in meaning can be very rapid or slow. The key is that the aim is connection between those engaged in the dialogue through the relationship that is created and being created. In such conditions paradigm shifts are possible. In conditions such as these we often have comments like: 'this is the only occasion in my work when I really have the time to think' or 'I don't think I have been really listened to with such intensity before'.

It is not just a question of reviewing existing work loads and reducing the time spent in formal lecture modes in order to provide time for reflective dialogue. The time space found for reflective dialogue tends to create a different quality in how that space is used.

Dearing (1997) suggested that learning at the level appropriate to higher education requires that students have the: 'opportunity to engage in "learning conversations" with staff and other students in order to understand and be able to use new concepts in a particular field' (para 8.6, p. 115). Such conversations are not closely defined but require the kind of time space for teachers and learners we have identified. Indeed, in justifying more attention to teaching and learning in the future they recommend innovative teaching strategies that promote students' learning.

In directly addressing the contemporary learning process Dearing asserts that teachers will have to plan for learning and this means 'designing the forms of instruction' which support learning is as important as the content of the programmes' (para 8.13, p. 116). They go further in recognizing that institutions will have to devise effective strategies to enable students to be effective learners, able to learn how they learn, to be effective lifelong learners.

Dearing goes directly to the time space issue when he suggests that all institutions encourage staff to plan for the learning time of the student by making 'planning for learning' an explicit responsibility of heads of departments, modifying staff contact time to include that time spent in support of student learning, considering how students can become active participants in the learning process and creating opportunities for teachers to examine and evaluate their teaching methods.

Thus though not unravelling alternative approaches to learning Dearing does grasp the need to shift the use of time towards the learning needs of students despite the pressure on resources. We wish to make an important corollary here. There is much emphasis on the use of technology to enable student learning that can be dovetailed to the learner's needs. This is particularly valid for the acquisition of material that may otherwise be transmitted in lectures. However, current technology is not yet a substitute for critically reflective learning that is achieved through reflective dialogue with others.

In the next two chapters we create the setting for reflective dialogue to take place, initially with teachers, then for students. This is followed in Chapter 9 with consideration of teachers undertaking a facilitative role that is conducive to reflective dialogue and critically reflective learning.

7

Developing Reflective Practice: The Teacher Using Reflective Dialogue with Colleagues

In order to facilitate learning teachers need to develop two aspects of their role as facilitators of learning. First, the ability to engage in reflective practice; and secondly, the facilitation skills necessary to enable others to engage in reflective practice, considered in later Chapters (9, 10 and 11). This chapter and Chapter 8 are designed to support teachers and learners in creating the conditions for critically reflective learning. This is based on the idea that effective modelling of reflective practice through reflective dialogue, by teachers, is a key to promoting effective learning in student learners. In Chapter 8 we convey how the teacher can then facilitate student learners to engage in reflective practice through reflective dialogue. We will finally demonstrate how the student learner, through reflective dialogue with colleague students, can become self-facilitating to support that reflection engendered by the teacher.

Our purpose in this chapter is to begin creating a structured means for a teacher in higher education to develop reflective practice in collaboration with colleagues. Although it is entirely possible for teachers to engage with colleagues informally, by following the 'applications' we outline below, a structured approach is likely to enable teachers to adopt the 'habits' of reflective practice, using the designated space and time in university life for scholarly and pedagogic development. We offer three applications of reflective practice. These are followed by a fourth application, a workshop format, where teachers skilled in reflective practice may facilitate other teachers to engage in reflective practice.

The teacher engaging in reflective practice

Each application represents a development on the previous application. Teachers may key into any of the applications depending upon commitments, time and inclination while recognizing that critical reflective practice is more likely to be achieved in the later applications.

  I Personal reflection
 II Reflective dialogue with another colleague – telling the story
III Reflective dialogue with another colleague – being part of the story
IV Reflective dialogue with other colleagues: enabling the development of reflective practice

The applications move from personal 'alone' reflection, Application I, through varying levels of involvement with other professional colleagues in dialogue. In Application II a teacher reflects *after* an event on her practice with a colleague. In Application III a teacher reflects with a colleague before, 'with' and after an event with her colleague. Application IV describes a teacher/facilitator enabling the development of reflective practice for a group of colleagues in a workshop format.

We will take as our basic example, a teacher in higher education, preparing for a lecture with students. The reason for this choice is that the lecture is the most typical practice for teachers in higher education. It is what we commonly do. Moreover, it requires some engagement with others (student learners) and usually has intended outcomes. For readers who have followed our critique of transmission approaches (in favour of transformatory learning) this may seem an apparent contradiction. Our choice is intentional. The lecture format is familiar territory which will provide the basis for reflective dialogue with another colleague. The reflective learning about the lecture format is the real material outcome of the engagement and there may well be useful outcomes for future lectures. Such a process offers potential benefits to the teacher as learner!

Application I: personal reflection

We will start with reflection engaged in by the teacher as shown in Figure 7.1. This first application of reflection we refer to as personal reflection.[1] We have elsewhere suggested the limited value of reflection on practice being undertaken by the individual reflecting in isolation. However, there is value in reflecting privately upon my practice. I can attend to what I intend to do in the lecture, then I can do it and subsequently take time to reflect upon it afterwards. This we would refer to as personal reflection on action after the event. I, as teacher, will endeavour to consider the content of what I have taught, the impact I think it may have had on the students, and whether what I intended actually happened. I may also attend to *how* I intended to teach the content and how it actually worked out. I may also have had some feelings before, during and after the event.

Thus I may, privately before and after the event, reflect internally upon the cognitive (the content), the conative (the action or doing – the how, or the process as well) and the affective (how I felt) aspects of the lecture as shown in Figure 7.1.

Figure 7.1   Application I: personal reflection

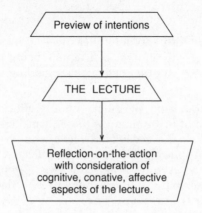

During the lecture I may have taken account of student behaviour during the session and afterwards via their verbal and non-verbal accounts, actions and behaviour. In addition I will not have ignored past experiences of mine and those of current and past students. We could add other factors that impact upon the session: teachers in higher education who have been 'one lecture ahead' of the students and the feelings that engenders; feeling unconfident with the subject matter; feeling over-confident with the subject matter and frustrated with students who are 'failing to grasp' the subject; using overhead transparencies and assuming the students can read them only to turn round and find the transparency is half off the screen. We could all add more no doubt!

All the above reflection is valuable to the teacher who is sensitive to her professional work. Indeed, the professional teacher will engage in reflection in action (see Chapter 5) during the event as practice is an organic activity with which the professional will interact in order to make the activity of value to the student.

The effect of all the above is that the teacher will develop her practice by reflecting on action against the parameters the teacher sets herself. Thus enhancement of practice occurs. New ideas on practice, comments made by colleagues, experience of staff development, reading of specialist journals, may also, given our curious teacher, add to her repertoire.

What are the limitations of this approach? As well as being enlarging of our repertoire, it may also be containing. To borrow and adapt Habermas (1974) on this: personal reflection requires the detachment on the part of self to look at another part of self. In this Herculean task there is a danger of self-deception (McGill and Beaty, 1995).

Let us examine self-deception more closely. There is what I, as, a professional teacher am conscious of yet wish to resist. For example, I may have a real fear that if I do not stick closely to what I am trying to 'get over' in the lecture, I may not cover it in time. Thus, I discourage questions or interaction on the part of the students. Reflection on my action after the event may still endorse my original position – getting through the syllabus is of prime importance. However, there may be self-deception of which I am unaware. I may not be aware that I have an unacknowledged fear of losing control in the session if student interaction happens. I may, however, only articulate this to myself in terms of concerns about time.

The question is how do I examine the overt and covert limitations on my practice through personal reflection? I am likely to deal with that of which I am aware, while by definition, neglecting that of which I am unaware. Thus some of the 'black box' (Chapter 4) about my own process may remain unknown, unexamined and therefore unexplored. Hence dialogue with others becomes important.

Application II: reflective dialogue – telling the story

Here we enter into reflection on practice as shown in Figure 7.2.

Figure 7.2 Application II: reflective dialogue – telling the story

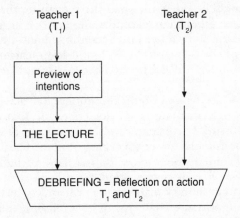

My self-reflection is supported and supplemented by dialogue with others such as a professional colleague, preferably chosen by me, *after* the lecture, shown as a debriefing in Figure 7.2.

Recalling the session after the event with another colleague will add to the potentiality for reflection over and above that undertaken on my own. This post-event dialogue will be useful as a colleague may well ask questions that I had not or would not have thought of. The key here is that structured discussion with a colleague may reveal some of the reasons why I screen out certain behaviours and actions. For example, a colleague may be able to help me after describing the session as I experienced it, to explain, through clarification and questions, what it is that makes me so concerned with the time factor related to 'getting through the syllabus'. Such questions may include: 'How might you ensure that the students get through the syllabus?' (based upon the reported anxiety about getting through the syllabus). This question is designed to help me, the teacher, to improve my practice within my existing framework or model of teaching/learning. This we have described in Chapter 3 as single-loop learning and we maintain is legitimate in enhancing practice within an existing paradigm.

To explain the next aspect of reflective dialogue promoting critically reflective learning we need to move to the third person from the above description in the first person.

Reflective dialogue which leads to critically reflective learning or double-loop learning is likely to include challenging questions to the teacher as follows: 'What do you think stopped the students asking you questions when they were invited to do so?' (following reporting by the teacher that the students were unresponsive).

The question may elicit the teacher's fear of student participation in a lecture situation and the resulting dialogue with her colleague may generate excitement as she considers alternative formats. This question has the potential to engage the teacher in an exploration of the lecture process which goes beyond her existing understanding of that process. For example, such a dialogue could be the point when she recognizes that the interaction with students can be other than transmission. Here we have the beginnings of potential paradigm shift in her understanding about the teaching/learning process, described in Chapter 3 as double-loop learning. In this latter response to questioning in dialogue, we have an example of critically reflective learning.

In addition, the act of describing intentions and actions may prompt further questions or statements from her colleague that elicits reflection about the timing issue. For example, within the issue of time are deeper issues about responsibility for encouraging student learning and the responsibility of the students themselves. Rather than telling the teacher what she should do her colleague may prompt her to look at the purpose of the session and the programme on the matter of student learning. Thus the teacher with the support and challenge of her colleague may move between improving the effectiveness of her lecture sessions in respect of time and depart into areas not previously considered by the teacher.

Application III: reflective dialogue – being part of the story

In this approach the teacher agrees to her colleague attending and discussing the session beforehand in a briefing about what she intends to do, and how she will do it (Beaty and McGill, 1995). This would be followed by a debriefing after the lecture to undertake the reflection on action. The colleague thus becomes part of the teacher's emerging story. This is the before/during/and/after the event as shown in Figure 7.3.

Figure 7.3 Application III: reflective dialogue – being part of the story

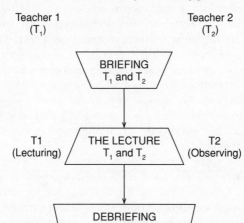

The teacher meets with a colleague before the session. This enables the teacher to explicitly consider what she intends to do in the teaching session and how she intends to do it. The process of the dialogue is intentional and conscious. The responsibility for the session rests with the teacher not the colleague. The latter may offer questions and ideas that the teacher may not have considered, but it is the teacher who will determine whether an idea about the session is to be incorporated. The teacher, at the conclusion of this briefing stage, will have a series of aims about content, process and relationship to the curriculum that she will be endeavouring to achieve in the teaching session, of which her colleague is now aware. While the initiative remains with the teacher, they will have agreed how the teacher will address her intended aims in relation to student learning. The teacher may also ask her colleague to highlight any aspects of the teaching session of which she is likely to be unaware.

The colleague then attends the session as agreed. Usually the student participants are informed ahead of the session of the anticipated presence of the colleague and reassured that they are not being tested in any way.

In the de-briefing session the dialogue is led by the teacher reflecting on the extent to which the intended outcomes were realized. Feedback upon the intended outcomes of the session and the extent to which these were realized is given by the colleague. In addition, the colleague may also observe outcomes that were unintended but are useful to give as feedback to the teacher and the latter has a choice as to whether she acts upon them.

The potential benefits of this before/during/and/after approach is that the teacher's colleague is able to hear the intentions of the session by the teacher before the event, observe what actually happened, and enter into a dialogue with the teacher based on a much richer story than one that is *only* conveyed by the teacher after the event.

Continuing, in the first person the story or picture set out for application II about time pressure and fears about student interaction, my colleague may have been able to observe my non-verbal behaviour and simply ask me questions about my manifest behaviour and how I felt. This may lead to more questions and perhaps elicit feedback about some of my actual behaviour of which I was not aware. In this dialogue I may learn about my behaviour, some aspects of myself of which I am unaware, as well as the potentiality to change my behaviour. Importantly, I now have a choice about how I shall continue to conduct my lectures. That choice is mine and not imposed upon me. My colleague, in dialogue with me, has enabled my learning about my practice.

Once I have made the choice, let us suppose I choose to engage with students more in my lectures. I will then embark on the challenging matter of how I will do it. I realize that my fears, now more explicit, remain and as I adopt a new stance towards the students, I will feel strange, uncomfortable, and less confident as I prepare for another session with students.

This discomfort is associated with the shift in understanding from within an existing paradigm and possibly towards another model of teaching/learning. The support of colleagues has enabled the shift but it does not necessarily remove the feelings of discomfort and dissonance, until I become more at one with the emerging model or new paradigm.

Thus, using the terminology developed in Chapter 5, I have been able to reflect on my practice myself with the support of a colleague. This reflective dialogue can in turn influence my future practice (what I intend) and my actual practice by bringing my new knowledge in use (what I have learned about my recent practice) in a teaching session when it next happens. In addition, while I am engaged in my practice I may internally reflect in action as it happens in the moment. This enables me to check to what extent I am modelling the new innovations I have introduced in my actions and behaviours. I am reflecting in practice.

The de-briefing dialogue with my colleague may also have considered issues about the content. My colleague recognizes and validates my concern about 'getting through the content' as being conscientious. This in turn leads on to what may be 'safe' to leave out or put in handouts and discussion about how students might 'fill the gaps' themselves.

What other differences are there between our teacher reflecting upon her own (Application I) and the dialogue between teacher and colleague (Applications II and III). Personal reflection (on my own) may or may not be intentional. I as teacher may create the conditions for reflection on my own. However, with a colleague in Application II, where we set out to provide the conditions for reflection on action after the lecture event, we are aiming to be conscious and intentional about my reflection and potential learning. Where my colleague is part of my emerging story as in Application III, the potential for reflective dialogue is deeper. My colleague will have evidence of my intentions for the session, experience of the reality of the session, and will participate in a dialogue in the debriefing, with which to share the experience and bring evidence of the session independent of my own.

Further we have recognized that reflection on my practice is about feelings as well as what I do and the content of what I do and these can be expressed safely in dialogue. Once we have recognized the potentiality of the event outlined above, we can continue to reflect upon our experience, form new ideas about our experience, create new intentions about how we will act in the future and put them into practice. A cycle of activity emerges that harnesses reflection on action. To state this as a cycle necessitates a caution that such a process is smooth and consequential. The reality may be much more messy with feelings and thoughts intermingled as the teacher struggles with and through her dissonances associated with the uncertainties of matching emerging ideas with those that have been part of practice until now.

In summary, with another colleague in real dialogue, I have reflected upon my action, learned about my action and can act subsequently upon it. I am 'ready for new experience' and can develop with that new experience. We emphasize the importance of the dialogue with other(s) in airing these applications which yields the potentiality and readiness at some stage to take on that which has, as until now, not been realized.

In addition, while I am supported by a colleague in dialogue, it is only myself that can learn and reflect upon my experience – it cannot be done for me by others. Hence, in the example above my colleague may have recognized my fears prior to my acknowledgement of them. But my colleague's recognition is not necessarily my learning! In addition, to have pointed out those fears to me may not have resulted in my learning! There is a subtle balance here between my 'stepping' into my own recognition and articulating the recognition and being challenged by my colleague.

Up to this point in the chapter we have considered the situation where a teacher is in dialogue with a colleague, enabling the former to reflect on her practice, and therefore creating conditions that can encourage critically reflective learning and development. In the application below we are overtly introducing the notion of the teacher as facilitator using a workshop format. At the workshop, the facilitator will be modelling a facilitation style appropriate for teachers who will in turn facilitate student learners. The workshop is thus also a potential model for student development of reflective practice.

Application IV: reflective dialogue with other colleagues – enabling the development of reflective practice

There are three main purposes for the workshop:

1. to develop and enhance an understanding and ability to engage in reflection on practice through reflective dialogue
2. to develop and enhance skills of facilitation

3. for the workshop to be a potential model for student development of reflective practice.

We describe the facilitation skills which can enable this group process to be effective in Chapters 10 and 11. For teachers who are skilled facilitators we recommend Chapter 8 for the student workshop.

The teacher as facilitator enabling a group of colleagues to engage in reflective dialogue is represented in Figure 7.4a.

Figure 7.4a   Application IV: teacher facilitating reflective practice with colleagues

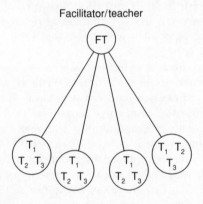

Facilitator/teacher

Note: FT: Facilitator/teacher T_1, T_2, T_3: Teacher

We will describe overall the stages envisaged in Application IV before outlining it in detail.

There are two distinct workshop sessions where a teacher as facilitator enables other teachers as a group to engage in reflective practice, the briefing session: workshop 1 and the debriefing session: workshop 2. In between the workshop sessions, staff undertake a teaching session, e.g. a lecture. The session before the lecture is the briefing session. The session after the lecture is the debriefing session. The whole of Application IV is, in effect, an enlargement of Application III which was between colleague and teacher alone. For Application IV we are describing a three stage process over time shown in Figure 7.4b.

Figure 7.4b   Application IV: the three stages process

workshop 1

teaching event

workshop 2

The teaching event is a lecture where the teacher engages with intentions derived from the briefing in workshop 1. The lecture is followed by workshop 2 where the teacher engages in a debriefing that creates the conditions for reflection on practice.

Thus Application IV builds on the core reflective dialogue between colleague and teacher. This application anticipates what can be undertaken with student learners to enable them to become reflective practitioners (Chapter 8).

Given appropriate set-up and conditions for the session by the facilitator, the teacher participants are asked to divide into groups of 3 which we will refer to as triads. In each triad teachers will take on one of three roles:

1. the teacher anticipating a lecture in the near future referred to here as the *presenter*
2. the colleague teacher, referred to here as the *enabler*, who will engage in dialogue with our presenter in a briefing session prior to the lecture and a debriefing session after the lecture. The enabler, in effect, is a facilitator for the presenter
3. another colleague, referred to here as a *reporter* will observe the enabler in his role as enabler of the briefing and debriefing dialogue. The reporter will also be able to provide insights into the presenter's intentions prior to the teaching session and feedback after the debriefing.

For the briefing, the presenter will give some individual thought and preparation to the intended lecture in the near future which the enabler will also be attending. The presenter and enabler will then conduct the briefing session for the anticipated lecture. By the end of the briefing, the presenter will have prepared the lecture in terms of aims, content and process, to her satisfaction and the enabler will have a picture of the intended session.

Following this dialogue, the reporter (who has observed but not intervened in the dialogue) will give the enabler feedback on the enabler's approach to how he enabled the presenter to prepare for the lecture. The nature of a dialogue that promotes reflection is dealt with in Chapters 4 and 5 and the skills are considered in Chapters 10 and 11. The key element to emphasize here is the role of the enabler in ensuring that the primary responsibility for the lecture, the teaching and the teacher's learning and development rests with the teacher (the presenter).

A similar process will take place for the debriefing session after the teaching session with the three parties to the reflective dialogue.

Application IV is important for four reasons. First, a number of staff can acquire and enhance their skills and abilities to engage in reflective practice and dialogue. In the workshop model described below teachers share with each other a briefing session, delivery of the teaching session (e.g. lecture), and reconvene to conduct a debriefing dialogue. This debriefing process is the key to reflective practice and enables staff to share their experience of professional work if they had not experienced Applications II and III above.

Secondly, the experience provides, in turn, a model for those teachers who wish to enable students to engage in reflection on their practice as student learners. Practising reflective dialogue develops teachers in this two-part workshop, which can then be applied with students.

Thirdly, academic staff when in the enabling role are able to practice their role as facilitators which can then also be applied in the student context.

Fourthly, there is a key difference between this application, apart from the workshop context, and that for Applications II and III. As in II and III, the teacher is supported in the reflection on practice by another colleague, the enabler. However with Application IV, the enabling colleague is additionally supported by a third colleague, the reporter, who will give the enabler feedback on the enabling of the teacher. Thus the presence of a third party, the reporter, provides the opportunity not only to give the enabler feedback, but also by being 'outside' the enabling, to be in a position to initiate reflection on the process that is happening between the teacher presenter and enabler in the two-part workshop. This 'objective' condition fosters reflection on the interaction in the triad (as well as the teacher's practice) that the two parties cannot as easily provide themselves. The parallel is the potential self-deception by reflecting oneself referred to earlier in this chapter. Here potential mutual deception is mitigated by the presence of another! It is an added bonus of reflection we do not have in one-to-one conditions.

There is another advantage in having the reporter in the triad group. When the reporter is conveying her observations on the interaction between the presenting teacher and enabler to the latter, the reporter is practising an important element of effective facilitation, namely, giving feedback. The enabler (and the presenter who also may receive feedback) is additionally gaining practice in receiving feedback. Both giving and receiving feedback are important attributes of effective dialogue. Without pre-empting the discussion on facilitation skills later, we can assert that the workshop mode, working in triad groups, can encourage the conditions for effective dialogue that promotes in turn the conditions for reflective practice. The reporter may well give feedback that challenges the enabler in the latter's role as facilitator and in doing so promote critical reflection on the part of the enabler.

Further, the workshop format allows colleagues to share their learning from impressions of the process that they have experienced. Here the teacher/facilitator who is conducting the workshop will need to deploy their facilitation skills (Chapters 10 and 11) in the process review of the workshop.

In summary, Application IV can be shown diagrammatically as in Figure 7.5.

Figure 7.5   Workshop 1: the briefing session

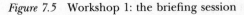

Workshop 1: The Briefing Session

T1: Presenter

T2: Enabler   T3: Reporter

leading to (outside the workshop)
A Teaching Session (T1 and T2 plus students)

Workshop 2: The De-Briefing Session

T1: Presenter

T2: Enabler   T3: Reporter

Note: It is not necessary for T3 to attend the teaching session.

We have created here a two-part workshop with a teaching session between each part of the workshop. The first part could be a day in length. This is an appropriate time to provide teaching colleagues with an introduction to developing reflective practice as well as undertaking the triad sessions within the day. Each of the teachers in the triads undertakes each of the roles once, for practice as well as having the opportunity to prepare for their teaching session to be undertaken between the workshops.

The second part of the workshop could be undertaken in a half day for the debriefing sessions and time for reflection on the whole process.

The workshop Part 1: the briefing session

The work undertaken in the briefing session is summarized in Box 7.1.

Box 7.1   Workshop 1: Developing reflective practice using triads: the briefing session

Divide into groups of three in the following roles:

Presenter: the teacher who is preparing a teaching session

Describe what you wish to achieve in the session in terms of aims, content and methods and/or an issue that you face in your role as a teacher and discuss it with the enabler. Try to be brief and specific. The 'issue' will be of *real* concern to you in your teaching role.

Enabler: the colleague who will be observing

You are to work with the presenter with her aims, etc., by enabling the presenter to think through how she will achieve her aims or tackle the issue. The purpose of enabling is to help the presenter:

- focus on the issues
- to take and maintain responsibility for making her aims happen
- to move to some specific action(s) that she will adopt in the session.

Ask open questions (How do you know? What does this mean?). The object is to enable the presenter to define or redefine the issue and their relationship to it in specific terms for *the presenter* to take some steps towards achieving her objectives and doing it effectively. Try to focus on what can be done *by* the presenter, not what she ought to do or what you would do. Some helpful questions may include:

- What do you want to achieve?
- How will you know if . . . . . ?
- How can you make it happen?
- How do you feel about that . . . . . ?
- What do you think would happen if . . . . . ?
- What could you do . . . . . ?
- What do you think really goes on . . . . . ?
- Do you think that . . . . . ?
- What would help?
- What might get in the way?
- What will you do . . . . . ?
- When will you do . . . . . ?
- What might happen?

Reporter: the person observing the above event

The reporter listens to what is being *said*, observes the interaction and considers what questions/responses were more/less helpful to enabling the presenter to move forward her issue(s). The reporter also listens to/senses what the *feelings* of the presenter are in relation to the issue(s).

Finally, the reporter also listens to/senses what the presenter has '*invested*' (or not) in the issue. What is the presenter's '*will*', '*commitment*' or *motivation* towards the issue and its possible resolution?

Further points the reporter may wish to consider include:

- is the enabler providing solutions for the presenter?
- is the presenter focusing on what she can do?
- is the presenter avoiding resolving the issue?
- is the presenter's proposed action specific enough?

In preparing for the dialogue the presenter will require some individual time in thinking about the future teaching session, say 10–15 minutes. During this time the enabler and reporter can discuss how such questions above may be helpful to the presenter. Then the presenter and enabler take about 20–25 minutes for the briefing session. After the session and a pause, the presenter and enabler convey within the triad how they experienced the session. The reporter then gives feedback for 10 minutes feedback to both parties.

These suggested times could be extended by agreement with the teacher/facilitator and participants. It will primarily depend upon the overall time available for the whole session.

Let us examine what is happening in this briefing stage of Application IV from the standpoint of each of the three roles.

The presenter
The presenting teacher is in real role. She is preparing a future session with a colleague who will attend the session in the near future. In thinking about that future session, she has the benefit of articulating her intentions and addressing issues and potential concerns about the session. In reflective practice terms, the briefing session will be the teacher's reflection on her practice *prior* to this briefing, with issues that she considers are important to raise that are central to her professional practice, with a view to attending to them in the session following the briefing. In this the briefing session is identical to that for Application III.

The enabler
The colleague is also in real role for he will be briefing with the presenter in advance of the anticipated teaching session. The term *enabler* is intentional. He is an enabler in the sense that his task is to enable the presenter to take the primary responsibility for the briefing. The responsibility of the enabler is to provide support, to pose questions and challenge that promotes the teacher/presenter's learning and development. The enabler is engaging in reflective dialogue with the presenter by reflecting on the latter's practice prior to undertaking the session following the briefing. In this briefing session the enabler is actually in the role of a facilitator for the presenter. Enabling in the triad is therefore useful practice for facilitation.

Further, the questions offered in Boxes 7.1 and 7.2 below may appear somewhat bland and ordinary. They are intentionally open but allow for follow through or more probing questions later in the dialogue. They are designed to enable the presenter to reflect and could be very challenging depending upon the context. The dialogue can thus become critically reflective for the presenter.

The reporter
The colleague who acts as reporter has a crucial role. As reporter she is making a note of, primarily, the enabler's contribution to the briefing dialogue. The main purpose is to ascertain and record the extent to which the

enabler is actually enabling the presenter to work through her thinking, feelings and potential action about the intended lecture. Once the dialogue has concluded, the reporter gives feedback to the enabler on the extent to which his purpose was fulfilled. In addition, the reporter may also give feedback to the presenter on how she responded to the enabling as well as how as reporter she 'sees' the issues as presented, e.g. around commitment as in the Box 7.1 example.

This essential task of giving feedback (see Chapter 11 on giving and receiving feedback) is important practice for the debriefing event which takes place after the teaching session. Developing reflective practice requires the ability and skill to give and receive feedback. The effectiveness with which feedback is given (and received) is a contributor to reflection, learning and development. For example, giving feedback that may be destructive may mean closure to receiving feedback at all, in which case there will be limited or no learning and therefore no development and potential change. The reporter is also utilizing qualities that are those of the facilitator and thus gaining practice in this role.

In terms of reflective practice, the role of the reporter is crucial. The reporter is watching the action as it is happening. The presence of the reporter provides the basis for reflection on the interaction between the presenter and enabler using the reporter's recording of what she observed. The reporter's role provides the enabler with insight through feedback about his contribution to the reflective dialogue. There is a second important contribution that is clarified by the presence of the reporter. By concentrating, mainly, on the interaction as reflective dialogue, the reporter is articulating the process. Thus there can be commentary on the behaviour relating to reflective dialogue and on the process of reflective dialogue – the meta level. Therefore there can be reflection on reflective dialogue. We refer to this in Chapter 5 where we show levels or ladders of action 'up to' reflection and 'down to' action in an interactive flow of reflection on reflection. The reporter, enabler and presenter can engage in learning about their learning in respect of reflective practice and reflective dialogue. This stage in the triad is, in effect, a process review.

Finally, the reporter in giving feedback and insights to the enabler (and to the presenter to a lesser extent), may also be able to offer a picture to each which is critically reflective that takes them beyond their existing ways of seeing their roles as teacher and facilitators.

Once this briefing has been completed, the three participants in each triad, can rotate roles for two more briefings. At the end of three briefings, every colleague has undertaken each role and in two of the roles exercised some of the skills and qualities of facilitation. All three will then be prepared for the next stage: the teaching session where the enabler for the presenter will attend the latter's session.

At the end of this part of the workshop, the facilitator will undertake a plenary review of the day for participants to reflect on their process collectively. We refer to this review in more detail at the end of the workshop.

The intervening teaching session

The briefings are then followed by the teaching session where the enabler is present. (The presence of the reporter is optional.) The agenda to which the teacher and colleague attend to will have been agreed at the end of the briefing session. The provisos about informing students of the presence of other colleagues apply. After an appropriate time period has elapsed to provide for the teaching sessions to be completed, teaching colleagues return to the workshop for the debriefings to take place.

The workshop Part 2: debriefing session

The format for the debriefing session is set out in Box 7.2.

Box 7.2 Workshop 2: Developing reflective practice using triads: the debriefing session

The debriefing session again uses the same triads as for the briefing session. The teacher as presenter and enabler in the debriefing session will adhere to the agenda agreed at the briefing and implemented at the teaching session. In addition, as before, the teacher undertaking the role of enabler can have feedback on the debriefing by the reporter in the triad following his debriefing with the presenting teacher.

Presenter: the teacher who has presented a teaching session

Describe what you achieved in the session in terms of aims, content and methods and/or an issue(s) that you identified in your role as a teacher and discuss it with the enabler.

Enabler: the colleague who attended the teaching session

You are to work with the presenter on the extent to which she achieved her aims, etc., by enabling the presenter to think through how she achieved her aims or tackled the issue(s) she considered important.
  Questions like:

- How do you feel the session went . . . . . ?
- What were you trying to achieve?
- To what extent do you consider you achieved your aims . . . . . ?
- What affected your session?
- What made you approach the content in that particular way . . . . . ?
- You say you thought the questions you asked were confusing. In what way were they confusing . . . . . ?
- What can you do about that?
- What specific changes would you make in the future in relation to this part of the syllabus . . . . . ?
- How can you . . . . . ?

And reflective questions, leads, on the process:

- What was the effect of the briefing on your teaching?
- What may you be doing differently from before?
- What has been the effect on what you think and feel about this?

The object is to enable the presenter to define or redefine the issues and her relationship to them in specific terms for *the presenter* to take some steps towards clarifying and reflecting upon her approach, possibly modifying her approach in the future. Try to focus on what can be done *by* the presenter – not what she ought to do or what you would do.

The enabler will also give feedback to the presenter on outcomes not anticipated at the teaching session of which the teacher may or may not have been aware.

Reporter: the person observing the debriefing event

The reporter listens to what is being *said*, observes the interaction and considers what questions/responses were more/less helpful to enabling the presenter to reflect upon the issue(s). The reporter also listens to/senses what the *feelings* of the presenter are in relation to the issue(s) and the extent to which the enabler picks up sensitively upon them.

Finally, the reporter also listens to/senses what the presenter has '*invested*' (or not) in the issue. What is the presenter's '*will*', '*commitment*' or *motivation* towards the issue and its possible resolution?

Further points the reporter may wish to consider include:

- is the enabler providing solutions for the presenter?
- is the enabler pressing for action when recognition is sufficient?
- is the presenter focusing on what she can do?
- is the presenter avoiding or unaware of issues emerging?
- is the presenter's proposed action specific enough?

In the debriefing dialogue the presenter and enabler engage in reflection on the teaching session and the presenter's practice along the lines agreed at the briefing. During this time the reporter will record the significant parts of the interaction, as perceived by the reporter. The debriefing between presenter and enabler may last up to 30–45 minutes. After the debriefing and a pause, the presenter and enabler convey within the triad what they felt and thought about the debriefing experience. The reporter then gives feedback for 20–30 minutes to both parties. For the enabler the focus by the reporter will primarily be the enabler's skills and effectiveness in giving feedback. For the presenter the focus will be on how effectively the presenter received feedback as well as insights about the behaviour of the presenter observed by the reporter.

These suggested times could be extended by agreement with the facilitator and participants – it will primarily depend upon the overall time available for the whole session.

Thus in this two-part workshop, teachers will have developed and enhanced their understanding and ability to engage in reflection on practice through reflective dialogue; they will have used the workshop as a potential model for student development of reflective practice; and they will have developed and enhanced their skills of facilitation.

With respect to the latter, facilitation, this will have occurred at two levels. The first level is primarily when the teacher is working as enabler. In acting as enabler, he can let the presenting teacher *off the hook* from taking responsibility for the briefing process while she concentrates on reflection on her practice. The enabler is then able to facilitate the process that is most conducive to the presenting teacher working on her practice. The second level is the facilitating of the workshop as a whole. Here the facilitator is modelling the process necessary for the workshop to effectively yield reflection on practice for a potential student group.

Review of the workshop: a plenary session
This second meaning of facilitation can be brought into a review of the process of facilitating the workshop so that participants can reflect together at a broader meta level about their experience of the workshop and how it may be programmed for students.

In addition, the review can be used for the whole workshop for participants to collectively reflect upon the main purpose of the workshop to enhance reflection on practice. Experience of the event – Application IV, as described above, provides a vehicle for examining reflective practice and its contribution to professional practice, learning and development. Users of Application II and III can include this review process in their format.

Application IV is a thorough and potentially rigorous means to address issues of reflective dialogue, reflective practice, facilitation and workshop practice to significant numbers of staff in a collaborative non-isolating format. However, we are conscious of the resource and time constraints in which teachers operate and the constraints that staff developers also face with the responsibility of launching such events. Application IVa is suggested therefore as a truncated version of Application IV.

Application IVa reflective dialogue with other colleagues: enabling the development of reflective practice

Application IVa has the same structure as for the workshop Part I: The Briefing Session using triads and Box 7.1 and should be a one day session. The presenter considers a session that she will undertake in the near future. The purpose of the enabler is to support the presenter in preparation for the session. The presenter and enabler still engage in the process of reflective dialogue. In preparing for the future session the presenter may highlight issues from her practice in the past upon which she wishes to focus. The reporter conveys her observations after the dialogue as in IV. Towards the end of the workshop in Application IVa the facilitator can hold a process review on what has been achieved in the workshop as well as supporting the participants in how staff may follow through from the workshop.

Following the workshop the presenter can then take one of the following steps:

1. as in Application I, reflecting alone after the event or
2. a variation of Application II, where the teacher invites the enabler to have a reflective dialogue after the teacher has completed the session but does not attend or
3. a variation of Application III where the enabler attends the teaching session and engages in a debriefing reflective dialogue after the session.

The last mentioned is nearest in approach to the workshop in Application IV. Steps 2 and 3 above leave the initiative to the parties involved.

Resourcing workshops on developing reflective practice and the training of teachers as facilitators are important to the continuing professional development of staff. We are conscious of the responsibility for resourcing and staff development and recognize that this is a policy issue requiring action at central and faculty levels. The suggested programme of development in Applications IV and IVa may also provide evidence for quality assessment purposes.

Finally, the experience of the two stage workshop provides a potential model for application with student learners – the subject of our next chapter.

Note

1. We could have preceded this stage with the teacher who engages in no reflection at all, who is content with her approach. Her teaching method has 'stood the test of time'. The danger is atrophy and hence the death of learning. Complacency is near it and it is tempting for many of us to say 'that will do today'. We recognize and experience that very human feeling. Dissatisfaction and boredom does tend to emerge, however, which wrests us from prolonged complacency.

8

Developing Reflective Practice: The Student Using Reflective Dialogue

In this chapter we describe the process by which student learners engage in critically reflective learning through reflective dialogue. Teachers can achieve this by facilitation of a process which is intended to create in students the conditions for understanding, as well as the ability and skill to engage in, the practice of reflective dialogue.

In Chapter 7 we have shown a path for teachers that moves through stages from personal reflection through to facilitating reflective dialogue for a group of teachers. First, to show how teachers can enter the reflective dialogue process as part of their own professional development. Secondly, to show how teachers can work with each other in reflective dialogue. Thirdly, to show how teachers as facilitators can enable groups of teachers to enter the process of reflective dialogue.

We can now add a fourth purpose. By experiencing the Applications, I–IV in Chapter 7, teachers are in a position not only to understand reflective dialogue for themselves, but to model both the understanding and the process for student learners.

Given that teachers are required to engage a significant number of students in reflective dialogue, the experience of teachers in being facilitated in reflective dialogue enables them to replicate the facilitation process (Application IV – the teachers' workshop) for students. Teachers thus have experience as participants of a workshop process which can in turn be used by those teachers to engage student learners in reflective dialogue.

Teachers also require (in addition to the ability to impart the understanding of reflective dialogue) the skills of facilitation and the modelling of dialogue skills so that students can acquire the skills which we believe are inherent in the process of reflective dialogue. In this chapter we make the assumption that teachers have acquired facilitation skills in order that we can give emphasis to the process by which students acquire the skills and ability to engage in reflective dialogue.

We are aiming to provide student learners with the means of engaging with each other in reflective dialogue as colleagues in the learning process. This reflects our view that learning is a social as well as an individual process. Our purpose is to promote learner autonomy rather than remaining learner dependent on teaching staff. The intention is also to promote learner inter-dependence or collaboration between student learners.

In this chapter for the student we reverse the applications described in Chapter 7. The reason for this is to ensure that students are introduced to the idea and practice of reflective dialogue through workshop conditions. With this experience students can then use the process of reflective dialogue with other student colleagues self-facilitating or in association with the teaching/learning strategy as part of their course. In addition, the teacher wishing to introduce reflective dialogue to students is more likely to be faced with the situation of a potentially large number of student learners. Therefore it is appropriate, initially, to assume a number sufficient for workshop conditions.

Once the student workshop has taken place, they can be introduced to the earlier models of reflective dialogue where students support each other, Applications II and III adapted to student need. We will refer to the student workshop as Application V, the teachers' workshop in Chapter 7 being application IV. Students can also be introduced to Application I, recognizing its value and its limitations.

Application V: teacher as facilitator enabling the development of reflective dialogue for a group of students

Context

Before embarking on the 'workshop' process it is important to set out the context in which the workshop will be a part. We would suggest that there should be a contextual requirement in the course design to ensure that the practice of reflective dialogue is implemented into the course. This requirement seeks to develop students' abilities and skills to practice reflective dialogue as a means of facilitating and deepening their levels of learning.

The requirement therefore forms part of the teaching/learning strategy to which the students will become explicit parties. The tendency is for the teaching/learning strategy, as a part of the rationale and implementation of a course, to remain in the documentation for validation, possibly in a student handbook about the course, and usually in the minds of the course leader, course team and teaching staff. One of the purposes of our writing is to help realize reflective practice in student learners as an active part of their course programmes.

For reflective dialogue to become part of the student's apparatus for learning, students will need an understanding. If reflective practice is espoused then students should be introduced to its practice, that is, reflective dialogue.

Course designers will need to decide whether reflective dialogue is to be intrinsic to the whole or part of a course or modular structure and consequently whether reflective dialogue can be introduced for the whole or part of the course. In addition, they will need to decide which aspect of the course content and what forms of continuing assessment are most typical, in order to determine where to slot a workshop that will be of most relevance to the student cohort. By relevance, we mean the practice that the student typically engages in which forms a key or central part of the course in respect of the content, practice and anticipated outcomes of the course from the standpoint of the student's learning.

In Chapter 7, the practice that teachers typically reflected upon in dialogue was their teaching. It could equally have been about their scholarship activity, research, or course responsibilities. We chose the most commonly shared activity which is also very tangible in that it can be observed and shared in reflection after the event.

In the case of students, what is equivalent activity or 'practice'[1] being reflected upon that enables their learning and development? For students to reflect on their learning they require an appropriate yet typical vehicle to use for their reflection. It could be an essay, seminar paper, project report, dissertation, design or product. The vehicle will vary according to the course and its intended learning objectives and outcomes.

A further contextual element is the potentially limited autonomy of the student to determine the chosen vehicle. The teacher/facilitator may determine the vehicle which the student will be using for reflection and to this extent the student is not so autonomous. However, within the chosen vehicle each individual student may determine her approach to her content and practice in preparation and execution of the task set for engaging in reflective dialogue. However, it need not limit the ability of the student to engage in the process. Indeed, we would suggest that the reflective process may well 'free-up' the student to have greater choice and creativity as a result of engaging in the reflective dialogue process. Evidence of reflective dialogue forms a part of the assessment criteria for a given vehicle or practice (see note 1) and we discuss this further in Chapter 6.

Finally, engaging students in reflective dialogue is not to be confused with the role of the teacher as assessor of the vehicle for reflection. For example, a vehicle may be an essay. In the following description of the process we will distinguish clearly the teacher's role for assessment and grading from that of the student's responsibility (shared with other students) for engaging in reflective dialogue.

The workshop

We are using the term workshop which may denote an event that is a 'stand-alone' outside the usual teaching sessions that students experience. This can be the case. However, there is no reason why the workshop cannot be incorporated into the prevailing teaching programme.

Adapting Application IV, is Figure 8.1: reflective dialogue for students.

Figure 8.1   Reflective dialogue for students

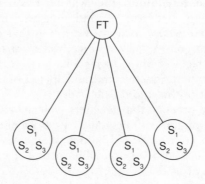

Note: FT: Facilitator/teacher S_1, S_2, S_3: Students

We could take for reflection a range of vehicles representing typical practice for many students, e.g. a project, essay, seminar, design, product. Because it is used so widely we will use the essay as the vehicle for student's practice. We would emphasize that a key feature at this stage is that it is an individual piece of work undertaken by the student. Students may need to be given 'permission' to overcome the cultural block to sharing ideas, as isolation and competition are prevailing norms in higher education.

Before conveying the detailed process for reflective dialogue we describe the overall workshop programme the student will undertake alongside completing a typical essay. Building on Figure 8.1 there will be three distinct workshop sessions where a teacher as facilitator enables students in groups of three (triads) to engage in reflective practice:

- *Part 1*: A briefing stage prior to working on the essay.
- *Part 2*: An intermediate stage following writing and presenting a draft essay.
- *Part 3*: A debriefing stage after submission to and assessment by the teacher.

At the beginning of Part 1 the teacher as facilitator introduces the whole group of students in plenary to reflective dialogue, including modelling the process and guiding students to enter the briefing stage to discuss and plan an intended essay that is to be undertaken by the entire student cohort. Necessarily, the teacher will have some requirements that students are informed of beforehand, e.g. topic of the essay and criteria for assessment. At this briefing stage students go into triads to plan each student's approach to the essay re objectives, content and process. Each student in the triad will take turns in deciding their approach in preparing to undertake the essay. On completion of this stage, students will depart to prepare the essay in draft, on the basis of the intentions determined at the first stage. After completion of their draft, students return to the workshop setting for the second stage (Part 2) in the same triads to review the draft. Ideally, the draft will have been presented previously to the two colleagues, and read. Failing this, the draft will be presented at the workshop. Following Part 2 each student completes the task, the essay and submits it to the teacher responsible for its assessment and grading.

Following the return of the assessed and graded essays (including the tutors comments), students meet in the third stage (Part 3) of the workshop to debrief. The purpose of the debriefing is for each student to articulate what they have learned from the task and what they have learned about their approach to learning. The debrief is not designed for a postmortem questioning or challenging on the tutor's grades.

Thus in summary the stages as shown in Figure 8.2 represent the stage for any one of the trio of students from Figure 8.1 with arrows to represent the link between the briefing, intermediate session and debriefing session.

We will now examine the stages or parts of the workshop in detail and explain the terms presenter, enabler and reporter.

The workshop Part 1: briefing stage

Teachers facilitating the workshop may refer to Chapters 10 and 11 for guidance on facilitation. The workshop will require a day for Part 1 and a half day each for the remaining parts. The aims of the workshops should be stated clearly at this stage. These can be:

- to develop and enhance an understanding of reflective dialogue
- to develop and enhance the skills and abilities necessary to undertake effective reflective dialogue
- to enable students to be able to undertake their own reflective dialogue with student colleagues
- through reflective dialogue, to promote critically reflective learning.

The initial stages, an introduction to reflective dialogue, detailing the process and conditions for the workshop and modelling the triad process, are essential to Part 1 of the workshop and are necessary to obtain the most effective use of all three parts of the workshop.

Introduction to reflective dialogue

We have considered reflective dialogue in Chapters 4 and 5. The aim in the workshop is to gain a minimal understanding – sufficient for students to grasp the concept and the importance of the process that will be experienced in the workshop stages. Modelling reflective dialogue by the facilitator with a colleague or volunteer student will aid this introductory stage. The

Figure 8.2 Workshop – developing reflective dialogue

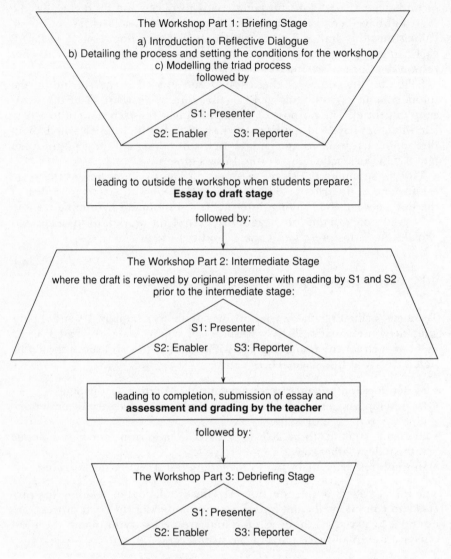

The Workshop Part 1: Briefing Stage

a) Introduction to Reflective Dialogue
b) Detailing the process and setting the conditions for the workshop
c) Modelling the triad process
followed by

S1: Presenter
S2: Enabler   S3: Reporter

leading to outside the workshop when students prepare:
Essay to draft stage

followed by:

The Workshop Part 2: Intermediate Stage

where the draft is reviewed by original presenter with reading by S1 and S2
prior to the intermediate stage:

S1: Presenter
S2: Enabler   S3: Reporter

leading to completion, submission of essay and
assessment and grading by the teacher

followed by:

The Workshop Part 3: Debriefing Stage

S1: Presenter
S2: Enabler   S3: Reporter

Note: S1, S2 and S3 defines the students in each triad

model for this can be drawn from Box 7.1 in Chapter 7 for the dialogue between presenter and enabler.

Following this introduction to reflective dialogue, the teacher/facilitator may wish to ask the students to consider what personal objectives they would like to achieve/have for the three-part workshop. These can be incorporated into the earlier stated aims provided they are within the boundaries of the workshop aims. An example of an inappropriate objective would be, say, discussion about assessment procedures which would be appropriate in another context – a course board.

Detailing the process and setting the conditions for the workshop

Here the facilitator outlines the stages of the workshop and the relation of the task, the essay, to the stages. She then explains the format for the triads and the role of each student.

The participating students will be divided into groups of three which we refer to as triads. In each triad students will take on one of three roles:

1. The student preparing to undertake the essay having been given the outline purpose. This student is referred to here as the *presenter*.
2. The colleague student, referred to here as the *enabler*, will engage in dialogue with our presenter in a briefing session prior to writing the essay, an intermediate stage and a debriefing stage after the essay has been assessed and graded. It is important to emphasize this role as a facilitative role and not a prescriptive one. This is a key role in the workshop which each student will have an opportunity to undertake. Teachers running the programme are recommended to ask the students in plenary to suggest and to record collectively the stance they should take in carrying out this role prior to and as part of the preparation for the triads. The shared stance here can be reflected upon and modified in the light of experience at the end of the workshop.
3. Another colleague student, referred to here as a *reporter* will observe the enabler in the role as enabler of the briefing, intermediate and debriefing dialogue stages. The reporter will also be able to provide insights into the presenter's intentions at the briefing stage and to give feedback after the intermediate and debriefing stages. Again the facilitator running the workshop may wish in plenary to ask and record what the reporter should be observing in the reporting role before going into that role.

Having given the introduction to and purpose of the triads and outlined the roles, the facilitator can then draw up the conditions or ground rules appropriate and necessary with the participating students to ensure the triads are implemented as effectively as possible (see Chapter 10 for workshop conditions).

If the student participants have not already done so they should be given some time individually to consider their initial plan, thoughts and intentions for the essay.

Modelling the triad process

Before inviting the groups to enter the briefing stage, it is important that the facilitator models the briefing stage either with a colleague teacher or, ideally, with a volunteer student on the lines suggested above. The facilitator will be the enabler and the colleague or volunteer student will be the presenter. This is crucial as it will probably be the first occasion that students have witnessed this form of interaction and dialogue. It is crucial in setting the approach to this first stage of the process of reflective dialogue. Chapter 7 is intended to set the bases for this initial modelling to be feasible. Where students are invited to volunteer it is important to emphasize that he or she does not require the skills prior to undertaking to act as volunteer.

Once the modelling is completed and the student has a plan, objectives and intentions regarding process, the facilitator or a colleague invites the students who have observed the dialogue to convey their insights and give feedback on the interaction. These are recorded on a flip-chart and discussed.

Following this shared reflection, students are then asked if they wish to add any more conditions that they wish to prevail when they will be working in the triads – drawing upon their own and shared insights from the modelling of the briefing process. This is an important part of learning about process and critical to reflective dialogue – the ability to 'stand outside' what is happening in order to 'see' and 'hear'. The students observing the dialogue between the teacher and the student have thus had their first experience of reporting on what they have observed and of giving feedback.

The resulting insights will include additions to the conditions they wish to add for the triads as well as initial reflections on the first stage of reflective dialogue all of which should be recorded under the headings suggested. The key here is that students are already experiencing practice in reflection and beginning to reflect upon it themselves. They are potentially involved at cognitive, conative and affective levels.

The combination of the introduction to reflective dialogue, explanation of the process, initial thoughts by the students on their essay, modelling of the triad briefing stage and emergent conditions provide the basis for the briefing stage to be undertaken by the students in their respective roles. At this point the facilitator will issue the briefing note set out below in Box 8.1 with attention, in particular, to the timing of the briefing stage to ensure that each student can undertake each of the roles within the triad. The total timing for the first student in dialogue with the enabler followed by feedback from the reporter is about 45 minutes. This excludes the individual time for initial thoughts on preparation that all the students have at Part 1 of the workshop before the first briefing. The 45 minutes interaction could be extended provided all the triads maintain attention to the overall time allocated by the facilitator.

The times suggested in Box 8.1 could be extended by agreement with the facilitator and participants. It will primarily depend upon the overall time available for the whole session.

The cycle of briefings continue within each triad of students until each student has undertaken the role of presenter, enabler and reporter.

Box 8.1   Part 1: The briefing stage

Developing reflective dialogue using triads: the briefing session.
Divide into groups of three in the following roles:

Presenter: the student who is planning an essay

Describe what you wish to achieve in the essay in relation to the aims,
content, process and approaches you may use to complete the task.
What particular issues do you anticipate or face in undertaking and
completing the task? Discuss it with the enabler. Try to be brief and
specific. The 'issues' you consider will be of *real* concern to you.

**Enabler: the student colleague who will support your briefing
preparation and intermediate dialogue**

You are to work with the presenter with his aims, etc., by enabling the
presenter to think through how he will achieve his aims or tackle the
issues that he raises. The purpose of enabling is to help the presenter:

- focus on the issues
- to take and maintain responsibility for making his aims happen
- to move to some specific action(s) that he will adopt in the preparations and execution of the essay.

Ask open questions (How do you know? What does this mean?). The
object is to enable the presenter to define or redefine the issues and
their relationship to the task in specific terms for *the presenter* to take
some steps towards achieving his objectives and doing the essay as
effectively as possible. Try to focus on what can be done *by* the presenter – not what he ought to do or what you would do. Some helpful
questions may include:

- What do you hope to achieve?
- What structure do you envisage?
- How long are you planning to take?
- What can you do to make this . . . . . easier?
- How will you control the length?
- What if you can't find out that . . . . . ?
- How do you feel about that . . . . . ?
- What do you think really goes on . . . . . ?
- What do you think would happen if . . . . . ?
- Do you think that . . . . . ?
- How would you know if . . . . . ?
- What could you do?
- How can you . . . . . ?

The questions are suggestions. Actual questions should derive from the presenter's thoughts and ideas. Questions are not to be mechanically delivered but to create and respond to the rapport being developed in the dialogue.

Reporter: the person observing the above event

The reporter listens to what is being *said*, observes the interaction and considers what questions/responses are more/less helpful to enabling the presenter to move forward his task and related issues. The reporter also listens to/senses what the *feelings* of the presenter are in relation to the issues.

Finally, the reporter also listens to/senses what the presenter has '*invested*' (or not) in the issue. What is the presenter's '*will*', '*commitment*' or *motivation* towards the issue and its possible resolution?

Further points the reporter may wish to consider include:

- Is the enabler providing solutions for the presenter?
- Is the presenter focusing on what he can do?
- Is the presenter avoiding some of the issues?
- Is the presenter's proposed action(s) specific enough?

In preparing for the dialogue the presenter will have had some individual time in thinking about the essay plans and preparations. The presenter and enabler take about 20–25 minutes for the briefing session at the end of which the presenter specifies his intended actions. After the briefing and a pause, the presenter and enabler convey what they have gained from experience. The reporter then gives feedback for 10 minutes feedback to both parties.

Let us examine what is happening in this briefing stage of Application V from the standpoint of each of the three roles.

The presenter
The presenting student is in real role. He is preparing for writing an essay but with the support and challenge of another student colleague in this briefing stage who will also share in discussing the presenter's draft at the next stage (Part 2). In thinking about the proposed essay he has the benefit of articulating his intentions and addressing issues and potential concerns prior to writing the draft. He is engaging in the first part of reflective practice.

The enabler
The colleague is also in real role for she is undertaking a briefing with the presenter in advance of the latter's writing of the draft essay. The term *enabler* is intentional. She is an enabler in the sense that her task is to enable the presenter to take the primary responsibility for the latter's reflection on

what he intends to do. This is a cardinal principle of learning via reflective dialogue. The responsibility of the enabler is to provide support, to pose questions and challenge that promotes the presenter's learning and development in relation to a typical vehicle for learning in the course.

The reporter

The colleague who acts as reporter has a crucial role. As reporter he is making a note of, primarily, the enabler's contribution to the briefing dialogue. The main purpose is to ascertain and record the extent to which the enabler is actually enabling the presenter to work through his thinking, feelings and potential action about the intended essay. Once the dialogue has concluded, the reporter gives feedback to the enabler on the extent to which her purpose was fulfilled. In addition, the reporter may also give feedback to the presenter on how he responded to the enabling as well as how, as reporter he 'sees' the issues as presented, e.g. around commitment as in the Box 8.1 example.

This essential task of giving feedback (see Chapter 11) is important practice for the intermediate event which takes place after the essay draft has been completed as well as for the final debriefing event. Developing reflective dialogue requires, inter alia, the ability and skill to give and receive feedback. The effectiveness with which feedback is given (and received) is a contributor to reflection, learning and development. For example, giving feedback that may be destructive may mean closure to receiving feedback at all, in which case there will be limited or no learning and therefore no development and potential change.

The reporter is thus not only *giving* feedback to the enabler. The reporter in *gaining practice* in giving feedback is therefore gaining practice for being an enabler who will be giving feedback to the presenter.

The enabler in *receiving* feedback from the reporter in the triad situation is *gaining practice* in receiving feedback which will be beneficial when she is also a presenter.

Thus all contributing students to the triads are able not only to *practice* the processes that contribute to reflective dialogue but also to *reflect* upon the processes they are using for reflective dialogue.

On completion of the above briefings the facilitator may ask the participants to hold a cross-group discussion so that students could be grouped into presenters, enablers and reporters to share the experience of being in specific roles. This could be followed by plenary discussion with the following themes suggested for students and the facilitator to share:

- What attitudes are appropriate for presenter, enabler and reporter?
- What qualities and skills do I need as an enabler, reporter and presenter?
- As reporters in what ways can feedback be given that can be useful and helpful? As presenters in what ways can feedback be received that can be useful and helpful? As enablers, in what ways can feedback be received that can be useful and helpful?

- Given the conditions we created at the beginning of the workshop what might you add or amend in the light of the experience of the briefing triads?

It is important to note that in this cross-group dialogue between learners there is the potentiality for shared understandings of critical learning deriving from the reflections on the reflective dialogue in the triads.

With the three briefings completed, all three will then be prepared for the next stage – preparing the essay to draft stage on the bases of the intentions agreed by the end of the briefing.

The workshop Part 2: intermediate stage

The workshop for this stage will take place following an agreed time for completion by all the students of the draft essay. We will assume that within each of the pre-existing triads arrangements have been made for all three students to have read each others drafts.

It is anticipated that this part of the workshop will require a three-hour session. The work undertaken in this intermediate stage can be summarized in Box 8.2 below.

Box 8.2   Part 2: The intermediate stage

Developing reflective dialogue using triads: the intermediate stage. Resume the same groups of three in the following roles:

Presenter: the student with the draft essay

Recall what you set out to achieve in the essay in relation to the aims, content, process and approaches you intended to use to complete the task. What particular problems or issues did you face in undertaking and completing the task? Discuss these with the enabler. Again, try to be brief and specific, focusing on what went well or not so well.

Enabler: the student colleague who supported you at the briefing preparation and in this intermediate dialogue

You are to work with the presenter with his stated aims, etc., by enabling the presenter to think through the extent to which he achieved his aims and dealt with the problems and issues that he foresaw and raises now. The purpose of enabling is again to help the presenter:

- focus on the significant current issues
- reflect upon the extent to which he is maintaining responsibility for making his aims happen

---

- move to some specific action(s) that he will adopt in the final stage for execution and submission of the essay.

The object is to enable the presenter to define or redefine the issues and their potential resolution in relation to the completion of the task in sufficiently specific terms for *the presenter* to take some steps towards achieving his objectives and doing the essay as effectively as possible. Again the focus is on what can be done *by* the presenter – not what he should do or what you would do. Some helpful questions may include:

- How are your aims being achieved?
- If you have modified your approach what are the reasons for this?
- Is the structure you envisaged appropriate?
- What can you do to make this . . . . . easier?
- How will you reduce the length?
- What do you think happened when . . . . . ?
- What do you think would happen if . . . . . ?
- How did you feel about that?
- What could you do . . . . . ?
- How can you . . . . . ?

Reporter: the person observing the intermediate dialogue

The reporter listens to what is being *said,* observes the interaction and considers what questions/responses are more/less helpful to enabling the presenter to complete his task and consider related issues. The reporter also listens to/senses what the *feelings* of the presenter are in relation to the task and its completion.

The reporter also listens, attends to and senses what the presenter is '*investing*' in the task. What is the presenter's '*will*', '*commitment*' or *motivation* towards the essay and its completion?

The reporter also prepares feedback including whether:

- the enabler is providing solutions for the presenter
- the presenter is focusing on what he can do or if the presenter is avoiding resolving some of the issues
- the presenter's proposed actions are specific enough to ensure completion of the essay and achievement of his aims.

The presenter and enabler take about 20–25 minutes for this intermediate stage, at the end of which the presenter specifies his actions prior to submission of the final draft. The presenter and enabler convey what they have learned as a result of the dialogue. The reporter then gives feedback for 10 minutes feedback to both parties.

Before ending this part of the workshop, the facilitator may wish to encourage broader reflection on the outcomes to date contributing to reflective dialogue with a group followed by plenary discussion such as:

1. What would you identify so far as the process?
2. What impact is this process having upon your approach towards your studies?
3. What does reflective dialogue mean to you now?
4. What have you learned about your learning?

With the conclusion of the workshop and given time for the submission and assessment of the essay, students are now ready for the final part of the workshop.

The workshop Part 3: debriefing stage

It is anticipated that this part of the workshop will also require a three hour session. The work undertaken in this final debriefing stage can be summarized in Box 8.3.

Box 8.3   Part 3: The debriefing stage

Developing reflective dialogue using triads: the debriefing stage.
Resume the same groups of three in the following roles:

Presenter: the person who has presented the essay

Describe and reflect upon what you consider you have achieved, gained and learned as a result of the essay's completion and commentary by the tutor. What impact did the briefing and intermediate stages have upon your approach to the essay?
What have you learned about the way you approach essays in particular and more broadly about how you study?

Enabler: the student colleague who supported the presenter

Listen to the presenter reflecting upon the above questions, suggesting where appropriate similar and/or more focused questions. Focus also upon what the presenter may do in future as a result of what he has learned about himself and his approach to his work.

Typical questions may include:

• What might you do differently in future?
• How will you do it in future?
• How do you feel about that now?
• Where do you go from here?

Reporter: the person observing the debriefing dialogue

The reporter listens to what is being *said*, observes the interaction as in the intermediate stage. The reporter also records the presenter's

---

feelings and commitment to the essay, its completion and his stance towards his reflections and intentions around his learning and future work.

The reporter also prepares feedback including:

- how the enabler supports and challenges the presenter to reflect upon the latter's learning
- on the presenter's focusing on what he can do
- whether the presenter's proposed future actions are specific enough to be able to make them happen.

Similar times are used as for the Intermediate stage in Box 8.2.

Reflection on the activities

The student participants have now reached a crucial phase in the three-part workshop. As in the two previous stages, the facilitator arranges for the student participants to form their triads for the debriefing events outlined in Box 8.3. This is followed by a reflection event after the debriefing triads have completed their work. The reflection event is designed to provide students with a means to reflect upon the whole process. In summary, the reflection process draws upon Figure 5.3 and the levels or dimensions of reflective practice set out there and reproduced below.

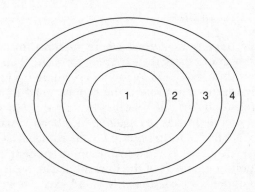

4	reflection on the description of dimension 3
3	description of dimension 2
2	r-in-a
1	action: prop k; k-in-u; k-in-a

Note: (Abbreviations: prop k = propositional knowledge; k-in-u = knowledge-in-use; k-in-a = knowledge-in-action; r-in-a = reflection-in-action)

Some of this activity takes place in the triads and some in plenary. There is a gradual build up of the levels of reflection in the triads, in cross-triads, and in plenary, and can be described as follows:

In the triads

(a) As presenter, the student will have described his experience of the task including any reflection-in-action (like changes he made in his approach, style and structure) that he may have instituted while engaged in the task. In addition, he will in interaction with the enabler have shared any feelings about undertaking the task. This represents level 3 above, a description, his thoughts and feelings, after the event, of the task or action that will include levels 2 and 1.

(b) Reflection on the task as described by the presenter, namely the deliberation and re-evaluation with the enabler in the debriefing, on his description. This represents level 4 above, reflection on the description at level 3, which can be referred to as reflection on action. It is in this process that the student presenter may well learn about his actions and behaviour significantly to enable a paradigmatic shift to occur, for example with regards to his understanding of his discipline. This contrasts with his previous understanding so that he 'comes to know' or 'really know' in a way that he did not before so that he now owns the meaning.

The presenter will record the outcomes and learning about his practice with support from colleagues in the triad.

In cross-triads or plenary

By cross-triads we refer to new triads where students form new groups so that students can begin to share the experience outside their original group. Facilitators may wish to use pairs or fours depending upon the size of the total group. It is appropriate to keep the groups small in order to ensure involvement. Cross-triads may be followed by a final plenary discussion.

(c) Reflection on the process of engaging in reflective dialogue. In Part 1 of the workshop, the facilitator set out to enable students to understand the idea of reflective dialogue as a contribution to student learning at the commencement of the first part of the workshop. The purpose at this point is to enable the students to ask themselves and each other what they have learned *about* reflective dialogue and what they have learned about how they learn.

The potential questions for each student to consider and to share with others could include:

- What is my understanding of reflective dialogue now?
- What have I learned about the process of doing reflective dialogue that promotes such dialogue?

- What skills and qualities have I developed and/or enhanced that promote reflective dialogue in myself and others?
- How does learning as reflective dialogue differ from my previous understanding of learning?
- What are the implications for my learning and development for the rest of my course and subsequently?
- What may you note about yourself, your understanding and your behaviour or actions that is different from the past?

The level of reflection being attained here is level 5 (Figure 5.4), reflection on the reflection on action or more simply, reflection on reflection. This is also equivalent to Bateson's Level III learning where the student is able to learn about the way she learns. With the explicit recognition of this by the student (really knowing) she can then utilize this acquired learning and skill across disciplines and domains, the latter including reflection and potentiality for the application of her learning across knowledge, self and world (Chapter 3).

An example of the presenter's learning about her learning would be the recognition of how she comes to realize that her discipline is bounded knowledge and that she can now critique the discipline from 'outside' the frame she has been locked in to date. Thus while she may have been engaging in an essay, the effect of reflective dialogue goes beyond the boundaries of the requirements of the task, and beyond her discipline to how she is learning about her own learning.

There is a potentiality for empowerment in the individual as well as emancipation in respect of how she may apply her knowledge (reason), self (being) and world (action) and be changed as a person with the capacity not only to understand but also to act. The means of achieving a position to be able to engage in critically reflective learning is not only instrumental (being able to work effectively) after higher education but is also about attaining an autonomy (often with others) to be able critically to act in the world.

After the workshop

The question to consider now is how can students incorporate reflective dialogue into their continuing progress through their undergraduate or post-graduate studies. Two scenarios can be envisaged. The first possibility is to leave the responsibility after the workshop to the student to collaborate with others once the workshop has achieved its purpose. Where the course design integrates learning through reflective dialogue into the course programme as part of the teaching/learning strategy, a second possible approach would be that after the workshop the students continue to engage in reflective dialogue, by self-facilitating the process through, say, a semester or academic year adapting Application V as follows:

1. *One-to-one format* where two students work with each other reciprocating presenting and enabling through the three stages outlined in Application V – briefing, intermediate, and debriefing.
2. *Triad format* where three students work with each other presenting and enabling and reporting through the three stages outlined in Application V – briefing, intermediate, and debriefing.

At the end of the period chosen the facilitator holds a review which evaluates the whole process and its relevance to student learning. A reflective document undertaken by each student that conveys the formative development of the student may also be required to assess the student. In addition, when the initial three-stage workshop has taken place each student could be asked to formulate a contract setting out their learning needs and aspirations that they will work on during the self-facilitating stage and at a review stage.

We can now bring the last two chapters together. We started with teachers conducting personal reflection (Application I) through to Applications II and III that created the conditions for reflective dialogue between teachers. We followed this with a workshop for teaching staff primarily designed to engage staff in reflective dialogue as well as model a workshop that could be adapted for student needs (Application IV). In this chapter we started with the workshop (Application V deriving from Application IV) to introduce reflective dialogue for students. Application V is designed to enable students to become self-facilitating in reflective dialogue which is an adaptation of Applications II and III for teachers.

The applications of reflective dialogue for teachers and students thus becomes mutually reinforcing. In Chapter 9 we link the ability of teachers to engage in reflective dialogue by attending to the role, value and purpose of facilitation, to support critically reflective learning. Teaching in the traditional transmittive mode is antithetical to critically reflective learning, hence the need to facilitate rather than teach.

Note

1. We are using the term 'practice' to denote the work or activities that students engage in during their course to use as vehicles for their learning. Their practice is the means by which they and their tutors have evidence of the progress the student is making on the course.

9

Becoming a Facilitator: Facilitation as Enabling Reflective Learning

In this chapter we explore what facilitation means, why it is needed for reflective dialogue, and how facilitation can be used by teachers in higher education to encourage critically reflective learning, through reflective dialogue. We describe the journey of the traditional subject teacher from the exclusively 'expert' role to a more balanced approach, incorporating the role of facilitator, while retaining her subject expertise, and we end the chapter with some of the barriers to, and benefits of, facilitation, for teachers in higher education.

What is facilitation?

For many people facilitation is just another way of teaching. The teacher behaves in a different way, encouraging the class or group to contribute, but ultimately tells them what to learn, how to learn it and how it will be assessed. The recognition and articulation of decisions about learning is part of facilitation and we discuss this below. The word 'facilitate', is defined (in the *Shorter Oxford Dictionary*) as:

1. to render easier or
2. to promote

and, when asked the questions

- 'to render *what* easier?' or
- 'to promote *what*?'

for staff in higher education, the answer must be 'learning'. Not just any learning, but critically reflective learning, defined in Chapter 5, is what is expected now in higher education, whereas traditionally, 'those undergoing higher education of any kind may find that they have learned successfully how to pass written examinations – and nothing else' (Salmon, 1980:12). Even where exams have been partially replaced by coursework, 'students adjust their study in terms of their understanding of what the assessor requires them to know' (Radley, 1980:37).

The traditional approach to learning in higher education has ignored the personal nature of learning and that 'people learn through relationship' (Salmon, 1980: 5), hence the social aspects of learning have been neglected. Radley (1980) maintains that, 'to understand a particular mode of learning . . . we shall need to appreciate the system of relationships to which it owes its expression' (p. 36).

Learning and relationship

Relationship in traditional learning in higher education has emphasized separateness and isolation, causing learners to be 'estranged' from each other, their teacher, and the material ideas they seek to learn about (Radley, 1980:34). As non-participants in the process learners have been presented with their subject as the teacher's 'product', often an alien 'buffet of ideas' (p. 40) and quite foreign to the student learner.

When relationship replaces estrangement, and learning is recognized as having implications in the realm of ideas, values, social interests and assumptions, then learning becomes, 'the expression of a social system . . . which is grounded in the ways in which student and teacher together work with their material' (p. 36), suggesting connection between teacher and learner, and, we would add, learner and learner.

Belenky *et al.* (1986:115) differentiates connected learning from separated knowing with reference to the deep relationships which characterize the former in contrast to the detachment of the latter. Connected learning, recognizes the significance of relationship as learners jointly construct knowledge for themselves and each other.

The significance of relationship in learning is underlined by Martin Buber (1994) who suggests that the human condition calls for what he describes as the I–thou relationship in learning, unlike the instrumental relationship, objectifying other, which he identifies as the I–it relationship. He claims that, 'the learner is educated by relationships' (Buber, 1965:90), and that the relationship which characterizes personal learning is the I–thou relationship, described thus:

> Relation is mutual. My *Thou* affects me, as I affect it. We are moulded by our pupils and built up by our works . . . We live our lives inscrutably included within the streaming mutual life of the universe.
>
> (Buber, 1994:30)

What mutual relationship will nurture the development of critically reflective learning? A relationship which has the potential to 'assist people to become aware of their taken-for-granted ideas about the world' (Shor, quoted in Brookfield, 1987:80). Such a relationship can accept an openness to outcome, making no presumption of answers or solutions: 'in the reflective classroom, both teacher and student will appreciate the fact that some problems may remain forever a mystery' (Meyers, quoted in Brookfield, 1987:71).

The unknown and unknowable outcomes of such learning relationships, in contrast to traditional methods of transmission, have enormous potential for enabling the critically reflective learning now sought in higher education, with all the uncertainty which that implies. Barnett (1997) in recommending a new approach in higher education, claims that, to date,

> academics have set themselves a limited set of tasks in developing students' critical capacities . . . higher education for the modern age has to do more than generate epistemological uncertainty, it has also to generate personal and ontological uncertainty and it has to produce practical uncertainty.
>
> (p. 175)

If this sounds a bit daunting we refer once more to Belenky *et al.* (1986) on connected learning:

> In a connected class no one apologises for uncertainty. It is assumed that evolving thought will be tentative . . . we can speak with certainty but . . . we can also try to construct a different sort of authority, based on personal individual experience and acknowledging the uncertainties implicit in an approach which values the personal.
>
> (p. 221)

The idea of learning as a social and collaborative process sits strangely on our traditionally competitive Western education system, with its emphasis on detachment and distance, particularly for academics in higher education. When the social context of learning is recognized, and collaboration is valued rather than penalized, the significance of relationship in learning makes sense, prioritizing involvement and connection, nurturing joint endeavours and stimulating the creativity of constructed knowledge, thereby encouraging movement towards higher stages of learning.

Also, such collaboration has implications for the student in terms of further learning: 'its effects extend far beyond that particular teaching session . . . it offers the student's appropriation of that mode of relating as a practice which he can subsequently initiate himself' (Radley, 1980:42–3).

We have described the possibility of students taking their learning about relationship in reflective dialogue into different contexts in Chapter 8.

In summary then, the relationship required to nurture critically reflective learning, is mutual rather than one-way, open to difference and uncertainty, rather than tied to inflexible outcomes, able to accommodate the questioning of established ideas, connected to the other by virtue of dialogue, rather than estranged, and, recognizing the existential reality of social and political contexts, rather than losing the value of tacit and personal knowledge in student learners. We discuss these issues in more detail below as we explore why teachers may choose to use facilitation.

Why use facilitation?

We have established that critically reflective learning is nurtured by relationships between teacher and learner, learner and learner and between both with the subject under study. We identified the optimal learning relationship above, as mutual, open, challenging, contextually aware and characterized by dialogue. Why use facilitation to inculcate such a relationship?

We turn first to Carl Rogers and Gerard Egan for some of the reasons for choosing facilitation to cultivate the learning relationship described above and thereby promote critically reflective learning for students in higher education. The Rogerian principles grew out of his recognition that relationship feeds learning and change, and this is why we start from these principles, having established that the critically reflective learning sought in higher education is based on connected learning, built on the basis of reflective dialogue in relationship with others. Rogers' thought, outlined in Chapter 3, established what has been called person-centred teaching. He set out the principles for person-centred learning and teaching in *Freedom to Learn* (Rogers, 1983) and we draw on these (noting that Rogers was writing prior to an awareness of gendering in texts) in Boxes 9.1 and 9.2.

Box 9.1   Some principles of person-centred learning

1. Human beings have a natural curiosity and potentiality for learning, and students learn when the subject has relevance and meaning for them.
2. Learning which involves change in self-perception is threatening and tends to be resisted, hence learning is more easily achieved when external threats are minimized and experience can be processed safely.
3. Learning is facilitated when the learner participates in the learning process and much significant learning is achieved by doing.
4. Self-initiated learning which involves the whole person, feelings as well as intellect, is most lasting and pervasive.
5. Independence creativity and self-reliance are facilitated when self-evaluation is primary and evaluation by others is secondary.
6. The most useful learning in the modern world, is learning about the process of learning, an internalization of the experience of change.

The principles of person-centred learning have implications for person-centred facilitation, and we summarize these in Box 9.2.

Box 9.2 Some principles of person-centred teaching or facilitation

1. The facilitator clarifies the purposes of the individuals and the general purposes of the group and relies on the desire of each student to implement those purposes which have meaning for him.
2. The facilitator endeavours to make available the widest possible range of resources for learning and regards himself as a flexible resource to be utilized by the group.
3. The facilitator remains alert to expressions indicative of deep or strong feelings and responds to expressions of feeling and accepts both intellectual content and emotionalized attitudes, giving each aspect the degree of emphasis it has for the individual and/or the group.
4. The facilitator, while recognizing and accepting his own limitations, takes the initiative in sharing feelings as well as thoughts, in appropriate ways.

The principles presented in Boxes 9.1 and 9.2 above, fulfil our requirements for critically reflective learning relationships as follows:

- the assumption that learning is natural when the learner's context is recognized
- a recognition of learning and change as threatening
- the importance of participation of learners and holistic attention to all three domains of learning, knowledge, feelings and action
- the possibility of reflecting on learning and appropriating that understanding, together with potential for self-challenge and other challenge
- mutuality.

The principles of person-centred teaching and learning declared in Boxes 9.1 and 9.2 provide the basics for the practice of facilitation which establishes a learning relationship within which reflective dialogue may occur, and hence, offer learners the opportunity to achieve critically reflective learning. Many of these principles are entirely familiar to teachers in higher education, and indeed, are adopted in course documents and teaching/learning strategies. We discussed in Chapter 2 the in-use status of such principles.

The development of Rogerian ideas by Gerard Egan has provided a particularly clear model of facilitation, suitable for use in higher education. Egan has provided operational definitions of Rogers' conditions, based on research findings (Carkhuff, 1969) with detailed examples for would-be facilitators. In particular, he identifies the failure of formal education to develop the whole person, that is, address all three domains of learning, and he recommends an 'intentional' approach to facilitation training for teachers, rather than assuming that the ability to relate comes naturally (Egan, 1973). In particular, he identifies the absence of reflexivity in education, so that incongruence between declared values and actual behaviours is unlikely to be explored (Egan, 1976). Egan's work offers a response to the criticisms levelled at Rogerian methods by some educationists.

The Rogerian approach, often incompletely understood, has been viewed as bland and 'quite unhelpful' (Salmon, 1989:232) in facilitating learners, as it is believed to preclude challenge and confrontation. The conditions established by Rogers in 1957, as necessary and sufficient for personal learning and change, included the existence of relationship and the communication of empathy, warmth and congruence. The potential for challenge in offering high level empathy from a congruent stance is recorded as being dramatic (Carkuff and Berenson, 1967; Egan, 1976; Mearns and Thorne, 1988; Rogers, 1957), and, where facilitators are properly trained in the requisite skills, there will be no possibility of the 'soft touch' version of facilitation, which is, unfortunately, what many have experienced in place of the real thing. A full description and definition of empathy and congruence will be given in Chapter 11.

The mistaken juxtaposition of 'person centred' or 'facilitative' alongside 'being nice', 'unstructured' or 'flexible standards' has not helped to promote the facilitation of critically reflective learning in higher education. The need for challenging assumptions and confronting embedded suppositions is a basic requirement for reflection. The adversarial method of challenging assumptions destructively, while traditional in academic life, is inappropriate for reflective learning. All the evidence suggests that the supportive challenge of empathic confrontation can enable a learner to consider contradictions or new material, as well as countenancing the possibility of change that disturbs their world view (Belenky *et al.*, 1986; Egan, 1990; Rogers, 1983).

The benefits of facilitative methods in higher education were established over 30 years ago, and some of the outcomes described by Ms Abercrombie bear remarkable similarities to the kind of learning presently being sought by practitioners in higher education, as the learner,

> [b]y comparing and contrasting his own judgements and those of his peers . . . could become conscious of some of the multitude of interacting factors that had profoundly influenced him but of which he had been unaware. Whereas in the didactic situation he is offered the teacher's judgement, the authoritative correct one, with which to compare his own; in the group, he is confronted with eleven others, made by his peers, which he must evaluate on their own merits.
>
> (Nias, 1993:11 from Abercrombie, 1984)

The value of facilitation methods for nurturing relationships where learners may engage in reflective dialogue with others and experience the realization of awareness through challenge, suggests that these methods have a place in higher education and teachers may like to consider using them, while maintaining their subject specialism.

Facilitation for critically reflective learning

Having presented a rationale for using facilitative methods, why should a teacher in higher education alter teaching practice in favour of facilitation?

Skilled teachers in higher education have always made judgements about the appropriate teaching approach for a given learning objective (Gibbs, 1995:22–3). For instance, to achieve the transfer of specific bodies of knowledge to learners who are motivated, lecture methods are likely to be cost-effective and rapid, and the required learning is achieved. We do not seek to undermine the function of such learning, where it is appropriate, and parts of the higher education curriculum are likely to include such bodies of knowledge to be transmitted efficiently. We note also that the lecturing process is familiar to many teachers in higher education, and is likely to present them with no problem.

On the other hand, for critically reflective learning as described in Chapter 3, facilitative methods of learning are likely to be more appropriate, and, for reflection to occur, some elements of facilitation *must* be present. For instance, our description of reflective dialogue in Chapters 7 and 8 implies involvement with others, exchanges with others, as well as action-linked-to-reflection.

Facilitative behaviours are linked with particular approaches to learning, and we have identified these as methods incorporating opportunities for reflective dialogue. We believe that exclusive use of lecturing approaches is less likely to lead to reflective dialogue and therefore may not always support critically reflective learning. The balance of lecturing and facilitation in a given course remains a professional choice of the teacher. Hence our contention that teachers in higher education need to be familiar with both approaches in order to enable their students to become critical and reflective learners.

Traditional teaching methods have been described as 'banking' because the teacher as expert 'makes deposits' of knowledge content into student 'containers' (Freire, 1974). This corresponds to the outcomes of surface learning, which, as stated above, has its place in parts of higher education courses. A discussion of the ideology of banking is beyond the scope of this book, suffice to say that the teacher operating as 'expert' or 'banker' does not, indeed cannot, encourage genuine dialogue. Why is this the case?

The seminar teacher may be skilful in questioning and stimulating discussion, but while primarily taking the role of expert or implicit banker, cannot enable dialogue. Students may remain passive and depowered by the yawning chasm between teacher knowledge and their ignorance. Some have described it as paralysis or exclusion from the academic club (barbarians at the gates again!). Most attempts at dialogue in seminars, with such an arrangement are disappointing, and many staff do not understand why. One reason for silent seminars is the relative inexperience of students in the form of dialogue we are advocating. The ability of students to create dialogue is an important variable here, as their educational histories may have silenced them, the existing learning environment may be experienced by them as oppressive, or their model of learning is one of transmission, perhaps driven by a surface learning assessment system. Teachers, too, may not have experienced reflective dialogue, formally, as part of their professional development.

So how can teachers in higher education enable reflective dialogue through facilitation?

How facilitation enables reflective dialogue

How can tutors facilitate students to become critically reflective learners through reflective dialogue, and how does this differ from traditional teaching in lectures and seminars? As part of our discussion, we reiterate the requirements for reflective dialogue, outlined in Chapter 4, namely intention, dialogue, awareness of process, awareness of personal stance, and modelling. We now establish how these requirements for teachers are fulfilled by facilitation.

Intention

Facilitation is intentional in the sense that the facilitator is conscious of what she is doing and why. She may also wish to declare explicitly her purpose and how she intends to achieve it, to colleagues and/or students. Such explicit articulation (naming that which is usually unnamed) enables the facilitator to be clear about what she is doing and whether it is appropriate. For example, if students are to be invited to engage in reflective dialogue, will a lecture about reflective dialogue facilitate this? (We recommend an alternative in Chapter 8.) Reflective dialogue has been identified as the key to reflective learning, and *intentional* reflective dialogue ensures that the condition is met.

To enable a student group to engage in reflective dialogue a teacher will need intentionally to alter her role as primarily expert, addressing the other two domains of learning, affect (emotion) and action. This does not mean that the teacher stops being an expert in her discipline. Her expertise in her subject remains, as does her authority within it. Her professional judgement with regard to the balance of content and process will direct her use of facilitative methods as and when appropriate. How tutors may move gently towards elements of facilitation in their work, without abandoning their authority as subject experts is explored below.

Many teachers describe themselves as facilitators, and rightly so, as they identify themselves as 'enabling learning to occur', and they do so in a variety of ways, known as modes or styles. Facilitator styles have been explored in detail by John Heron (1993) and include the traditional, *hierarchical* mode, where the teacher controls structure, content, method and programme, the *cooperative* mode, where decision-making is shared with learners, and the *autonomous* mode where decisions are taken by the learners. The facilitation modes or styles intentionally adopted by teachers are examples of process in teaching, and often may not be articulated to students, keeping the process hidden. We discuss transparency of process below.

Heron's work suggests that teachers in higher education need to be aware of, and competent in, all three modes of facilitation. At the start of a course/module the hierarchical mode is needed while structures and programmes are agreed or imposed (unless the course is totally self-directed). As the learners gain confidence, teachers may seek to include them in decisions about method and/or content, indeed this happens without articulation when students ask questions which divert the lecturer from his 'script'. For some teachers the prospect of total student autonomy may be too daunting, and indeed inappropriate, in award-bearing courses where qualifications are granted on the basis of externally laid-down criteria. Where teachers seek to offer a completely autonomous programme students are given clear criteria for achieving progression or graduation and left to design and create the course themselves (Charleton, 1996).

Intentional dialogue

We identified the characteristics of reflective dialogue in Chapters 4 and 5 as dialogue which: 'engages the person (who is in dialogue) at the edge of their knowledge, sense of self and the world'.

Assumptions about knowledge, herself and the world are challenged through the process of connection-with-others, in the realms of her mind, her feelings and her experiencing of the world.

Connection-with-others in dialogue provides the safety for voicing the realities of her world, and ensures that the implications for herself and her learning are attended to by means of what has been called 'inclusion' (Buber, 1965). We draw on Buber for an explanation of inclusion:

'Its elements are first, a relation, of no matter what kind, between two [or more] persons, second an event experienced by them in common, in which at least one of them actively participates, and third, the fact that this one person, without forfeiting anything of the felt reality of his activity, at the same time lives through the common event from the standpoint of the other. A relation between persons that is characterised in more or less degree by the element of inclusion may be termed a dialogical relation.

(Buber, 1965:97)

The power of inclusion for dialogue has been identified by David Bohm as sharing what is tacit with a view to developing meaning,

'The tacit process is common. It is shared' and 'meaning is not static – it is flowing. And if we have the meaning being shared, then it is flowing among us . . . From that form a meaning which is shared'.

(Bohm, 1996:40)

In addition, connection-with-others supports the perturbation or disturbance which may occur when existing assumptions are challenged, and effective dialogue deals with the emotional material flowing from such challenges. We discuss the management of emotion in Chapter 11.

The engagement with others at the edge of awareness, although sometimes painful, and possibly difficult to maintain, may generate new learning, forged from the discomfort and struggle of dialogue, which emerges as the critically reflective learning we seek to facilitate in higher education. The power of intentional dialogue to form essential relationships has implications for learning in every part of life, and we refer once more to the I–Thou relationship:

In all ages it has undoubtedly been glimpsed that the reciprocal essential relationship between two beings signifies a primal opportunity of being, and one, in fact, that enters into the phenomenon that man exists. And it has also ever again been glimpsed that just through the fact that he enters into essential reciprocity, man becomes revealed as man; indeed, that only with this and through this does he attain to that valid participation in being that is reserved for him; thus, that the saying of Thou by the I stands in the origin of all individual human becoming.

(Buber, 1965:209)

Awareness of process: the need for transparency

The move towards facilitation has encouraged teachers in higher education to invite students to contribute, while holding the power over what is to be learned and control over how it is to be learned. Thus the embedded process of hierarchy and control may remain unarticulated and hidden. The principle of transparency provides for the teacher making explicit the hidden processes within the learning programme, and facilitation begins from that principle. Making process transparent also 'comes clean' on the power relations which exist in the learning situation, and, in making them explicit, allow students to adjust their stance towards it, recognizing it and possibly working productively with it.

An understanding of the difference between task and process is helpful here, as both are needed for learning, and the balance is the key to successful facilitation. What exactly do we mean by task and process? In Chapter 4 we clarified the difference between task and process, and established that task is *what is to be done*, while process describes *how* a task is undertaken. Tasks serve the overall purpose, which in higher education is student learning in a given subject – mathematics, say. Each teaching session will address the purpose through a task, perhaps explaining double differentiation with a view to tackling differential equations, hence the task incorporates content, in this case, the differential calculus. Aspects of the subject may include analytical processes like differentiation in the teaching of calculus, or deconstruction in the teaching of literature, but these are still the content of the mathematics or English literature teaching session.

Clearly, facilitators in higher education also need to be subject specialists, having a firm grasp of the content part of the teaching session, so it hardly needs saying that academic credentials are essential for our kind of university facilitator. While recognizing the importance of the subject, we are 'doing' process all the time, whether we are aware of it or not, and our process has an impact on students whether we like it or not.

When teachers and learners become aware of this process they can then evaluate its relevance for the task in hand. Is one-way transmission the aim? It may be, and the process is appropriate. It may not be, and the teacher may like to consider an alternative process. Additionally, the teacher's choices will need to be shared with learners, making the process transparent. When the process is made explicit in this way, this empowers learners, enables them to take responsibility, and equips them to engage in reflection. Process, because it is often invisible, to both teacher and learner, is the factor in teaching and learning which has been most resistant to change. Curriculum development is only now incorporating teaching/learning strategies which recognize the significance of process in defining a subject area.

Facilitators need to be aware of process, and part of their role is to enable learners to analyse *their* learning process, to review, through reflective dialogue, what has occurred between themselves, other learners, teachers and the outside world. Such dialogue enables students to create understanding and meanings for themselves, which connect their learning to reality. An understanding of process for learners offers the possibility of grasping how their learning happens, and hence, how further learning may happen.

A student example

As part of our studies in mathematics at college, one of us was offered a weekly seminar diet of applied 'problems' which we learnt to depict graphically to aid our understanding (of forces and vectors, say). These diagrams were essentially a problem in geometry and figures were drawn in a traditional way with triangular shapes depicted as in Figure 9.1:

Figure 9.1   Vector diagram

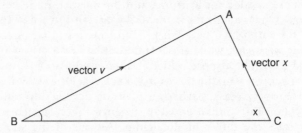

While struggling in a seminar session with my problem sheet, in conversation with my tutor, along the lines of 'how can we see this problem differently?', we chanced on the potential benefits of turning the diagram upside-down, enabling me to 'see the angular and spatial relationships in a new perspective. He responded immediately by saying, 'What a good idea – it looks quite different now.'

Figure 9.2   Vector diagram rotated

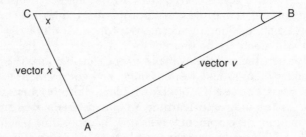

Afterwards, I engaged in a bit of rudimentary reflective dialogue (I didn't know the term then) with a fellow student in the tea break, and I realized that by talking in 'what if' terms with my tutor, who responded, I had found and articulated a process, i.e. the process of reversing a diagram in order to 'see' it differently. I had identified a way to help my learning, not only in the applied module but in other parts of the course. In realizing and articulating the process, I had learnt something about *my* learning through reflection. What I didn't know then, and only realize now was the significance of his encouragement, also part of the process, which might have emerged in reflection on reflection.

A *teacher example*
After facilitating a course recently one of us received (invited) feedback on our 'process' from participants. What had been observed by participants was a tendency to pose questions (see Chapter 11) and, if responses did not

come fast enough, supplying the answer (underlying this was the pressure of time and anxiety about covering the syllabus). While the technique of question and answer, where the teacher gives the answer, is a well-established method of making a subject accessible, it was not our intention to do this, and undermined our purpose, which was to enable adult learners, through *socratic* questioning, to experience the process of formulating the answers for themselves. So the invisible process was usefully brought to our attention.

After feedback, or reflection on process in reflective dialogue, and realization of what is happening, teachers can then choose what to do about it. Although in this case it destroyed my 'innocence' about my questioning style, it made me aware of the discrepancy between my espoused intentions and what I was actually doing.

Awareness of personal stance

We identified the teacher's awareness of personal stance, in Chapter 4 as: 'the position which each one of us takes up in life' (Salmon, 1989:231).

Personal stance influences our teaching (and our learning) by its impact on the learning context, and a teacher's personal stance is implicitly conveyed in her practice and learner's approach her from *their* personal stance, interpreting what they see and hear in order to 'place' her. This 'reading' of her will influence their understanding of the curriculum as 'knowledge-understanding – is no more separate from teachers than from learners' (p. 233). Awareness of personal stance is necessary but, as a desirable condition for reflection, we would add, the articulation of it, regardless of what that stance is. For instance, if a teacher's stance towards facilitation is negative her lack of enthusiasm will leak into her practice, just as a positive orientation to group work is likely to be communicated implicitly in her teaching method. Awareness of stance, whether positive or negative, towards aspects of the teaching process, enables a teacher to articulate her preferred process, justify it honestly to students, and thus make 'transparent' some of the unseen power in the learning relationship. We recognize that this may not always be possible and simply note that the teacher's stance will 'leak' anyway, as students are acute non-verbal observers.

Modelling

Modelling and the part it can play in enabling reflective learning in higher education has been described in Chapter 4. We have referred to intention and process – modelling is the intentional demonstration of process. Teacher modelling of dialogue is a source for students to see and hear the skills they will need to engage in dialogue with each other. The facilitation skills described in Chapters 10 and 11 are essentially the skills needed for effective dialogue. Bateson (1973) has explained the power of *schismogenesis*, the tendency of humans to imitate observed behaviours, and modelling seeks to use this tendency to support learning. The old adage, 'don't do as I do, do as I say' recognizes that, as learners, we 'pick up' the implicit process and copy it, thereby imitating behaviour rather than responding to spoken instructions, so we might as well model process intentionally. Another version of this can be found in moral education where the belief that moral behaviour is 'caught not taught' has not reached parents, teachers and priests, who may persist in preaching one thing and doing another, and then wonder why people tend not to behave 'morally'.

With the recent introduction of projects and self-facilitated group work to courses in higher education the possibility for reflective dialogue between students has emerged. However, without the skills of dialogue, students may lose the opportunities provided by such groups to engage in dialogue and achieve reflection on their learning. The assumption that group activity will automatically lead to skills development, particularly dialogue skills, is not borne out by experience (Assiter, 1995). Indeed, there is more than a suspicion that self-managed groups of largely inexperienced students may simply reinforce whatever power dynamics exist therein, without examination or reflection on process or indeed task. Without some model to work from, it seems unlikely that students will be able to develop the skills necessary for reflective dialogue, especially as the discourse of the wider society, which is likely to fill the vacuum, tends not to provide a model of mutuality in communication, and is not conducive to the dialogue situation described above. With little opportunity to reflect-with-others, students are likely to resort to the familiar lonely process of compiling their 'reflective document' about the group task/activity in comparative isolation. Teachers in higher education have been disappointed by the lack of critical reflection in such documents, perhaps forgetting that students are operating in a vacuum, without a model of reflective dialogue, either past or present, to draw on. We discuss the compilation of reflective documents in Chapter 6.

We describe facilitative behaviours, designed to promote reflective dialogue, in Chapters 10 and 11. Student learners, in observing such behaviours in their facilitator, can model their own behaviour for effective reflective dialogue. On the other hand, a teacher who is distant, dictatorial and unable to share the difficulties and struggles of their learning process, and presents material in its sanitized final version, is likely to be copied by students, who, in attempting to emulate, will lose the reality of struggling to construct their own meanings, while taking account of others, i.e. they are less likely to become connected, constructivist learners, as described in Chapter 3.

The importance of tutor modelling for student learning of the dialogue process should not be underestimated. Professional bodies encourage modelled behaviour for the development of professional practice, either formally or informally (Schön, 1987). We believe that offering students the opportunity to work in groups on projects or development, without also attending to process, has created a vacuum of responsibility. Who addresses the needs of students to develop their ability to engage in dialogue, to review their process, and develop their interpersonal skills and understanding of group process? If these needs are not attended to students are unable to benefit from the opportunity for critically reflective learning and their experience of higher education is consequently incomplete. Recent research findings from a medical practitioner in higher education puts it more bluntly: 'I think teachers need reflective skills . . . because if they don't have, it actually means that they are short-changing the students' (Miller *et al.*, 1994:23).

Retaining authority while moving towards facilitation

How can a traditional lecturer begin the journey towards incorporating facilitative methods into her/his existing practice? We look now at the journey, which many of us have made from 'subject expert' to facilitator. We draw on our own experience as well as academic sources, including findings from the participants at our workshop, SEDA 95,[1] where we explored the effects of such a journey, as well as some impressions of being facilitated. We emphasize the importance of personal, professional and institutional support, and we advocate how this can be provided. We also recognize that there will be losses and gains for the lecturer concerned and we mention some of them at the end of this section.

The key is that *all* need not be abandoned here. The tutor concerned is, and remains, an authority, both in terms of the academic discipline and also in terms of her/his role in the institution. Hand in hand with this authority goes the familiar responsibilities for assessment, standards and scholarly development. In point of fact our tutor would be well advised not to move from purely didactic methods to so-called autonomy in one jump, and she may never choose to go so far. Each tutor has a choice of at least three 'modes' of facilitation, Hierarchical, Cooperative and Autonomous, and there may be more, which span the spectrum of facilitation practice (Heron, 1993).

Using Heron's modes, the facilitator can be hierarchical about the structure and process of the interaction needed for promoting reflective dialogue, within a seminar, a group, action learning set, in supervision or mentoring. The facilitator in setting the structure and process, will create the conditions for a cooperative mode of interaction which creates some of the conditions for reflective dialogue. Moreover, the facilitator will then model the cooperative mode in her way of relating to the learner(s). Thus while hierarchical in respect of influencing the structure and process of the interaction for dialogue, the intention is to create the conditions for cooperative dialogue. Two points emerge here. First, the facilitator is establishing a relationship which is conducive to learning, and, secondly, she is creating the conditions for transformatory or critically reflective learning, which include containment within boundaries, and these are provided by the facilitator taking responsibility (in hierarchical mode) for articulating those boundaries and holding them, until the learners are familiar with the process, and can take responsibility for holding some of those boundaries for themselves. We note that it is often the failure in this responsibility when the teacher is moving into facilitator mode, that gives facilitation a bad reputation.

Facilitation does not mean an absence of structure or boundaries. An example of the importance of establishing right from the start, who will decide what, is offered by Jane Abercrombie, who used facilitative methods for educating scientists through her Associative Group Discussion method:

> the meetings were firmly structured in time and place. For twenty minutes or so the students worked individually at a scientific task ... There followed free discussion about the individual responses to the task ... I convened the groups, stated their purpose, fixed the time and place of meeting, arranged the programme of exercises, and opened and closed each session ... I tried to establish a group situation con-ducive to learning through the sharing of experiences of the initial individual task. This involved making a supportive, non-threatening climate in which constant challenge to habitual ways of thinking was tolerable.
>
> (Nias, 1993:10–11, based on Abercrombie, 1984)

We can identify here the use of hierarchical mode to provide structure and containment, and the cooperative mode to establish sufficient trust to enable reflective dialogue to take place in a supportive group.

Cooperative and autonomous modes of facilitation imply a redistribution of power, traditionally held primarily by the teacher. With the potential redistribution of authority/power goes a redistribution of responsibility, with learners being invited to take responsibility for their own learning. Learners taking responsibility for some of the learning process is still a relatively new phenomenon and when things seem difficult the temptation to revert to leaning on the tutor (maybe blaming her) can be irresistible. Teachers may need well-developed assertion skills when students abrogate their responsibility in this way, maintain the cooperative mode, and model conditions for reflective dialogue. Also for students used to transmission, their expectations of process are hierarchical, they may not be ready, experiencing the new way as harder, they may not like it to begin with, and therefore we recommend that facilitators attend to expectations and negotiation as part of their move into cooperative mode. Where students are enabled to take some responsibility for their own learning and engage in reflective dialogue, the outcomes include satisfaction with ownership of their learning, an awareness of taken-for-granted assumptions expressed as 'you made me think', and, the realization that they can 'begin to ask questions of (my)self and others', a good indication that critically reflective learning is in hand.

Moving towards facilitative methods from a traditional format implies some transfer of responsibility from lecturer to student, particularly responsibility for the student's learning, often implicitly carried by the teacher. Even a partial transfer of responsibility from lecturer to student is neither simple nor painless. The new, more egalitarian situation, demands capacities for living with uncertainty which traditional lecturing keeps well-controlled, and also there is a particular difficulty in assessing the capacity of the group at any given time. The new situation, for those who are adopting facilitative methods, is experienced as exciting and risky, expressed as 'I took a risk in dispensing with old ways', and 'I experienced scariness and took risks'. The learners experience the riskiness too, expressed as 'it felt safe – I could take risks'.

In the traditional model conscientious teachers took responsibility for their students' learning very seriously and to relinquish it, even partially, for some, may feel rather like not doing their job properly. However, with increasing commitments for teachers in higher education and diminishing resources, a reduction in uncalled-for responsibility can only be an advantage and a potential reduction in stress for the hard-pressed teacher.

Students cannot begin to accept responsibility for their own learning and development unless the tutor relinquishes some of what has been traditionally her responsibility. The tutor will need to do less telling and more listening, even though what she hears is not up to scratch! Part of the process is the student making his own mistakes and facilitators may choose to model this by openly admitting that 'I sometimes experienced not getting it right', and 'I can make mistakes'. The recognition that the facilitator can make mistakes has been expressed by learners as 'the facilitator admitted to not knowing everything' and this 'broke the cult of academic secrecy'.

Socratic questioning is a powerful way of highlighting errors without pointing them out, and open questioning allows for creativity and innovation. Learners experience such questioning as 'I was interested and the facilitator was interested' and 'I was honest and the facilitator was interested'. Teachers report 'positive feedback from asking questions' and 'profound satisfaction in students learning for themselves'. The skills which will encourage learners to voice their understanding, discuss their misunderstandings, and reflect on their learning in dialogue are those of establishing a solid relationship of trust, letting learners find their own way, even if their route is not the standard one or the preferred one.

We should emphasize here that less tell and more listen does not mean our teacher becomes a facilitator sponge. Effective facilitation, i.e. that which leads to critically reflective learning, includes challenge and feedback as well as listening and understanding. The facilitator is a valuable resource for students and must ensure that they use that resource. Teachers who have made the journey to facilitation find that, contrary to expectations of not covering the syllabus, they found that 'I got through more work' and expressed satisfaction with 'not needing notes any longer' as they were now giving 'less subject content – more of a tool kit to deal with learning blocks'.

The teacher will find that whatever she models will be picked up by her students and incorporated into their practice, as she is experienced by learners as 'a reflector or mirror of what is going on', and 'the facilitator provided a role model for me' and 'the facilitator modelled reflection'. Hence the facilitator is an important source of learning for students of the conditions for reflective dialogue, particularly the skills they will need in order to engage in reflective dialogue. Facilitators describe this as 'I worked in the here and now – I listened and asked questions' and learners say 'we shared different experiences but identified things in common', and, 'I was given lots of time' and 'I was not rushed'.

For those unfamiliar with facilitation of reflective dialogue, facilitating a seminar group is a safe place to start the transfer of some responsibility from tutor to student, and contain it within agreed boundaries. Teachers who have successfully adopted facilitative methods with small groups may, with confidence, feel able to handle facilitation of a large group. Supervision responsibilities, now carried by most teachers in higher education offer the opportunity to work in a facilitative way with a small group, and thereby optimize resources (see Chapter 13 on supervision).

The facilitation of groups requires some understanding of group dynamics, and the facilitator will be able to offer process comments to a group of learners. Such comments may assist learners to identify the intangible interactions which occur, often naming the 'hidden' dynamics which inhibit learners, like subtle dismissal of particular areas of work by members of the group, pairing of powerful members of the group, and domination by particular characters, as well as potential undercurrents of racism and sexism that may be present in any multicultural group in higher education today. Process skills require very well-developed observation skills and an understanding of group dynamics and these are dealt with in Chapter 11.

Support for facilitators

We noted above the 'risky' nature of making the change from traditional teaching to facilitative methods, and what has been described by some who have made the journey as 'using a new language'. The adoption of a new mode of teaching, even in a small way, is likely to engender feelings of strangeness and awkwardness, a familiar experience in learning anything new, and those teachers choosing to alter their practice in this way, may like to share their feelings with colleagues. Teachers who have become facilitators report that the support of colleagues through reflective dialogue, experience of others' practice, staff development and the adoption of a learner-centred curriculum, are key elements in a successful journey. Teachers who have adopted facilitative methods report the importance of 'sorting out' the facilitation process, 'before, during and after' their sessions. We refer to this kind of support as developing reflective practice in Chapter 7. We also discuss institutional responsibilities in Chapter 6, and other support mechanisms like action learning and mentoring in Chapters 12 and 14.

One way that facilitators can support themselves, whether they have made the journey or are making it, is through the process of co-facilitation. Many teachers in higher education have experience of co-teaching and such experience would form a basis for co-facilitation. We draw on our own experience here to suggest the conditions for successful co-facilitation:

- clarity about aim of session(s), e.g. do we aim to transmit knowledge or enable reflective learning? What outcome do we jointly seek?
- agreement about the process, e.g. how will we use our hierarchical mode to structure the session(s) and where will cooperative or other modes begin?
- shared understanding of complementary role, e.g. are we watching each other inspectorially or supporting each other professionally?
- agreed strategies for 'stuckness' or 'panic', e.g. some facilitators agree a code for communicating with each other without the student group's knowledge, simply to then take time to discuss privately the progress of the session and possible alterations
- agreement about 'who does what' and 'when' as this often causes confusion, in both students and facilitators!
- commitment to 'check out' each other while the session is running in a supportive way and be prepared to alter procedures if necessary
- awareness of differences in style e.g. pacing or type of intervention.

The intricacies and benefits of co-facilitation in higher education and other contexts are discussed in Pfeiffer and Jones (1975) and Davies and Sang (1997). If teachers are working together as facilitators, they will have opportunities within the teaching session to model with each other, the dialogue skills they wish to be imitated, and to demonstrate the conditions for reflective dialogue. For example, co-facilitators can model giving and receiving effective feedback to each other, so that students have something to imitate in their triads. Co-facilitators are also in a good position to comment and highlight the process for students, offering an additional opportunity for learners to 'see' dialogue in action.

Each pair of co-facilitators will discover their own preferred way of working and this will emerge through the preparation, processing and reviewing of sessions together. The minimum for this is a time set aside after the session to debrief it, checking out how each facilitator feels about their performance, their colleague's behaviour, and the students' response. Ideally, we recommend that co-facilitators prepare sessions thoroughly together, and, although this is time-consuming the benefits are enormous. In particular, co-facilitation offers teachers the rare opportunity to receive feedback on the way they interact with students. The relationship relies on trust and a willingness to learn, as well as a commitment to honest but supportive challenge. We discuss challenging skills in Chapter 11.

In preparing for co-facilitation teachers can use the reflective dialogue process together, and similarly allow time for debriefing each other in dialogue fashion. In fact, the process is not unlike the recommendations for reflective practice given in Chapter 7 except that *both* teachers need time to present and be enabled.

Gains and losses in moving towards facilitation

The gains are the prospects which bring most academics into the profession in the first place. These include the satisfaction of enabling students to develop and learn, the excitement of observing their progress as learners, as well as the satisfaction of seeing graduates, diplomates and doctorates leave our institutions with a capacity for independent thought and creativity which will equip them for the future. Teachers who have made the journey report profound satisfaction in students learning for themselves and becoming independent: 'At the end of the year, they flew the nest and didn't need me any more. I knew that they had done it themselves.'

The losses are associated with fears. As students are invited to take responsibility for their own reflection and learning, the teacher may experience fear of losing control of the situation. The facilitator is relinquishing total control over others, while retaining her personal authority as subject expert herself. The teacher who considers such an approach faces the fear of sharing power and control. What if students can't be trusted? The fear of taking the risk can be frightening. Learner-centred education is threatening to the student too, instead of conforming to instructions and complaining about the lecturer the student must take responsibility, make mistakes and live with the consequences. Years of being directed leads students to seek the security of being told what to do. Also their anxiety about teacher-centred assessment, over which they have no control, leads to questions like 'how will we be graded?' and 'how many exams will we have to take?' etc.

If power is thought of as zero-sum, then teachers have every reason to feel fearful. However, if power is thought of as a potential, then it is possible for the teacher to retain her power and authority, while enhancing that of the students, i.e. non zero-sum implies all gain. For example, the move from silence to connected knowing (Chapter 3) for a student is a potential gain for both teacher and student.

Other potential losses for the teacher include, the security of directing structure, content, method, assessment and evaluation; the control of meaning and challenge; the suppression of potentially problematic expression of emotion. These are some of the benefits she is being asked to abandon, benefits which tutors have enjoyed implicitly in traditional lecturing mode, without articulating the control therein. Many academics are disinclined to dilute their subject discipline for such potential difficulties and need to really feel sure that the benefits are worth it.

If the teacher regards herself as a professional in her role as a teacher as well as in the other roles she may have in higher education, such as research, then we regard it as incumbent for her to work on *how* she works as well as what she works with. This is a matter of accountability for professional practice let alone the responsibility towards learners by virtue of being a teacher, as well as notions of accountability to the community of peers, colleagues and the institution.

In addition, the journey to facilitation can bring isolation for teachers and suggestions for dealing with this by collaborating with colleagues, include: 'I shared a clear conception with colleagues of what I did which led to a model and a means of testing it in different situations' (SEDA 95, see note 1). Collaboration with colleagues is a crucial support for teachers wishing to 'become' facilitators. The experience of others at different stages in the journey to facilitation can help those at the beginning, particularly in relation to the doubts expressed above. Our experience suggests that *being facilitated* and *observing facilitation* are powerful ways of gaining confidence in the art of facilitation and we are still on our journey.

This chapter has clarified our views on facilitation, what it is, why it is appropriate in higher education today, and how facilitative approaches cultivate reflective dialogue, and thereby enable the achievement for learners of critically reflective learning. We have explored the experience of teachers making the journey from 'subject expert' to facilitator, and we have offered some strategies for supporting the journey. Facilitator behaviours are dialogue behaviours, so that teachers who facilitate are modelling the skills that student learners will need for reflective dialogue with each other. We move now to a detailed examination of facilitative behaviours in Chapters 10 and 11.

Note

1. SEDA 95: the Staff and Educational Development Association's 1995 Conference, entitled 'Developing Students, Developing Staff, Supporting staff in a Changing Environment'. Our workshop title: 'From Subject "expert" to Facilitator'. Quotations and material within the text of this section are derived from the contributions of participants at this workshop, a group of practitioners in higher education, interested in the journey from subject expert to facilitator.

10

Facilitation in Practice:
Basic Skills

We have suggested in Chapter 9 that facilitation, by virtue of the relationship it builds, will enable reflective dialogue, and lead to reflective and critical learning in students. We move now to an exploration of the actual behaviour of facilitation, i.e. what the facilitator does that is different from lecturing, supervising or leading a seminar discussion. In fact many of the behaviours are the same, although the emphasis or the order of use may vary. We note that facilitator behaviours are best learnt experientially, i.e. in a facilitative context, rather than from a book. These chapters are not meant to replace such an experience, but to supplement courses or workshops that may be already on offer to teachers in higher education who wish to develop their facilitation skills.

In this chapter, we explore the broad brush qualities of a facilitator, identifying what can be learnt, i.e. behaviours that teachers can acquire themselves in order to adopt facilitative teaching methods with their students, and we describe the basic facilitation skills. These basic skills form the building blocks for further skills which are discussed in Chapter 11.

The basic skills we discuss are, the facilitator's presence, her physical demeanour, as well as the environment she provides, the format of the session, her non-verbal and verbal communications with students, and the attention she offers them by listening and responding to them.

We have proposed a largely person-centred model, while maintaining that such a stance does not preclude conflict, challenge and confrontation, with an emphasis on the quality of relationships which are formed between teacher and learner, as well as between learners. We begin our discussion with some thoughts about the environment and format in which teachers in higher education meet their students and how this might affect these relationships.

Environment

As lecturing is still the most common interaction experienced by students at university (Dearing, 1997), we can expect many teaching rooms to be, at worst, tiered theatres, at best, arranged as rows of desks. We recognize that these facilities are necessary when lecturing is the chosen teaching method, but, where teachers wish to use facilitative methods, alternative room arrangements will be needed. Facilitative methods call for an arrangement where the learners may *relate* to each other, and, indeed, to their teacher. Hence we recommend that all parties in the enterprise are situated at the same level, in positions where they can see each other, and in reasonable proximity to each other. In order to facilitate the relationships needed for reflective dialogue and critically reflective learning, seating should be arranged in a semi or full circle if possible, and desks are less useful, as many institutions have found, replacing them with 'study' chairs.

A chair for each learner allows for students to work in twos, threes or fours, as well as the full circle for plenary mode. For many teachers this means limiting numbers to 12, 15, or at the most, 20, and we recommend small seminar numbers for teachers who are beginning to use these methods. With confidence up to 50 students may work in group format, but the session needs to be tightly structured and a good acoustic environment is essential. It is possible in such an arrangement to move between the modes of facilitation (described in Chapter 9) so that a mini lecture and group facilitation may occur within the same session. Indeed for the kind of process review we recommend in Chapter 8, some elements of facilitation will need to be present in any kind of teaching session.

Group format

Group working has inherent characteristics which differ markedly from the traditional lecture or seminar. The significance of group work in higher education has been explored at length elsewhere (Brown and Atkins, 1988; Jaques, 1990; Nias, 1993) and here we simply recognize that, when we arrange a group in the way described above and facilitate communication within it, group effects, known as group dynamics, affect the individuals in the group and the group as a whole. We are told that a group behaves rather like a person, with distinctive and recognizable characteristics, as well as having a significant impact on the individuals within it (Bion, 1961; Egan, 1976; Foulkes, 1975). We recommend David Jaques' *Learning in Groups* (1990) for teachers who would like to know more about group dynamics in higher education, and we discuss group issues further in Chapter 11.

The most dramatic effect experienced by individuals in groups is feelings of fear and lack of safety and we recognize, that the degree of these feelings will vary with membership of the group, and between individuals. This effect exists in ordinary seminars, though not articulated, and accounts for much of the silence many teachers experience. In order to facilitate learning using group formats, the facilitator may need to accommodate the fears of group members, by establishing very early, an atmosphere of trust and safety, so that learners can contribute and all can benefit. One way to promote such an atmosphere is the process of agreeing, as a group, on guidelines or rules for working in a group.

Guidelines for facilitative working in groups

When students are arranged in group format, and are offered the possibility of being real (a necessary condition for reflection) then it is necessary to also protect students from psychological harm. By this we do not mean nervous breakdowns or the like, but we do recognize the potential for group dynamics to trigger the hurt child in every human being (Miller, 1990), and this may include the facilitator. Hence when launching a facilitative programme with students we advise that the teacher begins by discussing the model of learning she proposes, gaining agreement to it, and establishing with group members a series of guidelines for group behaviour. We are aware of a variety of versions of such guidelines and below we list some of the items which may appear when students are invited to contribute (usually in brain-storming style) to the question: 'What conditions would you want to pertain in a group with x aims, using facilitative rather than traditional methods?'

Clearly, students will need to understand what these words mean, as outlined above, clarifying that responsibility for learning lies with the student rather than the teacher, and this can be a revealing moment for everyone. Some students want to be passively fed, as they may have been for 20 years, while others are familiar with experiential group learning techniques. Providing the course material has been clear and there is not a negative issue about group work in the institution then this process should produce some of the following (and this list is not exhaustive):

Guidelines for group activity

- confidentiality
- equal time to speak
- listen to others when they speak
- be honest and open
- don't attack others
- give constructive criticism
- no compulsion to speak
- feelings may be expressed
- feelings not dismissed
- awareness/acceptance of diversity
- observe time boundaries.

A number of these items will require discussion to agree their meaning in the group. There is no right or wrong meaning. Providing persons are respected, difference is recognized, and context is articulated, then whatever the group decide is the meaning to be observed and this conforms to the person-centred model we recommend.

The guidelines stage of a group life can be the first chance for students to engage in dialogue, as the process of agreement may be carried out in small sub-groups or pairs. In addition, the teacher may introduce the process of review at the end of the session, where students, in twos or threes, review the *process* of the session and identify their learning from it, using the reflective dialogue structure outlined in Chapter 8. As part of that review students may consider the guidelines they have agreed and make alterations they feel are appropriate.

So when the guidelines are established what does the facilitator do then? What skills are needed to facilitate safely and effectively? We begin with a medical education source in higher education, when asked about facilitation skills:

> Patience, I think that's the main one you need; patience and encouragement, and also interpersonal skills – being open, being approachable, showing that the student's contribution is valued however minor or major that contribution might be; not showing favouritism, being seen to be fair within the group – I think those are the main skills.
>
> (Miller *et al.*, 1994:26)

We endorse the above and stress the patience required, especially if the teacher is used to fast-paced wordy interactions. Facilitative methods seem slower at first and the teacher may wonder if anything is happening at all. Patience will reward her with results! The facilitator will use behaviours which we call skills, although they do in fact incorporate cognitive, affective and active components. The basic skills to enable a group to begin to feel safe enough to consider the prospect of reflective dialogue are as follows:

* facilitator presence
* self disclosure
* attending and accurate listening
* basic assertion.

Further skills, e.g. managing emotion, questioning, challenging and providing feedback will be described in Chapter 11, together with behaviours, specific to groups, for facilitators. We begin now with facilitator presence.

Facilitator presence

The first thing a facilitator brings to a session is her presence. She comes into the room and is instantly present to her students by virtue of her posture, gesture, facial expression and relative position, even before she uses her voice or hearing to communicate. We have discussed (in personal stance) the immediacy of impressions gained by students of their teacher and the ensuing stance they take towards her and the curriculum she offers.

Her non-verbal messages are already in the room, as are some of the students. Non-verbal channels like body language, facial expression and voice are thought to deliver meaning quite independently of words (Argyle, 1975; Ekman and Freisen, 1975; Morris, 1977; Pease, 1981). In fact non-verbal and vocal channels often carry a bigger proportion of meaning than the verbal message. For instance, communication of approval has been explored and found to favour the non-verbal channel (90 per cent), leaving the spoken words with only 10 per cent of meaning (Mehrabian, 1971). Where the non-verbal or vocal channels are inconsistent with verbal messages, i.e. spoken words, receivers accept the meaning carried by the non-verbal channels. A clear example of this is sarcasm, where, whatever the verbal message, the voice tone is the message received. Clearly, cultural factors influence how far meanings carried by non-verbal channels are universal, and this point receives a thorough treatment, as do all non-verbal communication issues in Bull (1983). Of particular interest are the findings on dominance and status and how they are communicated by interpersonal distance and posture (op cit.). Suffice to say that a teacher communicates, whether she knows it or not, a host of messages through non-verbal and vocal channels and of course, students will communicate through the same channels, e.g. yawning, sleeping, glazed eyes are all indications that students have stopped listening. Awareness of these non-verbal communication channels is likely to enable the facilitator to make sense of responses from students about their learning. For instance, a student who keeps his head down in seminars, avoiding eye contact, and fidgets while others talk, is clearly preoccupied with his own concerns, which may relate to his learning in the subject, and facilitated sessions may enable him to voice those concerns.

One key aspect of non-verbal behaviour that affects the facilitator is her physical stance. If we consider the likely stance of a teacher giving a lecture, many would say that standing, pacing or leaning on a lectern are the favoured poses, and that lecturers are mostly unconscious of their physical stance. What physical pose is appropriate for facilitation? Heron (1993) suggests that a facilitator's personal presence enables her to be in 'conscious command of how she is appearing in space and time' (p. 32).

He suggests that many facilitators crouch in defensive positions, slumped in chairs with ankles crossed and head jutting forward. Heron suggests that in such a position the facilitator is 'about to talk too much, exhibits anxious control, and is missing a lot of what is going on in the group' (p. 38).

Figure 10.1a   Facilitator posture – crouched and defensive

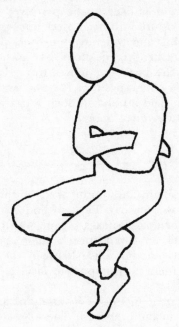

Figure 10.1b   Facilitator posture – open and potent

When crouching in the way shown in Figure 10.1a), awareness is reduced, and the facilitator is likely to be perceived as a talking head. A simple adjustment to posture with head, neck and spine rearranged with a sense of lift, lengthening and widening the back, pelvis, thighs and legs grounded through contact with the floor, as shown in Figure 10.1b), is suggested by Heron. The facilitator moves from slouch and impotence, into a commanding and potent posture. The body wakes up and is ready to receive energies in the field around it. Such a facilitator posture projects presence, and the posture *can be learned*.

Facilitator speech time

The vocal channel is significantly influenced by the facilitator's pace of speaking, which we now consider. First, we look at the pace of delivery when the teacher or facilitator speaks. Again, we draw on Heron (1993) who differentiates between rapid speech time and facilitation speech time. An awareness of the difference between the two and a sense of when and how to use them is an important facet of personal presence in facilitation.

Rapid speech time, used in most conversations and teaching, is often hurried, urgent, non-stop and over-tense. There are no gaps or silences, the speaker may say too much for too long, and continuous activity displaces anxiety about performance in the teacher. Skilled public speakers have improved their delivery by incorporating some of the characteristics of facilitator speech into their material.

Facilitator speech time is slower, with intentional pauses and silences, free of urgency or tension. It is likely to be warmer, deeper and rhythmic in delivery. It is appropriate for interventions which touch on matters of human significance, e.g. teacher disclosure, responses to participants, matters of importance like group guidelines. The facilitator will not use either mode exclusively – a balanced style enables free movement between both modes.

The test of competence in facilitator speech is toleration of silence, with the ability to remain fully present, without anxiety during intentional (or, indeed, unintentional) silence. In silence the facilitator can tune in to her listeners and generate unstated meaning. Some facilitators learn a 'rhythm' of counting to six or 10 before intervening into silences.

We would say, however, that students are used to rapid speech within traditional lecturing where the tutor is the undisputed expert, and, where the facilitator is moving between modes she may need to alert the students to her intentions. For example, in a typical seminar, the opportunity for key input may arise, when the tutor may stand and adopt rapid speech or lecturing mode momentarily. The resumption of her seat is the signal that she has returned to facilitator mode. We believe these signals should be made explicit for students so that processes are clear.

Self-disclosure or 'really talking'

Belenky *et al.* (1986) have described 'really talking' as characteristic of constructivist learners (described in Chapter 3), as the ability to really talk enables learners to engage in reflection through reflective dialogue. They differentiate 'really talking' from the holding forth of traditional academia, where there is no intention to share ideas, only to transmit them one-way (p. 144). We shall explore what 'really talking' means in terms of the skill of self-disclosure as it is a key dialoguing skill.

We define disclosure as the conscious sharing with others of previously unknown material, and *self* disclosure when this material relates to the discloser. We note the obvious point that 'all relations which people have to one another are based on their knowing something about one another' (Simmel, 1950:307).

Our approach to learning demands connection and relationship through reflective dialogues and this implies a potential for some disclosure between learners. The idea of relationships in learning situations may concern those with narrow, possibly sexual, interpretations of the term 'relationship' and may seem strange in the context of higher education. We need only return to our stories at the beginning of this book, and invite our readers to do the same, to realize that relationship was the key to our most productive learning. Many tutors in higher education are only too aware of the importance of relationship in learning and regret the loss of resource 'space' in which to nurture relationships with students. While recognizing the loss we recommend that teachers/facilitators can enable their students to relate with each other through the process of reflective dialogue, thereby providing an all-important relationship factor in learning.

What exactly do we need to know about the other, and more to the point what does he need to know about me? Just how much disclosure is needed for learning relationships?

We call attention to the diagram known as the Johari Window to illustrate the process of self-disclosure in Figure 10.2.

Johari Window

A useful insight into how we may relate to people is the diagrammatic representation known as the Johari Awareness Model or the Johari Window (the name being coined from the joint authors' names) (Luft, 1984). The model rests on humanistic, holistic and psychodynamic assumptions as follows:

- subjective factors dictate our impressions of each other
- emotions influence behaviour more than rational reason or logic
- human beings have limited awareness of self, and benefit from information from other sources
- change promotes the possibility of learning and development
- experience is fluid and ever changing.

Figure 10.2 'The Johari Window'

	Known to self	Unknown to self
Known to others	1	2
Unknown to others	3	4

The four panes, or quadrants of the Johari Window represent one person in relation to others, with each quadrant revealing awareness of behaviour and feelings. Some awareness is shared, some is not. Material is allocated to a quadrant on the basis of who knows about it. We examine each quadrant in turn. The window relates to a person we will call A.

Quadrant 1: The Open Quadrant – Behaviour and feelings known to self (A) and known to others. The Open Quadrant, refers to the behaviour, feelings and motivations that 'I' (A) know about myself as well as others who see my behaviour. This is the window that A (and all of us) open to the world. It is the basis of most interaction that we willingly display.

Quadrant 2: The Unaware Quadrant – Behaviour and feelings known to others but not known to self. The Unaware Quadrant is that which refers to behaviour, feelings and motivations that others see but which 'I' do not. This is the window A 'displays' to others without being aware that he is displaying it. In an interaction person A displays himself as quadrant 1 – his public self. The person to whom he displays himself, person B, sees the public A but may also get an insight into A through quadrant 2 that A cannot 'see' or be aware of. For example, A may not realize that he inadvertently uses a racist expression to another colleague. If B points out the remark to A then A may become aware of his behaviour. How B conveys the message that A has made the remark and how A reacts to it will influence how A gets to know about that part of his behaviour where he is unaware.

Quadrant 3: The Hidden Quadrant – Behaviour and feelings known to self but not to others. The Hidden Quadrant is that window which refers to behaviour, feelings and motivations which 'I' know about but which I am unwilling to convey to others. For example, A may be unwilling to disclose to C that he is pleased about a good grade even though C may observe manifestations of that pleasure through A's window 2. When A offers disclosure to C then quadrant 3 'reduces' in size, while increasing the size of quadrant 1, as the material which was previously 'hidden' is now shared by others, in the Open Quadrant.

Quadrant 4: The Unknown Quadrant – Behaviour and feelings known neither to self nor to others. The Unknown Area is that window that we do not know about ourselves and is not known about by others as well. We may get insights into them through our dreams when we sleep or even in the occasional day dream. This window will contribute to our behaviour but we do not, as others do not, normally see that part of ourselves. We may get insight into this part of ourselves through therapy and that is the place for it.

The total window is drawn to scale for ease of representation, but Luft (1984) suggests that quadrant 4 is much larger than displayed. Using the Johari Window, we can see how disclosure works in a group situation in Figure 10.3.

Figure 10.3

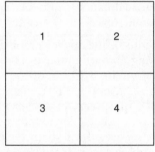

(a) A's window: new group

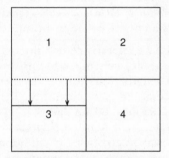

(b) Window after A's disclosure

In window a) we have a starting point, say in a new group. In window b) the person begins to disclose some of that which is hidden from the view of others from quadrant 3, thereby enlarging the size of A's open quadrant 1.

Clearly, such a transfer is managed as a choice by the discloser and is relevant to the context. For instance disclosure in a family situation differs from disclosure at work or with friends. In higher education the context is reflective dialogue with the purpose of enabling reflective/critical learning. We know that reflective dialogue involves disclosure as the learner seeks clarification of their learning processes through sharing them with others. The personal component of learning will need to be communicated in reflective dialogue or the opportunity for reflection is being missed. Hence students will be asked to self-disclose to each other and indeed to their tutor, as appropriate. As tutors are models here we therefore recommend that aspiring facilitators acquire the skill of appropriate self-disclosure, so that students are given an idea of how to proceed.

When a group first forms and members are asked to speak, they often *don't know what to say* and they may be frightened of speaking in case they say the wrong thing and make a fool of themselves, so they may remain silent (another route to seminar death), or gabble nervously. The facilitator can control the level of contributions by a very simple procedure, i.e. by starting off, that is, speaking first about herself, the skill of disclosure, sometimes called self-disclosure. The act of self-disclosure is a direct example of trust behaviour, where the facilitator takes the risk of disclosing and thereby encourages others to do the same.

The facilitator can provide a model of what is appropriate disclosure in terms of duration, level, depth, etc. We are talking here about *appropriate* self-disclosure and this has been defined firmly by Egan (1976) as authentic statements about self, taking into account the following criteria:

- *breadth* – the amount (how much do you want to tell?)
- *depth* – level of intimacy (how deeply do you want to reveal yourself?)
- *duration* – the amount of time (frequently overdone in lectures with lengthy anecdotes)
- *target person* – to whom is the information to be disclosed?
- *the nature of the relationship* – friendship, acquaintance, work colleague?
- the situation – corridor, private room, public place?

We all have experience of a myriad of versions of the above combinations. For example, someone who insists on talking about themselves constantly and at length (duration) is deemed inappropriate as is the over-discloser who reveals intimate details (depth) to almost anyone (target) on any occasion (situation). So we have a true sense of appropriate self-disclosure and moderately well-adjusted persons disclose appropriately for human contact and social intercourse. In addition to the above, the literature on self-disclosure reveals that women are higher disclosers than men, and that disclosure is reciprocal in effect (Cozby, 1973).

The facilitator also models authenticity by demonstrating the crucial characteristic of 'owned' statements (which begin with 'I' or contain 'I' statements). Such statements are likely to be real disclosure while use of the distancing 'you', 'they' or 'one' serves to mask disclosure.

The term itself holds fearful connotations for many. The fashion for over-disclosure in some groups has given the term a bad name, and horror stories abound about learners being 'taken apart' in T-groups, etc. We do note that the stories are almost always recounted by *another* member of the group, suggesting that most of the distress was engendered in the observers rather than the learner concerned. However, we do recognize that the association with nakedness, exposure and stripping are connotations which may concern facilitators, either for themselves or for their students.

We have strong cultural imperatives against self-disclosure and this may inhibit the students' behaviour, especially in conditions where they perceive themselves to be under test. For many, self-disclosure implies revealing weakness – rather a lopsided view as we hope to show below. The reverse halo effect and fear of shame and rejection are strong inhibitors, especially in a group where no trust has been established. And here we have the conundrum. A sure way to establish trust is minimal self-disclosure in the group, while group members may fear self-disclosure until they are confident of trust in the group.

The first person to take a risk is the facilitator, who, we recommend, discloses first. This is essential as she will model the breadth and depth of appropriate self-disclosure for the group. For instance, she may begin by saying that this is a new way of working and although she is confident of the process as useful for learning, she is unsure about the students' response.

Because self-disclosure is reciprocal in effect, this gives permission for everyone in the room to express some positive feeling about what they are doing and some negative feeling too. In particular, it allows students to say 'I don't like the sound of this. I've never done it before', 'it feels like counselling'/'AA'/'evangelical meetings' or whatever it triggers for them. Note that the example given above, the teacher's disclosure about method, includes some emotional material, namely her mixed feelings of confidence and unsureness. These feelings, expressed openly, although fairly superficial, are the hallmark of trust-building self-disclosure. We discuss the management of emotion as a facilitator in Chapter 11.

Another useful idea in the literature on self-disclosure is Egan's distinction between 'history' and 'story'.

Telling it like a story

The distinction between an account which resembles a story and that which is more like history, has been developed by Egan (1973) and adapted to a group context.

'Story' is involvement; 'history' is non-involvement. History is a statement or message which is analytical, factual – it ticks off the facts of experience and even interpretation of these facts but leaves the person who is the speaker, untouched, relatively unknown, and her style may be tedious and even boring. The speaker is detached and uninvolved, taking no risks. The speaker treats herself as *object*, who is 'there and then', rather than subject who is 'here and now'. Generalities may be disguised by the use of words like 'we', 'one' or 'it'. History does not reach or engage the listener. It is flat or boring because it is divorced from the person. It is not really disclosing of the person.

'Story', on the other hand, is not analytic. It is authentic self-disclosure – an attempt to reveal myself as a person and to reach the listener. Story involves emotion. Story is a signal of invitation. The speaker is opening the door to others in the group. It is a story if it is a description by the speaker about themselves expressed, for example, as 'I'. For example, 'I feel pleased with myself; I've managed to get the reference I need from the library at last'.

Another way of categorizing the difference is contrasting the words below:

Story	History
I	Them; it; people
Feeling; affect	Fact
Actual	Abstract
Real	Abstract; detached
Interesting	Boring; a turn off

Readers may like to identify to what extent our stories given at the beginning of this book are quintessentially 'story' or 'history', by checking out our use of 'I', the presence of feeling and emotion, the realness or immediacy of the accounts, and whether they were interesting or boring!

In other words, when we are expressing our feelings (the affective part of us) as well as the cognitive and conative we are likely to be in story mode and disclosing something about us that has the basis in a real meaning that will make connections with the listeners.

Story is selective in detail – not necessarily complete in communicating fact, but complete in communicating self. The 'story' teller is taking a risk and knows it. By so doing the speaker requests support from colleagues. In a group self-disclosure is a leap of trust, and demands dialogue 'here and now'. It is unusual not to be engaged when someone is telling their story. It is usually interesting. The speaker may have taken a risk, made herself vulnerable in the process but will not lose her colleagues' attention. The group will seldom be bored by such a story with sincere self-disclosure, but they may be embarrassed.

The embarrassment can be a cultural bias against self-disclosure and the expression of emotion – seen in some contexts as a weakness at one extreme or exhibitionism at the other. Self-disclosure peaks in childhood and is seen as a passing phase that goes with oncoming maturity. In the fullness of time we become fully locked-in mature adults! However, as human beings we do not lose our emotions, they remain in us and can either be a barrier to our development or can enhance that development. Self-disclosure is often associated with the psychiatrist's couch; we must be weak and in need of 'treatment'. Fortunately, this model is becoming outmoded with our increasing understanding of ourselves as having subjective feelings which impinge on our everyday lives.

As illustration of the difference between 'story' and 'history' we offer three samples of text in an academic context moving from 'history' to 'story' in three stages as a staff member modelled appropriate self-disclosure to her students:

1. 'A validation meeting was held this week for the new modular degree. The reflective skills module was identified as an exemplar for courses of this kind.' (pure history, factual, abstract, impersonal, and detached)

2. 'My expertise was acknowledged at the recent validation meeting for the new modular degree. Questions were addressed to me about the Reflective Skills module and considerable interest was shown in it by academic colleagues.' (moving towards story with use of my, some reported emotion, some action, less detached)
3. 'I am feeling very pleased because, this week, at a validation meeting, I was asked to respond to questions about the Reflective Skills module, part of the new modular degree. I am also glad that my contribution has helped to make the degree so successful and highly regarded by academic colleagues.' (pure story, personal, use of 'I', expression of owned feelings, involved and interesting)

Thus telling it like a story is more likely to convey congruence between what we are saying and what we are feeling and what our thoughts really are. It is more likely to create bridges of understanding than a 'history' version which takes no risks and may lead to misinterpretation. The test of authenticity in self-disclosure is boredom. If the listener's attention is wandering then the discloser is probably in history mode. So what about the listener? Isn't that an important facilitator skill? We move now to how the facilitator attends and listens to students.

Attending and accurate listening

In order to listen it is necessary that we first attend to the other. The reinforcement power of attending means that attending can alter another's behaviour (quoted in Egan, 1976:96). Indeed, the withdrawal of attention has been described as psychological punishment (Nelson-Jones, 1986) and likely to damage development (Bowlby, 1969). Certainly, the effects of never being listened to have been summarized in the statement: 'A riot is at bottom the language of the unheard' (Martin Luther King).

Attending is how the facilitator is personally present, physically receptive, calm and grounded without anxiety, ready to tune in to verbal and non-verbal messages. Attending refers to the way in which we can be *with* our speaker in the context of a group both physically and psychologically. The body stance and orientation of the facilitator will influence the quality of her listening, and Egan (1990) offers a mnemonic to assist facilitators to adopt an attentive posture. Many facilitators have begun their training with SOLER, shown below, as the minimum requirements for a listener to attend to a speaker:

S Face the speaker *squarely*, that is with a posture that conveys involvement, reflects the speaker in a positive manner and indicates that you wish to be with the speaker. This is not meant to be in a threatening manner but just one that suggests you wish to be with them, inclining towards the speaker. The posture shows that you are not distracted and provides stereophonic reception.

O Adopting an *open* posture to signify 'receive' mode. Crossed arms and legs may convey a closed stance towards the speaker. Such a posture may not necessarily mean that you are closed towards the speaker, but it may convey it non-verbally to her. The key question to ask is to what extent is my physical posture conveying an openness and availability to the speaker?

L At times it is possible to *lean* towards the speaker in a way which suggests engagement. We can see this when viewing people in pubs and restaurants by observing how people lean forward, lean back or lean away without losing a grounded stance (see facilitator presence above).

E Maintain *eye* contact with the speaker. This is a useful indicator of involvement with the speaker which does not have to be continual to be effective. It does not mean 'eyeball to eyeball' either!

R Be relatively *relaxed* in your behaviour so as to minimize distractions to both speaker and listener. This means not being physically distracting or fidgety. It also means being comfortable with the speaker so that your body can convey non-verbal expression.

A commitment to listening to the speaker, utilizing SOLER ensures authenticity. Artificially contriving a physical stance will convey messages that are counter-productive for the speaker. Negative or uncomfortable messages might include staring, getting too squared up where it becomes threatening, looking out of a window continuously or tapping a pencil on a table! Being aware of the effect of your physical and emotional presence is the key. SOLER is useful to convey the basic features of attending. To the reader unfamiliar with the approach it may appear that to adopt the features could suggest a lack of genuineness or manipulation. It is designed merely to highlight what we all do naturally when we are authentically attending.

Having established an attending posture, facilitators need to be aware that many factors inhibit accurate listening. There is a tendency for us to lose a significant part of what a person has said simply because the act of verbal communication is itself complex even though we take it for granted. We illustrate what happens when A communicates with B in Figure 10.4. When A communicates with B in five stages, accuracy may be compromised, and the message reduced or distorted at every stage in the process:

1. A formulates an idea and creates a message which may or may not signify exactly the original idea.
2. A transmits a message: the message in the form of sounds and visual signals travels through space and time to B and may be distorted by external factors like noise, light, wind.
3. B hears approximately 50 per cent of the message as B may make judgements, creates arguments, perhaps while A is still speaking and may miss part of the message.
4. B decodes the message, and may decode incorrectly for all sorts of reasons including lack of understanding through different forms of discourse which can be influenced by, for example, class, gender or culture. B may also be confused by conflict between verbal and non-verbal information.

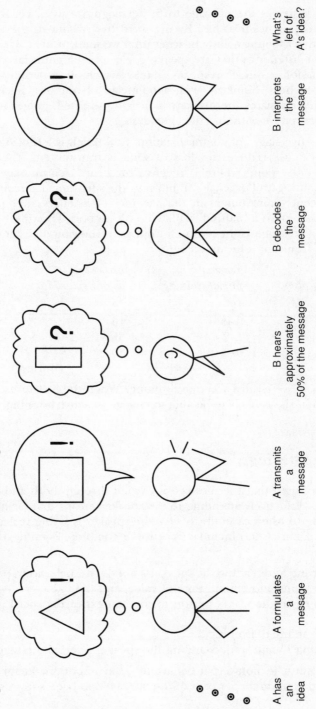

Figure 10.4 A communicates with B in five stages

5. B reconstructs the message to fit her cognitive map, i.e. B may have a negative or positive 'fix'. By the word 'fix' we mean the tendency for selective listening – only hearing what we want to hear. We often evaluate the listener as they are speaking, e.g. when a politician of a different persuasion to ourselves speaks we may 'switch off' and only hear what we want to hear. Similarly, with a politician of our own persuasion! The listener evaluates the message as it is transmitted, judges it and rejects (or accepts) it without critical analysis.

After the five stages of communication, how much is left of A's message?

How can we reduce this loss of what is transmitted? The largest loss occurs at the point where B receives or 'hears' A's message and this is where training and practice can improve the situation. There are records of 25 per cent improvement in the accuracy of listeners after training. But surely listening is a 'natural' skill? Weren't we born knowing how to listen? Burley-Allen suggests the reason for our poor showing on listening lies in its absence from our education:

Mode of communication	Years of formal training	Estimated % of time used
Writing	12	9
Reading	6–8	16
Speaking	1–2	35
Listening	0–1/2	40

(Burley-Allen, 1995:39)

So how can we ensure accurate listening? When the listener is attending as above then she is likely to be able to engage in active listening, to which we now turn.

Active listening

We have noted that the message is carried through both audio and visual channels. Effectively attending to the speaker means that facilitators are in a position to listen carefully to what the speaker is saying verbally and non-verbally. Egan (1990) includes in active or complete listening, the following components:

1. observing and reading the speaker's non-verbal behaviour; posture, facial expressions, movement, tone of voice, and the like.
2. listening to the whole person in the context of the social groupings of life
3. tough minded listening
4. listening to and understanding the speaker's verbal messages.

1. Attention to non-verbal behaviour is an important factor in accurate listening, as up to 90 per cent of the message has been shown to be carried

by the non-verbal or vocal channels. Over half of the message may be communicated by facial expression or body language, while over 30 per cent travels in the tone, pitch, volume, para-language of the voice. (Argyle, 1975; Mehrabian, 1971) In relation to non-verbal behaviour it is important to recognize that we seek to listen to speakers in a way that deepens our understanding of what they are trying to convey in overall terms. It is inappropriate to fix on an expression of non-verbal behaviour and then to create a total impression from that single piece of information.

2.   At this point the listener does not form his responses to the speaker but listens. For example, where a speaker is telling the group what it is like for her as a student, as her family commitments prevent her having the time and space to study, the listener may have some views about how he would cope in such an environment. For example, he may reflect to himself: 'I could cope with that' or, 'It would not be a problem for me'. But if he listens to his own thoughts on *his* way of coping he may detract from how she is thinking, feeling and being in *her* environment. The key is for our listener to 'put aside' his own responses to her situation and listen from the speaker's standpoint – where she is coming from. As we shall see below, even when he responds, it is necessary to work with where she is and not put his solutions to her predicament.

Our listener above in listening to her story will, if effective, place himself (as far as is possible) as a man in her social context. He will endeavour to understand what it is like to be a woman in a family situation, to tackle a prevailing norm within which she feels oppressed. Rather than get trapped in his own contextual picture, what is it about *her* picture that he needs to understand to enable her to deal with it? In this way he will be endeavouring to get into her personal context – how life is for her.

Issues relating to the social grouping of a speaker's life may not be part of the verbal message. However, a student who is a member of an ethnic minority is visibly living with issues of exclusion and her message will convey something of her struggle, and may be very relevant to her learning and reflection. For example, black students in an all-white law school may be marginalized in group work and informal support groups. Cultural factors may provide important cues for an active listener, who will need to be alert to the cultural context of the speaker, and provide what is known as cultural-care in his responses (Leininger, 1987).

3.   Tough-minded listening requires that our listener places himself in the frame of the speaker so that he really understands her context. It also means that he picks up what is perhaps being distorted by the speaker. For example, our speaker may be talking about completing a piece of coursework. However, she is also conveying less explicitly through her voice tone, demeanour and some of her words that she may feel that she is not confidant to do it properly. This in turn may affect her will to get down to it. It is for the listener to pick up this inconsistency and hold it until it is appropriate to offer it as an observation. We discuss challenge in Chapter 11.

Hearing, active and passive listening

Contrast the distinction between hearing, active listening and passive listening. If you close your eyes you can hear what is going on around you (unless you have a hearing impediment) as well as inner sounds inside you. Even though we close our eyes we may well be interpreting what we are hearing from the sensation of the sounds; we will place meaning on the sounds through our listening. Even when we close our eyes we may listen by paying attention to what we hear. We could also be passive in simply not trying to grasp meaning from it or not really caring what we hear. Now with our eyes open we listen to somebody such as our speaker.

Listening actively is not just hearing what she is saying but is a two-way process involving both sender and receiver skills. Active or effective listening can only be assessed by the listener. So that in the example of our speaker conveying her message about her work, I as listener need to convey to her that I have received what she has tried to communicate. This is why active listening is a tough-minded process. We have to really work at it, and if we are really listening it shows! The sender (speaker) is aware of the listener really listening.

Active listening also involves listening to the whole person not just the words they may be using at the level of intellect. Our culture emphasizes listening to what people *say*. We tend to listen at the level of our intellects. But active listening also includes listening to what a person's non-verbal messages are saying – *body* messages. In addition, as senders of messages we convey our *feelings*, that is the emotional content of our message. Lastly, we have another level which can be called our will, commitment or *spirit*. Let us take our example of the speaker talking about her coursework.

She is saying that she intends to complete the work. Her body is sending out messages that convey something about her feelings towards the work, as is her tone of voice. Underlying these messages is another that is transmitted about her will or spirit. If as listeners we merely went by what she said we would conclude that all she needs to do is to get on with it. However, by actively listening we are picking up more complex messages.

Contrast passive listening and the signals that are conveyed between the sender (speaker) and receiver (listener or facilitator). With passive listening the listener conveys, often non-verbally, that he is not really listening. As a reader you may wish to go through SOLER and think of situations in which you have been on the receiving end of passive listening. Recall situations where you have given out the signals of passive listening to a person who wanted your attention!

Further aspects of effective listening

Apart from being passive towards the speaker there are other ways, which can overlap, that can impede the effectiveness of our listening.

Evaluative listening

When we listen evaluatively we may impose our own values upon the speaker's message. In our example where the speaker is talking about her coursework, we may do any of the following while apparently listening:

- think that she really can't do it (or she'll do it easily)
- feel annoyed (why can't she just get on with it?)
- I wouldn't be making such a song and dance about a piece of coursework
- that she shouldn't be at university if she's got a family anyway (if a person with sexist views).

The listener is judging what he is hearing while it is being transmitted instead of putting the thoughts to one side in order to hear what she is conveying. It is very difficult to put judgements aside entirely. It is important to recognize where they are coming from, however. Evaluations of the situation may be helpful at a later stage provided they enable her.

Inattentive listening

This occurs when as listener we are distracted by tiredness, our own emotions, or our difficulty with differences of culture, gender, race, sexual orientation or disability differences which 'gets in the way' of listening.

Filtering listening according to the listener

Similar to the above, but more specifically, the listener is filtering what the speaker is saying according to the listener's view of the world.

How shall I respond?

A listener preoccupied with this question (and it is understandable when we first become conscious of our responses), may stop attending and therefore listening to the speaker. However a really active listener will not require any preparation for his response as he is likely to be congruent with the speaker.

Listening with sympathy

A common and human response, but sympathy can get in the way for the speaker. For example, if at a later date our speaker reports that she has still not completed her assignment, we as listeners could offer our sympathy and collude in this or even foster it, and in the process, we, as listeners are merely getting in the way of the speaker moving on to future action. We could be disabling in our effect. Being with her empathically is different as we shall see in Chapter 11.

Being listened to without interruption

Interrupting a person who is conveying her thoughts and feelings is a common trait in conversation arising from enthusiasm, boredom, having something to say ourselves, not being able to wait, emotion, through to insensitivity towards the person speaking.

Listening with 'silence'

At times the speaker may pause or not want to express words. There may be a tendency for a facilitator to fill the silence or space with a question or a response. There is, in fact, no silence – it is just that the speaker has stopped using words! That 'silence' can be precious for the speaker and should be respected.

Reflecting back

Retaining the verbal content of a message can be learnt by facilitators. The technique of 'reflecting back' is one way of discovering what you do hear and improving your accuracy, and is recommended for enabling critical reflection:

> one of the most useful tasks we can perform as we seek to develop critical thinking in other people, is to reflect back to them their attitudes, rationalisations, and habitual ways of thinking and acting.
>
> (Brookfield, 1987:75)

This section is distinguished from the last one in that the listener now responds to the speaker in order to clarify and confirm that what the listener has received is an accurate reflection of what the speaker conveyed. Dialogue is enabled when the speaker's contribution is affirmed and confirmed by an active listener. A group's activity is killed off when members' contributions are attacked or ignored (a possible reason for seminar death). The skill of 'receiving' contributions from group members without evaluation is the basis of facilitation and probably the most valuable skill for aspiring facilitators to learn.

Once the speaker has conveyed her statement, the facilitator or any member of the group may respond. Initially, the facilitator may need to model responding and gradually encourage others to join in. Indeed, when used effectively it can mean that the speaker benefits from having a group of people attending to her with what may be called a collective wisdom. One member of the group may attune to the speaker more closely than others and follow it through with reflecting back what has been conveyed followed by clarifications. In the beginning the first responder is likely to be the facilitator.

Given that the facilitator will wish to reflect back what he thinks he has heard he may wish to start with phrases like:

> 'What I think you said was that your essay is incomplete because you are unsure about referencing?'

> 'If I have understood you properly, you want to discuss the criteria for the assignment as you are unsure what they mean?'

The purpose here is to *accurately* reflect back to the speaker what as listener he thought she said. Using the speaker's exact words in 'reverse' may be helpful if it is unclear, i.e. changing 'I' to 'you' and changing 'my' to 'your', etc. An inappropriate response would be to:

- give an interpretation of what was said rather than an accurate response
- make and convey an assumption beyond what was said.

This description may appear simple, obvious or even banal as set on this page. It is stated here because of our social tendency to assess and interpret and think what we are going to say even before the speaker has finished. It is simply an important process to disentangle so that we really are attending to the speaker and not imposing our own view of her reality. The listener in responding should aim to respond in a way that is not pedantic or inter-rogative. The tone of voice is important. A tone which suggested criticism or uncaring or agreeing is not helpful. The aim is to reflect back what is being said – her words and her meaning; her emotions – her feelings; her will or spirit.

The reflecting back does not have to repeat the words our speaker used exactly, although use of the speaker's key words is useful for accuracy. It is useful to paraphrase so that she can respond with say, 'yes, that's it' or 'not quite, I would put it like this' until there is assent between speaker and listener. Moreover, by paraphrasing the listener is also going beyond simply saying, 'I understand' when in fact he may not and he has not demon-strated to the speaker that he has and she does not really know he has understood. The use of the notorious phrase, 'I hear what you say' may also convey the same lack of real understanding between listener and speaker!

For instance, when a student has expressed concern about their work, with a sense of panic, an appropriate response might be: 'you are getting rather concerned about the deadline for your work', and an inappropriate one might be: 'well we can't change deadlines just for you', or, 'yes the deadline is next week – you should be concerned'.

Many people find the prospect of 'reflecting back' embarrassing and are uncomfortable with it, possibly resorting to an inappropriate response be-cause of that discomfort. The speaker is unlikely even to notice that you are reflecting back – the luxury of being responded to is so rare and precious that speakers are likely to move on enthusiastically. The discomfort is in the listener and, with practice, the awkwardness dissolves as the increased potential for understanding the message becomes obvious.

Summarizing

Reflecting back builds material for a competent summary, so often missing or inaccurate in seminar sessions. A facilitator who has reflected back key points will be able, with or without notes, to give a résumé of the session for the benefit of students, and they will learn the skill from her modelling of it. As part of the reflective dialogue process summarizing is a key skill for the review session.

In particular, when the facilitator is able to pick up some of the emotional content of the speaker's message and respond empathically as well as accurately, then the 'easy' meaning of facilitation comes into its own. We deal with empathy under management of emotion in Chapter 11.

One final point about listeners who are inert and non-responsive, preferring to listen in silence. Listening in silence has its place, especially where high levels of emotion are being expressed (e.g. weeping). However, in the initial stages of facilitation, group members are seeking a response from the facilitator, and this is where the tone of the session is set. If the first response is silence, which may be perceived as negative or critical, then the scene is set for a silent seminar. If, on the other hand, a listening response, is given, i.e. reflecting back, then the climate of support and safety is established from the start.

Where a student refuses to or is unwilling to speak in seminars, the facilitator may judge that the student has made a conscious choice and that choice should be respected (see guidelines). We would urge facilitators to ensure that every member of a seminar group is enabled to speak at least once, early in the group's life, thereby ensuring that student's choose silence rather than being silenced. The learning group is likely to be embedded in a number of oppressive social systems, e.g. sexism, racism, ageism, and in universities, possibly intellectualism and academicism. The silencing of minority groups becomes very clear in facilitation situations and the facilitator may like to address the issue when agreeing guidelines at the very beginning.

In summary then, the basic skills of facilitation are therefore the basic skills of human communication, disclosure, listening attentively and responding accurately with understanding. We identified the effects of disclosure on the Johari quadrants, and established the criteria for appropriate disclosure. The technique of reflecting back to a speaker was introduced and examples provided. We have also examined the significance of environment and facilitator presence in teaching sessions, as well as the importance of non-verbal channels in communication.

We move now to further skills used in facilitation, managing emotion, challenging and feedback and we explore these in Chapter 11.

11
Facilitation in Practice: Further Skills

In Chapter 10 we described the basic skills of facilitation, disclosure, attentive listening and responding, as well as the non-verbal factors which influence the learning relationship.

In this chapter we explore the further skills of facilitation which enables the formation of relationships within which reflective dialogue and critically reflective learning can take place. We have established in Chapter 9 that such facilitation should include the core conditions of empathy, warmth and congruence, as well as aspects of all three domains of learning, so that knowledge, self and the world are integrated through the process of reflection.

Our emphasis in this chapter is with the affective and action domains, so that emotional expression, empathy, conflict and congruent challenge are examined. The further skills of questioning, immediacy, feedback and confrontation, are also described, as well as some techniques for dealing with the group dynamics which emerge in student groups in higher education.

Emotion, as we have seen, has not featured in the academic tradition. In introducing reflection to higher education we need to address the management of emotion because of its key role in reflective dialogue, double-loop learning (see Chapter 3) and critically reflective learning.

The three-stage process of reflection begins with 'uncomfortable feelings and thoughts', discomfort or surprise, and moves on to analysis of these feelings and thoughts; leading to potentially new perspectives (Atkins and Murphy, 1993). To enable learning through reflection the learner needs to be in touch with those feelings, aware of their significance, and be able to: 'describe these verbally and/or in writing' (p. 1190).

We note the implicit devaluing of emotion in some interpretations of reflection, with traces still of the mind/body dualism discussed in Chapter 2, and we support the movement towards recognizing emotional and experiential knowledge as itself contributing to transformational learning (Michelson, 1995).

We have also seen that interpretations of reflection almost always present it as an isolated activity, undertaken by the learner inwardly, with only self-report of the process through reflective documents and the like (Atkins and Murphy, 1993; Barnett, 1997; Harvey and Knight, 1996; Mezirow, 1990). We are suggesting that, while intrapersonal dialogue is valuable, it may be insufficient to break through to the critically reflective learning required in higher education, and we discuss this fully in Chapters 4 and 5. Reflective dialogue provides the space and opportunity for learners to examine safely their 'uncomfortable feelings', analyse them and use them to fuel their learning towards double-loop learning (see Chapter 3 for details of double-loop learning).

In other words, for reflection-with-others, our learner needs to be able to articulate her own feelings, and receive other's expressions of emotion. It follows therefore that the teacher/facilitator will need to model similar behaviours, managing emotion in herself and others in order to enable learners to respond to challenges and opportunities. The stimulation and 'disturbance' created by articulation of emotion provides the energy for change, and learners will need support in their move. Challenging is most effective when it includes support in relationship, and empathy provides that support.

The teacher/facilitator is an important model of relationship and supportive challenging as students may carry histories of experiencing destructive confrontation. Further, the provision of feedback in a skilled and supportive manner is the key to productive challenge, as opposed to destructive criticism, as well as being part of day-to-day practice in academia.

Management of emotion in self and others

We begin with emotions experienced by the self, i.e. the facilitator. Traditionally seen as irrational and the part of humans associated with 'bodily humours', emotion has been largely ignored in higher education. As explained in Chapter 2 the educational philosphies handed down to us have dismissed emotion (some might say denied it) and hence the facility for dealing with feelings has been absent from education, particularly higher education. This resistance to emotional intelligence mirrors the inadequacy of emotional matters in the wider (Western) society (Orbach, 1994).

The expression of emotion is socialized on cultural and gender lines, e.g. privileging particular emotional expression to females but not to males, such as weeping. Some emotions are more acceptable than others, and this is inculcated very early in life and there is no further training in the handling of emotions (Skynner and Cleese, 1983). People who declare that they feel no emotion have just got the lid on tighter than the rest of us and will reveal 'leakages' in some way. Emotion in itself is a fact. We are living human beings for whom emotion is an integral part of ourselves. Facilitation offers us the chance to express feelings safely.

Being socialized to discourage the expression of some of our emotions is partially useful. I may be angry with someone. That does not mean I can hit out physically or abuse them emotionally. That is useful socialization. However, some forms of socialization may result in inhibiting the display of emotions so that we become fully 'locked-in' adults.

Jourard (1971) suggests that persons who are 'known' by others are healthier and happier than those who are not. The suppression of emotion in Jourard's view is a major component of stress in modern society. In our role as facilitators we have often heard a student say that being able to give voice and express their emotions has been a major breakthrough in tackling a major task in work or in life, confirming expert findings on stress management (Cooper and Payne, 1988; Rachman, 1980).

If a person does not express their emotions verbally there will be a tendency to 'leakage' – the expression non-verbally of the emotions. Both can of course be expressed together as congruent behaviour. Non-verbal expression of emotion may include tone of voice, gesture and body language. Verbally emotions may also be expressed inadvertently when the words belie the stated intention as in Freudian slips!

The root of the word 'emotion' suggests movement, and can be recognized therefore, as a strong motivator. In fact it is recognized in some countries as mitigation for a crime (*crime passionnel*), but in the UK citizens have to be declared insane to be helpless in the grip of passion!

Given our cultural heritage how can we deal with expression of emotion and what is its value in higher education?

Expression of emotion

First, emotions are part of being human, in themselves neither right nor wrong, and though we can suppress or even repress 'unacceptable' emotions they are not so easily controlled and may be released verbally and/or non-verbally. Secondly, the motivating power of emotion provides the 'fuel' for the adventure of double-loop learning (see Chapter 3). Emotion is an important source of energy to support and sustain the learner through the 'dip' of the learning curve. In addition, an ability to deal with emotional material is necessary if we wish to 'unpack' the blocks to learning which emerge in reflective dialogue.

We recognize our heritage and seek to identify where our difficulties may lie. The difficult–easy continuum shown in Figure 11.1 is based on the work of Egan (1977) and indicates how awkward we find emotional expression, under a variety of circumstances.

We find it easier to express negative emotion and this is borne out by our lop-sided emotional vocabularies which incorporate more negative feelings than positive ones. Further we are able to express emotions about people in

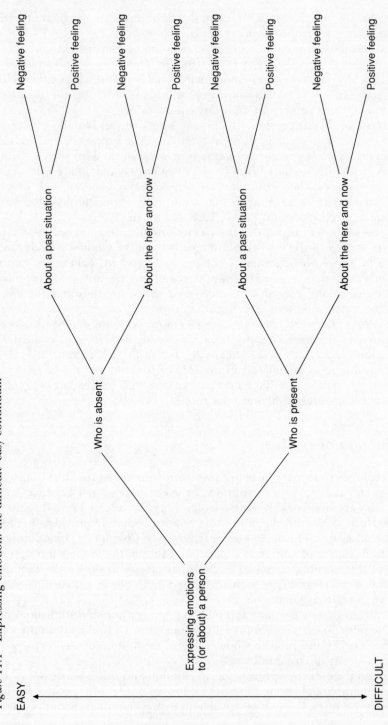

Figure 11.1 Expressing emotion: the difficult–easy continuum

Source: adapted from Egan, 1977 p. 81

their absence more easily than to their face, what we call the gossip syndrome. The facilitator, to enable reflective dialogue, is an important model of emotional expression in the here and now, so how might she express emotions appropriately?

Responsibility for emotion: owning it
We are each responsible for our emotions. If, say, someone lets me down I may feel angry and disappointed. What do I do with my anger? I can respond with an accusation: 'You are making me feel angry' or 'I feel angry because you have let me down . . . I'm disappointed.' With the latter I am taking responsibility for dealing with my own anger and disappointment. This is important. If I make the former statement, the person to whom I am making it may feel accused, threatened and defensive, while the latter statement relates only to me.

Storing up emotions
Saving or storing up emotions is not helpful for when they eventually erupt they may explode. It is better to express feelings as they arise even if they are negative. We may need a little time to identify what the emotion is and how we feel but that is different from putting the emotion into storage.

Assertiveness and expression of emotion
Assertiveness has its place in emotional expression. If someone's behaviour is upsetting you – say so and why in terms of your own feelings – taking responsibility for your feelings as suggested above. Asserting feelings is congruent behaviour, mentioned in Chapter 9 as one of Rogers' conditions for facilitating personal change. Assertiveness as an interpersonal skill is beyond the scope of this book, and we refer readers to existing texts on assertiveness, e.g. Back and Back (1982), Dainow and Bailey (1988), Dickson (1982).

Knowing your own emotional states
Awareness of our emotional states enables us to express clearly in words what it is we are feeling and why. Students and facilitators may have difficulty expressing some emotions or express them indirectly. For example, students may feel inferior or inadequate, while the facilitator may feel frustrated or impatient, the first likely to be revealed by the student's lack of eye contact and drooping body language, and the second may be leaked in the tone of voice used by the facilitator.

Parking it
We may decide, having identified our feelings about an issue or person, to 'park' the feeling until the situation arises where it can be dealt with. The person concerned may not be available or the time may not be right and

emotional intelligence means judging when to deal with and when to 'park' emotion.

As noted above, feelings and emotions are basic human characteristics. They are neither good nor bad, right or wrong. However, we may seek to control the expression of our emotions even though we may feel them. In fact, how we handle our emotions is a learned style of behaviour. We may be socialized not to show some of our emotions, e.g. hurt or anger. As a consequence we may not be able to handle these emotions either in ourselves or in others. An example of the first would be a reluctance to cry if another person makes me feel angry or hurt because it may be seen as a sign of weakness. An example of the second would be if another person is in tears, I might feel embarrassed and avoid the situation.

Whatever the emotional expression in a teaching session, how should the facilitator respond?

Empathy

The purpose of this section is to suggest that a facilitator can, with care and respect for each student, enable the expression of emotions in a helpful way, using primary and, where necessary, advanced empathy, and we define these terms below.

If we wish to respond to another's feelings with understanding we use the skill of empathy, the genuine response to an expressed feeling. The word *empathy* is a recent creation, being coined in 1904 by Vernon Lee from the German 'einfuhlung' or 'feeling – into'. The word is defined as: 'Projection of the self into the feelings of others. It implies psychological involvement' (*Fontana Dictionary of Modern Thought*). This particular skill requires careful handling as it *is* so rare in modern life. An empathic response from a facilitator may be the first such response ever received by some learners and the effect can be dramatic. We recommend that teachers in higher education restrict themselves to the simplest form of the skill, i.e. primary empathy, in the first instance, leaving advanced versions to therapists or counsellors (see Conflict, challenge and confrontation and Egan, 1976 for detail).

Primary empathy responds to feelings which have been expressed explicitly, while advanced empathy endeavours to 'read between the lines' or respond to feelings which may have been expressed obliquely. However, because we inhabit an environment which largely devalues feeling and emotion, some advanced empathy skills may be called for where learners are suppressing or denying what they are clearly feeling. This is particularly important when the facilitator is dealing with conflict, and the skill of assertion is valuable here, as well as confrontation skills and we will discuss these below.

What exactly is empathy?

By empathy (either primary or advanced) we mean an ability to project oneself into another person's experience while remaining unconditionally oneself. Carl Rogers expresses it well as follows:

> Being empathic involves a choice on the part of the facilitator as to what she will pay attention to, namely the ... world of the speaker as that individual perceives it ... it assists the speaker in gaining a clearer understanding of, and hence a greater control over, her own world and her own behaviour.
>
> (adapted from Rogers, 1979:11)

In summary, empathy is: 'an understanding of the world from the other's point of view, her feelings, experience and behaviour, and *the communication of that understanding in full.*'

So *feeling* empathy for someone is fine, but this is not the skill of empathy-in-use. For true empathy there needs to be a communication of under-standing from the listener to the speaker. Egan (1976) built upon Rogers' ideas about empathy and developed a model of the skill which we adapt below.

Primary empathy is based on two pieces of information:

- what the speaker is feeling (expressed in words or non-verbal behaviour)
- the experience and/or behaviour which is the source of that feeling (revealed by what the speaker has already said).

When these two pieces of information have been identified the next step is communication of that awareness of the listener to the speaker. For example, the speaker might say: 'This essay is really bugging me with all the other work I've got to do.' The listener if empathetic may respond with something like: 'You feel pressured about the essay, because of all your other work.'

In starting to use empathy it may be helpful to use the form of words given in Box 11.1 below:

Box 11.1

'You feel . . . . . because . . . . .', or

'You feel . . . . . when . . . . . because . . . . .'

Using this form of words can be a useful way to get into using the skill. Once familiar with the approach, using the skill will be less mechanical. We give examples below in our words and recognize that a facilitator will use her own words in her own way.

Egan (1976) describes a number of ways in which listeners have problems engaging in accurate empathy. We will refer to his headings and adapt them to the student learning context. Let us take the following statement made by the speaker: 'I see myself as so ordinary. I'm not up to this reflective stuff. I don't relate well to others. I'm ordinary.' Her statement can be followed by a number of less than appropriate responses including: the cliché; the question; interpretation; inaccurate; too soon/too late; parroting; incongruent.

For instance the facilitator may respond with cliché like: 'I hear what you say', 'I understand', which in themselves are of no help to the speaker. Such statements do not convey to the speaker that she is understood. Such statements or clichés are more likely to convey to the speaker that she is *not* understood and that the facilitator is responding in an automatic and inauthentic manner.

A questioning response to our speaker's statement might be: 'In what ways are you ordinary?' The question does not take account of the fact that our speaker has taken a risk in disclosing how she feels. The question does not convey empathic support about how and whether the facilitator is understanding her.

Interpreting the speaker's words occurs when the facilitator responds by trying to guess what is implied in the speaker's disclosure. An example might be: 'This ordinary thing is the outward problem. I bet there's something else behind it that's upsetting you.' The facilitator may just be plainly inaccurate with a response to the speaker like: 'You're not very happy with the way the course is going.'

The speaker may be taken off-track or stop or hesitate because accurate empathy has not happened and she may be blocked by what has been said. The facilitator may be listening to his own agenda about the speaker rather than attending to her.

Giving the speaker a chance to express herself gives the facilitator time to sort out feelings and content. However, spontaneity is valuable and 'interrupting' may be necessary if the speaker is beginning to ramble. Care needs to be taken here in order not to convey impatience.

If the facilitator merely repeats back to the speaker what has been said she is parroting. The facilitator needs to 'own' what has been said and then respond. This shows that the facilitator has got 'inside' the speaker in a way that conveys accurate empathy. Egan (1976) compares parroting with a tape recording where there is little mutuality or human contact. An effective response gets to the speaker in a way that parroting cannot.

The facilitator may use language that is incongruent with the speaker's. Using similar language in response to that used by the speaker encourages rapport provided the language the responding facilitator uses is authentic to him. He then conveys that he is in tune with the speaker.

We offer now an example of an accurate empathic response (primary) to the student's statement about being ordinary (in our words):

'You say you feel rather ordinary. You're not confident about the way you relate to others, and you seem concerned about the reflective dialogue which I've mentioned'. (We have assumed here some non-verbal evidence of anxiety.)

We note some misunderstanding about empathy and stress here the variety of responses which are not empathic. This is not to say they are not appropriate responses, we simply clarify *what empathy is not*.

Empathy is not:

- giving advice
- giving an evaluation
- making a judgement
- giving an interpretation
- making a challenge
- engaging the speaker in a reorientation.

When a student expresses a feeling it is not necessary for the facilitator or other students to treat them as a problem, go into 'rescue' mode, or offer advice. Your solution may not be appropriate anyway. Understanding of the speaker's problem or issue is much more useful – provided the facilitators communicate that understanding. We know from the work of Rogers (1992) and Egan (1990) that communication of understanding allows a speaker to move on to a discovery, in time, of her own solutions and find ways of handling them, and taking with her the knowledge of her own ability to learn and reflect. We offer some examples of non-empathic responses, (often described as empathic) below:

- evaluating what the speaker has said, e.g. 'Oh dear, you mustn't worry about your essay. Its only the first assignment.'
- judging what the speaker has said, e.g. 'Nonsense, you'll easily get it done on time.'
- interpreting what the speaker has said, e.g. 'You want an extension really don't you?'
- challenging the speaker, e.g. 'I bet you can do it if you try.'
- reorienting the speaker, e.g. 'What about those of us who have to do lab reports?'

Each of these responses has its place but none of them is empathic.

Empathy commits the listener to the speaker and commits her to stay with the speaker. That is a sign the speaker is valuable and worthwhile, to be respected. The skill of empathy is rather rare in social interaction – few people experience it. When students experience empathy, they recognize the power of an understanding response that builds trust, establishing the basis for a relationship within which it is safe to engage in reflective dialogue, and thus enables critically reflective learning.

Advanced empathy

As mentioned above, advanced empathy differs from primary empathy in that the feelings to which we respond are not necessarily expressed explicitly. They may be revealed obliquely, through verbal or non-verbal codes. For instance, a speaker may be talking about his coursework and asking a lot of aggressive questions about assessment in a puzzled tone of voice. The facilitator may 'sense' that the speaker is actually rather worried about the work, and not clear about what is needed for the assignment.

The process of advanced empathy is the same as for primary empathy, only in this case, because the feeling is not clearly displayed by our speaker, and, more important, *he may be unaware of the feeling himself*, then care is needed in communicating what we think we understand about his world. A tentative approach using qualifiers like, 'perhaps', 'it seems', 'I wonder if' and 'it sounds like', means that the speaker may dissent if they so wish. Offering advanced empathy needs care so that the speaker does not feel trampled on.

So for advanced empathy, the definition, as given above, for primary empathy, is valid, with the addition of some hesitancy and caution, as the facilitator may be mistaken in her 'sensing'. So for advanced empathy, the facilitator will, *in a tentative and careful manner*, offer, 'an understanding of the world from the other's point of view, her feelings, experience and behaviour, and *the communication of that understanding in full.*'

For instance in response to our speaker above, the facilitator might say:

> You have some queries about assessment John, which we can talk about shortly. I am also wondering about how you are getting on with the coursework. It seems that you might be feeling a little confused about what is required, you know, the criteria.

An experienced teacher in higher education is well placed to 'guess' a lot of what is going on for students. What is unusual is for teachers to offer empathy before, and possibly instead of, judgement. Students are often their own harshest judges and offering empathic understanding may provide them with a basis for tangling with their problems.

Facilitators may also 'hunch' about their student's feelings, being prepared to be mistaken. In this case, a tentative response may have hunched as follows: 'You seem very angry John, perhaps you are angry about the grade you got last time; I know you were shocked when you got your feedback.' The student concerned may not agree with your hunch, and, whatever the facilitator thinks is really going on, she may prefer to return to the 'safe', primary version of empathy, based on expressed feelings, giving the following response: 'You were asking some questions John, and you sounded puzzled about the assignment. Perhaps we can explore the criteria together today, if that's all right with you.'

The facilitator's skill in summarizing (based on reflecting back) also offers an opportunity for advanced empathy, as the sum of a person's statements may reveal a consistent feeling, like resentment or lack of confidence, and, in summary, the facilitator may be able to draw the threads together and, tentatively, comment on the overall feeling being communicated, albeit obliquely or in code.

Questioning

The place for questioning comes after contributions have been received without judgement, so that some trust and confidence has been established, through the use of the skills and techniques described in Chapter 10. Questioning too early can be experienced as interrogation, and may halt the process of rapport-building. Why should this be?

Common uses of questioning carry connotations of status and control, and many situations involve questioning by persons with power in relation to the person being questioned. For example, teachers, doctors, lawyers, police, job interviews, etc. The person with 'authority' is asking the questions, usually with a view to making a judgement/diagnosis in relation to a selection promotion, etc. The style of questioning is interrogative rather than enabling.

Enabling questions are different in kind from interrogative questions, but may be equally probing. The main purpose of enabling questioning is for the facilitator to enable a student or group of students to learn and develop, to reflect upon their actions (their academic work) generate their own plans, and implement their own solutions. In other words the questioning forms part of reflective dialogue as described in Chapters 7 and 8. The facilitator, while modelling the skills of reflective dialogue is also enabling the student learner to struggle with the issue under consideration, challenging embedded paradigms, encouraging consideration of possibilities, without restricting the range of possible solutions, and without providing a ready-made solution.

The use of open questions allows learners to develop their own agendas. Open questions begin with one of the following: What, how, why[1] who, where, when. On the other hand, closed questions may close down their willingness to speak or speculate, thus limiting opportunities for reflection. Affect questions invite emotional expression, probing questions need to be open, and reflective questions are challenging to the learner. Rhetorical or leading questions may divert the learner from their own learning path, and multiple questions just confuse everybody. We give some examples below:

- *Open* – What do you understand by reflection?
- *Closed* – Have you done reflection before?
- *Affect* – How do you find reflective dialogue?
- *Rhetorical* – You know how to do it don't you?
- *Probing* – What exactly did you do last time?
- *Checking* – You said you'd like to do x and y. Is that right?

- *Multiple* – Which tutor did you have and how much reflection did you do, can you remember what you did?
- *Reflective* – What would help you to get the coursework done in time?

Socratic questioning was the device used to enable the slave boy in the Meno dialogues (Jowett, 1953b) to understand Pythagoras' famous theorem about trigonometry. Using Socratic questioning, the teacher offers minimal information and then stimulates the learner to work out his own solution. Patience is required! Of particular note here is the use of socratic questioning in reflective dialogue, where learners may be developing preferred scenarios, a term borrowed from Egan (1990) to envisage the future as it would be if the possible visions were realized. For example, when a student says he 'wants to get a first' the questioning may go something like this:

1. What do you need to do to get a first?
2. How can you achieve that?
3. What might stop you?
4. What could help you?
5. Who could help you?
6. When will you be able to do this?

When facilitators question assumptions, e.g. 'what is the benefit of a first for you?' it can feel like an attack and the student may withdraw. Encouraging inspection of taken-for-granted assumptions need questions that are encouraging rather than threatening. Also the follow-up must affirm the speaker, there is no point in asking insightful questions and then destructively critiquing the answer. Non-verbal responses to answers are notorious here and teachers may communicate negative views or even contempt through, for example, sighing, a tired smile, raised eyebrow, inflected voice or inappropriate laughter.

Conflict, challenge and confrontation

Conflict is inevitable in human interaction. We experience conflict as causing pain and loss of trust. We usually receive no training in dealing with conflict in our lives so we are left with whatever we learn at home. Many people tolerate conflict and can use it productively, but there are those of us who dread it and avoid it at all costs because our early experiences of conflict were frightening and painful. So we can fear conflict but we may also use its benefits to build trust, create intimacy and derive creative solutions. When we deal destructively with conflict we feel controlled by others, seem to have no choice, we blame and compete with others, and we hark back to the past rather than grappling with the future.

Nelson-Jones (1986) offers a formula for dealing productively with conflict – in another mnemonic, CUDSA:

- C – Confront the issue
- U – Understand the issue from both sides

- D – Define the difficulty
- S – Search for solutions
- A – Agree on a plan

So to deal with conflict productively we need the courage and the skill to confront. We draw on Egan (1976) to place confrontation into the context of challenging skills, an absolute requirement for reflective dialogue. These skills 'lay the ghost' of so-called 'niceness' in facilitation. Egan puts three challenging skills together: (advanced) empathy, confrontation, and immediacy. The use of advanced empathy is 'strong medicine' and we discussed its use above.

The manner of using advanced empathy as defined above, i.e. tentatively and with care, is the manner needed for confrontation. In addition, Egan stressed the importance of a strong relationship in which to challenge, an established right to challenge (by being prepared to be challenged yourself) and appropriate motivation, i.e. who am I challenging for? Is this for me or them? The state of the receiver should also be considered – is it the right time? What else may have happened to the speaker today – does he look able to receive challenge today? And one challenge at a time please!

Confrontation

The word confrontation denotes 'put-in-front-of', so that when I confront I take someone by surprise, hence again I need to do it with care and tentatively, as I might be mistaken. The word confrontation inspires fear due to the common experience of destructive confrontation, known as the MUM effect (keeping Mum about Undesirable Messages), the primal memory of what fate awaits the bearer of bad news (Rosen and Tesser, 1970). Experience suggests that a great deal of time is spent on unresolved conflict due to people being unable to confront and deal with it productively (Magnuson, 1986). Because it is a fearful behaviour, for both confronter and confrontee, we sometimes avoid it and then do it clumsily. For effective confrontation we need to speak directly, assertively and then listen with empathy to the response we get. Note here that confrontation is in the 'eye of the beholder'. Anything can seem confrontational if I'm in that mood, and what may appear low key can seem outrageous to others.

Confronting is the process whereby the facilitator seeks to raise consciousness in the learner about resistance and avoidance which blocks, distorts or restricts learning.

Note that confronting here has nothing to do with the aggressive combative account of confrontation that is sometimes applied to legal, political and industrial disputes in our society. However, the confronting effect of identifying taken-for-granted assumptions can be perceived as threatening, and may be threatening in reality. The revolutionary nature of breaching paradigms implies a threat to existing models and this can have real negative repercussions. For example, where learners are attached to a particular learning paradigm, e.g. learning is a lone activity, achieved in isolation, without connection to others, the introduction of reflective practice using reflective dialogue presents a huge departure from previous practice. The prospect of communicating with others about learning, when up to now it has been a private affair, may lead to discomfort and some distress. Hence care is necessary as learning is unlikely when threat or distress is present.

Effective confrontation is non-aggressive, and non-combative, deeply supportive of the confrontee, with the intended outcome of *enabling learning* in the confrontee. In particular, the power of confrontation for learning lies in its 'surprise' element – the fact that what was previously unknown is now known to the learner (quadrant 2 in Johari Window). If the learner can be 'held' and supported in her 'surprise' then she is free to consider how she might use the information. Facilitators may like to point out or suggest in Guidelines (see Chapter 10) that the learner has a choice, i.e. to act differently or seek further information from other sources – a kind of second opinion option. We discuss responses to challenge below.

Impending confrontation generates anxiety in the confronter (Rosen and Tesser, 1970). Because confrontation is necessarily revealing that which was previously unknown, the receiver will experience shock, even if they are prepared. A simple preamble is a good way of warning the confrontee that a surprise is coming up! Confronting takes nerve to cope with the natural anxiety of causing shock, and this natural existent anxiety may be confounded by archaic anxiety from past distressing experiences of confrontation.

There are two options traditionally available to the facilitator/confronter. Either the *pussyfoot*, the so-called 'nice' facilitator who avoids the issue; or the *sledgehammer* who is aggressive and wounding. We are proposing the third option, of skilled, supportive and enabling confrontation (Heron, 1989:81).

Our earlier comments about challenging pertain here. Who confronts and why? Confronters may like to consider whether they have earned the right to challenge by being open to challenge themselves. Self-disclosure offers the invitation to challenge by others. What motivates my confrontation? Sometimes there are murkier motives than the benefits to the learner operating and we need to be aware of possible contamination along the lines of 'its for his own good' (Miller, 1983), where discipline is enacted for the benefit of the parent or teacher, masquerading as a concern 'for the good of' the child or learner.

Has there been sufficient listening and understanding to justify the confrontation? Will the relationship support a confrontation at this point in time? Does the confronter have a history of accepting confrontation herself? Is this the right time/place? Is the confrontee in a good state to receive a confrontation? These are just some of the points to consider before launching into confrontation.

So how is this difficult operation to be done, particularly in the context of learning in higher education? We offer some types of confrontation based on Egan (1976) which might be used in higher education, with some examples:

- *Didactic* – checking previous information, e.g. 'Correct me if I'm wrong but didn't you say you'd have the draft ready today?'
- *Experiential* – discrepancies, e.g. 'You seem anxious about your draft, and you have said it's not good enough; having read it and appreciated the quality of it, I'm wondering why you are worried.'
    - distortion in what X says, e.g. 'X, you say that your essay is nearly finished and yet I haven't heard a word about it, and I'm wondering how nearly finished it is.'
    - games (being played unconsciously by Y) e.g. 'Y, I realize that you have asked for help with this essay before, I'm beginning to feel like a rescuer here.'
- *Strength*, e.g. 'I got a sense of your understanding last time in review and I suppose I wonder why you keep it well hidden in seminars. It seems a pity that others here can't benefit from your understanding.'
- *Weakness*, e.g. 'I know you believe in the right to silence, but I feel a bit deprived of your contribution here, especially when I know you could offer a lot.'
- *Encouragement to act*, e.g. 'Is there any reason why we can't share our learning on this issue so far? I'd like to propose that we dialogue on our progress so far and then pool what we've learnt.'

We note that confrontation is not always necessarily negative, and Heron (1986) has offered some ideas on the 'how to' of confronting. We offer some examples:

- Interrupting and identifying the agenda, e.g. 'Can I just check if you realized John, that you've cut across Jane while she was speaking just then?'
- Explain relevance and give space, e.g. 'We were discussing the social context of this particular novel, where the female author used a *nom de plume*, and I suppose I saw Jane being silenced in a similar way.'
- Open questions and silence, e.g. 'When can I hear about *your* review Karen?'
- Educational information, e.g. 'I am getting the impression Jen, that you are unaware of the literature on grounded theory, could there be a gap there?'
- Correcting, e.g. 'I heard what you said Peter, about the median average, in comparison with the arithmetic mean. I would like you to look at that again as what you said was incorrect. Can you do that please and review it with us?'
- Disagreeing, e.g. 'I recognize your view here Mark and I'm afraid I don't agree with your reading of Freud. I would like you to read Webster on this issue and review it with us. Can you do that?'
- Moving the discourse from 'what and why' to 'how and when' and from 'then and there' to the 'here and now', e.g. 'You are saying what you want to achieve James, in terms of making a new start on your learning programme and you've told us why. I'd like to hear today how you

will operate differently here in review and when you think that might happen.'
- Mirroring, e.g. 'You say you want to complete your project by the 15th.'
- Validating, e.g. 'I noticed that your grade on the last assignment was a distinction based on your understanding and critique of theory plus your innovative method of applying theoretical principles to your actual practice as a scientist. I would like you to reflect on how you gained your grade so that you can work as effectively next time.'
- Attending, e.g. Silent attention after someone has spoken can operate as a confrontation as the speaker considers her own words in silence.
- Moralizing, e.g. 'You said you had mixed feelings about learning from Mark's draft – perhaps you went beyond sharing resources and it felt unfair?'

Immediacy

Immediacy is an operational form of congruence, one of Rogers' requirements for personal change, mentioned in Chapter 9. Egan (1976) identifies this as 'you-me' talk, reminiscent of the process of constructing our humanity through interactions of the 'I-thou' kind (Buber, 1994) where realities are forged in relationship and the interplay from you to me.

Immediacy is defined as: 'the ability to discuss with another person what is happening between the two of you in the here and now of an interpersonal transaction' (Egan, 1976:201).

We remind readers of the difficult/easy continuum in expression of emotion in Chapter 10 and note that saying a feeling to a person who is present about the here and now is the most difficult and challenging way of expressing emotion. For example: 'I sense you're feeling resistant to doing this dialogue process, Eddie. I can feel you withdrawing from the group and I feel disappointed.'

Immediacy is a complex skill, and far more daunting than any technique associated with the traditional lecture. In terms of reflective learning it is 'strong medicine' and may have powerful effects. The facilitator needs to be aware of what is happening internally and externally, and make a judgement about what is appropriate to express and what is appropriate to 'park'. The skill of immediacy takes courage, there is no knowing how the receiver will react. For many, its a shock but our experience is that when the receiver recovers from the shock immediacy is incredibly appreciated and the relationship moves into a new plane. However it is daunting and the facilitator may wait too long.

Another example:

I'm aware that you resent me, Peter, although you haven't said so. I see by your look and your tone of voice that you are angry. I feel confused and I would prefer you to say how you feel out loud.

Really, immediacy is high-level self-disclosure and feedback wrapped together – 'what is happening to me right now' disclosure which relates to the
relationship and the purpose of the seminar. We move now to feedback as
a facilitation skill needed for reflective dialogue.

Feedback: giving and receiving

We begin our discussion on feedback with some evidence from the Dearing
report:

> Feedback and assessment are important in helping students to progress
> and learn from their mistakes. Fewer than half the students responding
> to our survey were satisfied with the feedback they got from staff about
> their work. Planning for learning will require teachers to consider care-
> fully how best to provide useful feedback to assist the student's ability
> to think about their work and develop their understanding of the area
> of study.
>
> (Dearing, 1997:117, section 8.17)

We note the preoccupation with mistakes and refer to it below. The Dearing
findings suggest that, although written feedback is almost always provided
when coursework is returned to students, the majority are not satisfied with
it, and we suggest some reasons for this. First, the feedback may be vague
and couched in a discourse with which the student is unfamiliar, and therefore difficult to understand. Secondly, the balance of positive and negative
feedback may overwhelm the student so that he is unable to 'take in' the
message of the feedback. Thirdly, what the student seeks is *dialogue* about
their work, and we have explained why this should be and what this means
for student learning in previous Chapters 3, 4, 5 and 9.

Realistically, teachers in higher education are unable to offer each student the personal feedback dialogue that they may desire. However, the
proposals for student dialogue in Chapter 8 offers an acceptable alternative. In addition, the quality of written feedback from teachers can be improved by observing some simple principles, and we discuss these below.

As the facilitator is providing a model for students who will be engaging
in reflective dialogue, an important behaviour to show students is that of
giving feedback, as they will do in triads, in their role as reporter. In addition, as students will need to receive feedback in a way that will enable them
to achieve critically reflective learning, the facilitator may wish to model
reception of feedback too.

The traditional role of an academic has emphasized giving feedback rather
than receiving it, and the focus of relationship in critically reflective learning necessitates that facilitators embrace the two way process of both giving
and receiving feedback. It is our experience that students become adept at
preparing concrete and specific feedback, and delivering it responsibly,
when they are invited to do so.

To understand the role of feedback in reflective learning we look again at the Johari Window, the details of which were given in Chapter 10 and shown below in Figure 11.2.

Figure 11.2 'The Johari Window'

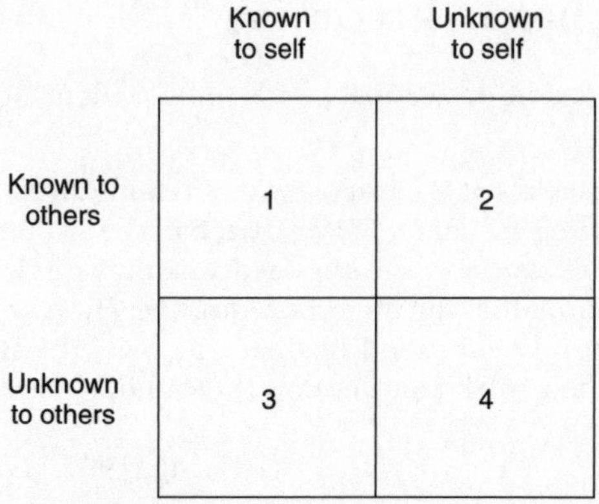

	Known to self	Unknown to self
Known to others	1	2
Unknown to others	3	4

This time we are considering movement of information from quadrant 2 to quadrant 1, after A has received feedback. If the window represents person A in interaction with B and others in a group, A will, if there is trust in the group, receive feedback about himself about quadrant 2 which he is unable to know without the insight of others. The result may be that A may present, a new more informed self represented by the enlargement of quadrant 1 as shown in Figure 11.3.

Figure 11.3 A's window after feedback from B and others

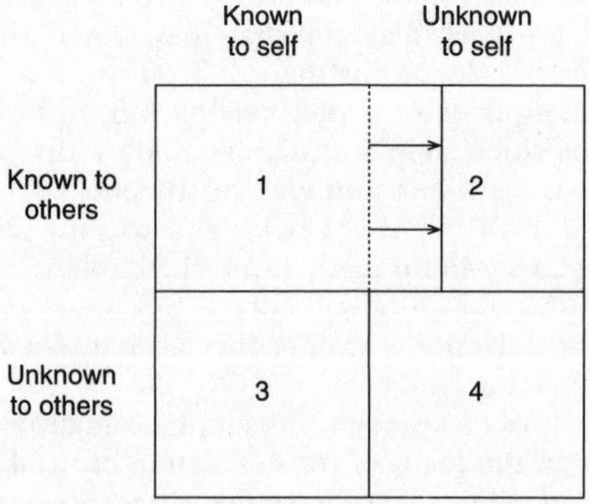

	Known to self	Unknown to self
Known to others	1 →	2
Unknown to others	3	4

The combination of A's disclosure shown in Figure 10.3 *and* the effects of A receiving feedback can be seen in Figure 11.4 below.

Figure 11.4 A's window after A's disclosure *and* after receiving feedback

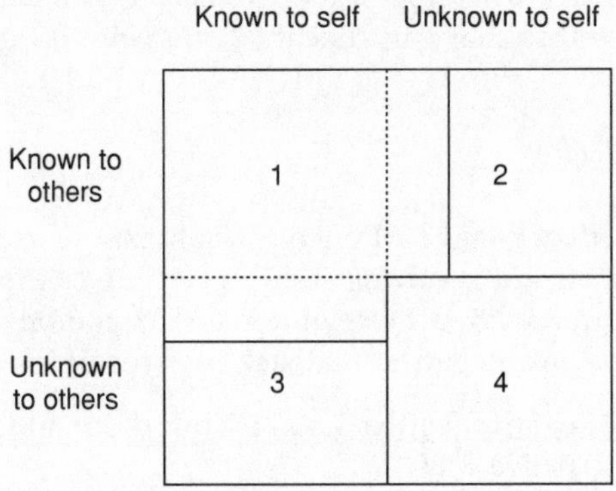

Known to self   Unknown to self

	Known to self	Unknown to self
Known to others	1	2
Unknown to others	3	4

Effective feedback on our actions and behaviours is a way of learning more about ourselves and the effect our behaviour has on others. Constructive feedback increases our self-awareness, offers us more options to how we can act, relate to others and the opportunity to change our behaviour. We describe the characteristics of effective feedback below.

Effective feedback does not only mean positive feedback. Negative feedback, given skilfully, is just as important. Destructive feedback is unskilled feedback that leaves the recipient simply feeling bad with little to build on. The most commonly voiced complaint is lack of feedback or feedback which cannot be used by the recipient.

Feedback is of little value to the recipient unless:

- the recipient can understand it
- the recipient can use it.

What if the feedback is negative? How can I give positive feedback without sounding sloppy? We look at some of the difficulties below and identify the skills needed to give feedback properly.

Positive feedback

Often we may not give positive feedback because:

1. we may forget to do so in taking a person's qualities and skills for granted when something has been done well. We may be more likely to draw attention to those aspects that have not gone well
2. we may be embarrassed to say something positive to others for fear that it may be misinterpreted or may not seem genuine or that the receiver may be embarrassed
3. we may be brought up to think of self-effacement as better than too much self-confidence.

Some or all of these reasons may inhibit the giving of positive feedback, which is an important part of learning. Students need to know what was effective about their work so that they can repeat it, otherwise it is a guessing game.

Negative feedback

Giving negative feedback may feel uncomfortable to do as we fear it may be distressing for the person receiving it. We referred to the fears associated with being the bearer of bad news under confrontation above. However, persistent failure to give negative feedback may result in:

- the tendency for negative feedback to be 'stored up' and, under pressure, explode in a destructive way
- no change in the person's practice because they are unaware that it is causing any difficulties
- a continued use of practice that is less effective.

What are the skills in *giving* feedback?

Be clear about what you want to say in advance
In order to achieve clarity, first observe and listen carefully (or scrutinize written material). Secondly, record observation in concrete and specific terms, i.e. what was seen and heard, e.g. details of behaviour and observed effects on others. For written material record where criteria have been met or not met.

Before delivering feedback verbally, it may help to practice beforehand, possibly with someone else, and/or write down what it is you want to say.

Start with the positive
Most people need encouragement, and students need to know when they are doing something well. Do not take the positive aspects for granted. When offering feedback, it can really help the receiver to hear first what they have done well, for example:

> I liked the way you structured your essay – it made it clear and easy to follow. *And* I felt that the second example you gave did not appear to relate to your main proposition or the evidence you set out earlier.

Note avoidance of the word 'but' when linking positive and negative feedback, as 'but' tends to devalue what has just been said. The use of a feedback 'sandwich' has been recommended, where a negative piece of feedback is sandwiched in between two positives. This pattern may be used in written feedback quite easily.

Be specific not general
General comments are not useful in feedback when commenting on a person's behaviour, actions or written work. For feedback to be useful (i.e.

it can be used by the recipient) it needs to be specific. Statements like: 'That was brilliant' or 'You were awful' may be pleasant or dreadful to hear but they do not enable the person to learn what was brilliant or awful and act upon it. Written comments like 'not good enough' are equally useless.

Select priority areas
Highlight the most significant feedback especially if it is negative feedback that you are giving. If possible, don't let it build up into one great bundle! Many people can only 'take' one piece of negative feedback at a time, even when sandwiched between two positives.

Focus on behaviour rather than the person
Reporting what was seen and heard (or read) ensures that the focus is on behaviour (or written material) rather than the person. For example the comment, 'You dominated the session' is potentially damaging and less useful to the recipient than: 'I think you interrupted each person when they spoke'. For written work comments like, 'you haven't answered the question' is less helpful than 'X and Y do not address the question and Z does because . . .'.

Refer to behaviour that can be changed
It is not very helpful to give a person feedback about something they can do nothing about, e.g. a personal attribute, dialect or accent.

Descriptive rather than evaluative
Telling the person what has been seen or heard and the effect it had is more effective than saying something was merely 'good' or 'bad', e.g.:

> When X asked the question, I noticed that you looked away without speaking. I felt it would have been more helpful if you had given her eye contact and responded to her directly with your reply.

For written work, a comment on the 'weight' given to A rather than B might be: 'you have devoted three pages to A, and a paragraph to B. The assignment relates to B so there needs to be a different emphasis in your work.'

Own the feedback
Effective feedback is 'owned' beginning with 'I' or 'in my view' rather than with 'you are . . .', which may suggest that a universally agreed opinion is being offered about that person. Starting with 'I' means that the person giving the feedback is also taking responsibility for what they are saying. For written work the comment 'you have dealt with X over two pages of text. I would have preferred less emphasis on X and more on Y'.

Give the feedback as soon as you can after the event
Students want feedback on their written work as soon as possible, and

immediate feedback should be given (by the reporter) in the case of reporting in reflective dialogue. The exceptions to this would be:

- if the learner/group is feeling very emotional about the behaviour or the
  session
- the feedback would not be constructive and/or
- if it is inappropriate, e.g. others do not need to hear it.

Feedback should be based on observation rather than inference
Based on what is seen, heard, or read, rather than on interpretations or
conclusions made from what is seen or heard which may contaminate observations and therefore affect the quality of the feedback.

Value to the recipient rather than to the provider of feedback
Givers of feedback may need to check out who this feedback is for. Is it for
the benefit of the giver or the receiver?

'What is said' rather than 'why it is said'
The aspects of feedback that relate to the what, how, when, and where of
what is said are observable characteristics. Why something is said goes to
the inferred rather than the observable motive or intent. 'Why?' questions
can be received interrogatively and lead to defensiveness and attack (see
Questioning section beginning on page 199).

Leave the recipient with a choice
It is usually more effective for the recipient if they have a choice about
whether to act on the feedback or not. Making *demands* that they must or
should change may invite resistance, so feedback should not include imperatives for change, but may include suggestions.

Limit negative feedback
Limit feedback to one or two areas if you are giving feedback on weak-
nesses, as after two pieces of negative information, we suggest the receiver
may 'switch off' and hear no more of the feedback being offered.

   The prospect of receiving feedback often inspires fear as most people
expect negative feedback and are not in a receptive listening mode. The
person giving feedback should take into account the receiver's state and
check out if the feedback has really been heard and received, possibly
ensuring that it is recorded, especially if it is positive. So having given feedback, can I receive it?

What are the skills in *receiving* confrontation or feedback?

Be clear about what is being said
Clarify what it is you understand has been said without jumping to conclusions or being defensive before responding. A useful device is to repeat

what it is you think you have heard to check for accuracy. This also gives you time to consider how you will respond. If the written feedback is difficult to understand ask for an explanation.

Listening to the feedback rather than immediately rejecting or arguing with it
Feedback may be uncomfortable to hear but we may be poorer without it. People do have their opinions about us and will have perceptions of our behaviour and it can help to be aware of these. However, we are entitled to our opinion and can choose to ignore, agree, or modify their view. Written feedback allows us to re-visit comments which seemed difficult to accept initially, and, after considering them, possibly in dialogue with others, change our feelings about them.

Check it out with others where possible rather than relying on one source
In a triad, the third person may have a different view. In a group others may give another perspective. The reflective dialogue process outlined in Chapter 8 offers an opportunity for students to compare written feedback from a variety of sources.

Ask for the feedback you want if it does not occur naturally
Feedback is an important part of learning. Learners have a right to receive effective feedback, and should ask for it assertively.

Decide what you will do because of the feedback
'It takes two to know one' is the meaning of the Johari Window, rather than relying only on our own view of ourselves, offering instead multiple views for our consideration.

Should we always give feedback? The person offering feedback must make a judgement about appropriateness. *When* – is this the right time; *where* – is this a good place; *who* – am I the right person to give it; *how* – how can I do it most effectively?

Group process skills

In Chapter 10 we referred to the power of group effects when students are invited to participate and contribute to the learning process. We noted the impact of group dynamics on the feelings and behaviour of those in the group, as well as the facilitator. A full treatment of group dynamics is beyond the scope of this book. However, we do recognize that facilitators will need to have some idea about the unconscious forces at work in their student group and we introduce the basic concepts below.

The group dynamic is dominated by feeling, and group behaviour may be conducted according to 'habeas emotum' (Jaques, 1990) recognizing members' right to have and express emotion. Hence a facilitator needs to be aware of emotion in the group as potential energy for learning or potential blocks to learning if unexpressed. We have discussed emotion above.

The facilitator can anticipate much of the group defences by declaring values of support, trust and safety. Facilitator behaviour sets norms of disclosure, owning, honouring and respecting choice. Modelled behaviour is picked up by group members, consciously or unconsciously, and imitated.

An effective facilitator will have the ability to observe, identify and describe such dynamics in a group of learners, through process comments, enabling reflection on that process by articulating it, e.g. where a student is dismissive of another's work, the facilitator may be the only person able to identify what is occurring, and 'name' the oppression for the victim. Process comments, if accepted by participants, are the trigger for reflection, and may be the first time the process has been highlighted.

Facilitators may attract aggression from learners where the process alluded to has exposed them in some way. The unconscious forces within a group (large or small) are well understood by group analysts, and their training includes the capacity to deal with transference, counter-transference, projection, displacement and other dynamics of group behaviour.

Where feelings experienced in the past are 'transferred' unconsciously into present relationships, the term transference is used (Jacoby, 1984). These feelings are not just memories they are alive and can deeply affect current relationships. In addition, they may not be all negative, and can take the form of undiluted admiration *or* hostility. We are type-cast or propelled into the matching pre-prepared script, where we respond in role, and this is called *counter-transference.*

The teacher in higher education does not need to 'work with' these dynamics as an analyst would, but she will feel more confident when she understands what is happening in a group when these unconscious forces are at work, e.g. it is quite common in a group where freedom of expression is granted, for members to attack the perceived leader or authority figure. Indeed a leaderless group will create such a figure primarily for the purpose. The psychodynamic roots of such transference are well understood, and the lay-person would easily identify a problem with authority. A skilled facilitator will be aware of the likely counter-transference which may occur, and monitor their own response to the situation (Bion, 1961; Egan, 1976; Foulkes, 1975).

Group members may '*project*' their own feelings onto others, especially if they are unacceptable feelings, so a person who has been discouraged from showing anger may accuse others of being angry with her. *Displacement* defences are often described as 'X took it out on Y' meaning that X 'displaced' her feeling about Z onto Y. When group members imitate behaviour they admire this is termed '*introjection*' and 'pairing' may occur in the group.

The facilitator can help group members to unlock these defences, usually by interruption. Where the facilitator is part of the defence, i.e. transference, where group members project feelings from the hurt child within, about a parent or other authority figure from the past, then the facilitator needs to resist the temptation to offer a punitive response. Similarly, the facilitator may need to resist being carried away by the undiluted admiration given by some students and alternatively perhaps, dare to reveal the cracks!

The facilitator needs to be aware of the effects of defences in a student learning group. As mentioned above, there is no need for the facilitator to 'work with' any of the psychodynamic issues raised by anxiety (as a therapist would); the facilitator's awareness of them is sufficient. When appropriate she may use non-technical language to gently point to what is occurring in the group. For example, the facilitator may observe that the group is in flight from the task by means of distraction or displacement. She may note the challenging behaviour of group members who seek to confront authority. The student who 'pairs' or introjects can be encouraged to value their own contribution, and so on.

Defensive forms of behaviour in groups are usually triggered by anxieties, and these have been identified as Existential and Archaic Anxiety (Heron, 1993). Existential anxiety triggered by being-in-a-group may take the form of 'self-talk' like: Will I be accepted, wanted, liked? Will I understand what's going on? Will I be able to do what's required? Archaic anxiety is the echo of past distress and comes from the repressed grief of emotional rejection, fear of being overwhelmed and repressed anger at constraints on freedom. These anxieties are real for anyone who takes part in a group where all members are given voice, and 'jokey' put-downs can cause hurt when they trigger damaging self-talk.

The facilitator may encounter any or all of the above dynamics in the session itself, as well as in the plenary reflective event, the process review, as described in Chapter 8.

Facilitating the process review

The process review offers participants the opportunity to reflect (in plenary) on their reflective dialogue for example in triads. This has been identified as the students' reflection-on-reflection or the process of learning about their learning. The process review is itself another instance of reflective dialogue so the same facilitation skills described in these two chapters are appropriate. The facilitator in reflective dialogue mode, will additionally need to become a chairperson, ensuring that contributions are heard, and that the group does not get drawn into detail.

The material for the process review relates to *the learning process*, as it has been discovered in triad dialogue, not the details of any one person's reflective dialogue. For example, a student may have identified, in dialogue with colleagues, that a method (new to her) of tape recording has enabled her to organize material for her essay. When reflecting on the learning process in plenary this may be reported as a reorientation towards how academic material is ordered, not in terms of the detail of her essay.

The facilitator's clarification and summary of what has been said is an opportunity for the whole group to take part in reflection-on-reflection. The facilitator's role includes ensuring that a record is kept (not necessarily by him) of the process review, as contributions represent evidence of critically reflective learning and the students may wish to present such evidence for assessment.

Towards the end of the process review the facilitator ensures the psychological safety of the group by conducting a wind-up session, basically a closing down of the group, where students may express any feelings that remain and they wish to voice. Such a wind-up session, which may take no more than a few minutes, is likely to be important as a time for 'healing' the group. Through reflective dialogue, learners may discover inadequacies in themselves or others and may be hurt or angry. These feelings may be expressed obliquely so the facilitator will need to have advanced empathy skills at the ready as unfinished business can block the future learning process. The facilitator should allow all the fears and worries *relating to the session or the course* to be expressed and received, but stop discussion about other courses or other people.

In this chapter we have described the further skills needed for facilitation in higher education as a requirement for engaging in reflective dialogue and leading to critically reflective learning.

We have explained how managing emotion, offering empathy, questioning, challenging, as well as giving and receiving feedback, can contribute to reflective dialogue. We have offered examples of the skills in a higher education context, and briefly considered the facilitation of groups.

We now turn in Part 3 to some of the ways our approach to facilitation can be used in higher education in order to promote critically reflective learning for both teachers and students.

Note

1. 'Why' questions are likely to be ineffective in facilitator situations, unless and until the relationships are resilient. They have been perceived as intrusive, like an interrogation, led by the questioner, for the questioner's benefit, and may cause the learner to lose their train of thought (Dainow and Bailey, 1988).

Part 3

Exemplars

In this part we introduce exemplars to promote reflective dialogue and learning which can be used in higher education. The exemplars in the following chapters adopt approaches to facilitation that embrace dialogue and reflective practice, potentially leading to critically reflective learning. The three exemplars – group learning in the form of action learning, supervision and mentoring – are chosen because they also represent specific relationships as facilitator, supervisor or mentor.

Underlying each of these roles (which in many respects are synonymous) is the idea of transition from dependence to independence in learning. The facilitator in action learning enables participants to use reflective dialogue to take ownership and responsibility for their learning with other learners as colleagues; the supervisor seeks to 'launch' his student as an independent reflective researcher; the mentor aims to foster autonomous learning and reflective practice through facilitative methods of reflective dialogue.

However, this independence of learning is not our only aim. While moving from dependence we highlight another attribute of the emerging relationship between teachers as facilitators, supervisors, mentors and learners as well as between learners as colleagues – that of an interdependence that derives from the nature of reflective dialogue that lies at the heart of these relationships. Interdependence implies collaboration in learning and development.

12

Action Learning

Action learning is a group-based approach to learning. Our purpose in this chapter is twofold. First, to convey and demystify the meaning of this approach to learning. Secondly, to show how the approach can be used to foster reflective dialogue and critically reflective learning.

The term, action learning is sometimes criticized as a jargon phrase that misleads and hides meaning. We use the term to acknowledge the origins and core practice embraced in the term. The term 'Learning Set' is increasingly used synonymously with action learning in higher education to denote the same form of group based learning. The word 'set' conveys the notion of a group of the same members who meet over a specific time period. The set is led, at least initially, by a facilitator who has some appreciation and experience of the process by which the group operates and may also have expertise in the field of study with which the students are engaged.

This chapter is necessarily an abridged version of what we could say about action learning but will be sufficient, with other parts of the book, to embark on using the approach in higher education. Indeed, we would suggest that when included with material on facilitation, reflective dialogue and reflective practice, action learning may provide the basis for the beginning of a new approach for teachers in higher education. For readers wishing to further their understanding of action learning we recommend, McGill and Beaty, 1995; Morgan, 1988; Pedler, 1992; Revans, 1980; Weinstein, 1995.

Action learning has only recently been introduced to higher education (McGill and Beaty, 1995). The origins of action learning rest with Reg Revans (Revans, 1980) who introduced the approach in organizational contexts after the Second World War. It remained in industrial and public sector use, e.g. the National Health Service until the early 1980s when introduced into postgraduate courses in higher education. The delay in application to higher education was due largely to the consideration that because it was used primarily for practical applications in industry and particularly at senior managerial levels it had limited use in universities and, as they were then, polytechnics. The approach also suffered from the perceived stigma of being managerialist in its uses. The other problem inhibiting its entry into higher education is that Revans used terms like 'working with and learning from experience' that were, at the time, anathema in many university contexts.

Introduced, initially into polytechnics, the approach has now spread across a number of universities. Following the growing acceptance in higher education of learning centred on the learner and the increased use of experiential learning methods, ideas about reflective practice have made action learning increasingly appropriate in higher education settings. The relevance of action learning has been furthered by the use of project-based learning as an important component of undergraduate programmes.

We will now describe what action learning is and how it works in the context of higher education. As defined in McGill and Beaty (1995), 'Action learning is a process of learning and reflection that happens with the support of a group or "set" of colleagues working with problems with the intention of getting things done.' The participants in the set each take forward an important issue with the support of other members of the set. The process helps people to take an active and responsible stance towards learning and helps overcome the tendency towards passivity in the learning process.

How action learning sets work

What we are about to describe may be said to be a typical template for enabling learning using action learning sets. The template can be varied to suit particular purposes.

Drawing upon the quotation above, what are the key components within our definition?

- Individuals meeting together in a group (known as a set). For ease of working, about five to seven people make up the set in addition to the facilitator (the term set advisor is sometimes used).
- Each individual other than the facilitator brings a real issue/problem or project to the set that they wish to progress.
- The whole set works on the issue for the benefit of the person presenting the issue.
- The aim for each individual presenting their issue is to be able to take action on some aspect of the issue, to reflect upon and learn from the actions as the issue is progressed.
- Typically, the action learning set meets for three to four hours (or one day) every four to six weeks for a cycle of meetings over an agreed period (for example, six, nine months or one academic session).
- The set will create explicit conditions, 'ground rules' on which to operate to ensure effective working.

Thus over an academic year the set may meet on eight to ten occasions. Within each meeting each set member (the name used for each participant other than the facilitator) will have roughly equal time to work with the set on their issues. Alternatively, the set may determine to use the time depending upon the needs of the set members. The proviso here is that over a number of set meetings each set member has quality time to work on their issues.

We will consider a typical meeting in a university course to convey the nature of the activity with which students, as set members, may be engaged. The example is drawn from a model used by one of us in undergraduate courses with a three-hour session every four weeks.

The facilitator will ask who among them will take time at the set meeting today. Three colleagues want and need time today and the set agree each will have about one hour devoted to their issues.

The first set member to take on the role of 'presenter', starts by conveying the issue as she sees it, listened to by the others. Set members and the facilitator will then seek to clarify what they have heard in order that they have as full a picture themselves as possible. Then they will ask questions that seek to enable the presenter to consider, define, or re-define the issue and her relationship to it.

The set will offer her empathic understanding and support, without being collusive as well as being challenging. We elaborate in much greater detail the facilitation skills implicit in this sentence in Chapters 10 and 11. The purpose here, as in all the interaction and dialogue in the set, is to enable the presenter to understand her issue, own the issue, take responsibility for it and to learn from it following the set meeting. In addition, the set members will help the presenter take some steps towards action on it. She will be invited to be as specific as possible about her intended actions as this will make them more feasible to achieve.

We will take as an example an issue a set member may bring to the set. Many students undertake live projects during a placement year. The student has difficulty in obtaining support within her placement organization to carry out research requiring interviews with staff within the organization. There is resistance to her planned formal interviews. She feels blocked by the situation and unable to make progress. This she presents to the set.

So what is so different about action learning from usual interactions between colleagues? The presenter is given concentrated time and attention by the set members and the facilitator, though the latter will not dominate the interaction. This is quite different from a conversation between colleagues with quick moments of thought offered from our repertoire of individual past experience. Such thoughts tend to be based on what *we* would do if we were dealing with the situation. It is not our situation. It is the presenter who will have to take responsibility and any subsequent action. What I might do is not necessarily relevant for someone else! In action learning we do not prescribe or say what the presenter should or ought to do! She may want ideas and pictures of how set members see her situation, but the purpose is for her to re-frame or re-conceptualize her own situation. Ownership remains with her as does its resolution and potential action, in contrast to imposed or directed solutions which may lead to incomplete or partially owned commitment.

Through action learning the presenting student takes responsibility for her issue, asks for what she needs from the set, really listens and reflects on the questions and statements made by colleagues and then concludes with actions – important next steps that are specific, clear and feasible.

Another key difference is pace and time for real reflection. The student will have the undivided attention of the set for an hour and be able to use the time between set meetings to work on the implementation of her actions and continued reflections. As presenter, she is not only working on an appropriate action that she will seek to implement in the placement context following the set meeting, she will be bringing back the results of her intended actions and reporting upon the effects of implementation. She will be invited at the next or a subsequent set meeting to reflect upon what actually happened, the extent to which what happened was congruent with her intentions, what was different about her actions from those undertaken earlier, how did other people in the organization respond. These are just a few of the potential questions that could be asked to enable her to really *reflect* upon her continuing issue.

The object is not only to enable her to progress her project for completion of the course, but to provide the conditions for her to reflect on her actions and to ascertain what she has learned from the changing situation. In addition, because the project is taking place within the context of an academic programme, she can reflect upon how her understanding of relevant theory is related to the live situation she is experiencing thus relating theory and practice. The work in the set is not only important for her – her reflections may also be providing insights for other set members and the facilitator!

Other set members replicate the approach when it comes to their time in the meeting.

There is also the added value of finding that set members are likely to share the same or similar concerns and problem searching and solution. One person may effect critically reflective learning in others including the facilitator!

Action learning sets provide the structure, process and time for learners to struggle with and reflect upon their existing knowledge, their relationship to particular situations that may be familiar or novel and the context in which they are happening. Learners undertake this reflection with and through the support and challenge of others in the set. There are the conditions here for reflective dialogue and critically reflective learning in that existing ways of understanding and knowing and thinking about the world can interact with that which may be emerging.

Thus a cycle of learning and action is built into the process for every set member: intended action *leading to* learning in and from the experience of the action (between the set meeting) *leading to* the set meeting where the presenter reflects and questions with others that experience *leading to* a reframing of the picture and/or new way of seeing the situation *leading to new action* . . .

The above looks very neat suggesting a cycle of action, reflection, learning. The situation is not necessarily like this, but often more messy. On occasion, a student may have a vague notion of discomfort or unease in relation to some aspects of his work and have difficulty articulating what those feelings represent. As a set member he should not be discouraged from taking time to struggle with and explore what may emerge.

Ground rules or conditions for action learning sets

Action learning sets are a particular stylized form of group based learning. Sets enable their participants to explore issues that are personally relevant to them that they relate to at cognitive, affective and conative levels, that is at the level of thinking, feeling and doing. To be effective in enabling set members to explore their existing and emerging learning across these domains requires some basic conditions to prevail. We set out some of the following conditions recognizing that it is important that each set creates its own conditions and works on what each condition means for each person and the set as a whole. This ensures that there will be a greater chance of ownership and commitment.

The following are some of the basic conditions:

- confidentiality. What individual set members bring to the set remains with the set (more on this under 1. below)
- one person speaks at a time
- one person is presenter at any one time
- set members really listen to each other
- when speaking use the first person, 'I' rather than 'you' or 'one' (more on this under 2. below)
- be genuine and honest.

1. What can be taken outside the set meeting and be discussed elsewhere? Obviously, a presenter can take her issues and discuss them outside the set at her discretion as opposed to taking someone else's issues outside the set. There will be ideas and thoughts about the process in which the set operates that the set member may wish to discuss elsewhere provided that she does not link a particular aspect of a process to a specific set member other than herself. For example, the one person at a time rule is clearly important to maintain the sense of dialogue within the set. For someone to continuously breach that condition breaks down the quality of real dialogue for the presenter. To refer specifically to the person who breaches that condition would be inappropriate. Indeed, a no referral rule may be included in the conditions. The purpose of the confidentiality condition is to encourage trust that will in turn encourage openness and disclosure in the set

2.   The benefit of using 'I' is that it becomes clearer that what the set member is saying is not only about her, but that she 'owns' what she is saying. An example could be: 'If you get to the set late, you feel that you have let others down', which can be contrasted with: 'If I get to the set late, I feel that I have let others down.' Not only have the words changed but we are clear that she is talking about how she feels rather than pushing 'out there' where she can avoid actually expressing her own feelings and create ambiguity about whether she is talking about herself, the set members or both.

There are also conditions that are obvious and perhaps the responsibility of the facilitator initially. These include:

• finding space where the set will not be interrupted by phones, people who are not members of the set or other distractions.
• creating space where the set and facilitator can sit in a circle of similar chairs.
• taking a little time at the outset to enable each person including the facilitator to express thoughts and feelings about themselves. This helps to break any formality.
• having a natural break about half way through a session of three hours.

Contrasts with traditional forms of teaching

Traditional forms of teaching may be characterized (though this may not always be the case) as didactic, hierarchic, with control in the hands of the teacher, dependency on the part of the student, lecture and tutorial based and with a cognitive bias. Action learning starts from a different base which is reflected in the values and methods we are bringing to this publication. The teacher as facilitator of a set will be in hierarchical mode initially by informing the student learners how sets work and, initially, in modelling the process to ensure the format is effectively used. But the set is from the outset, highly participative. Once the students *do* action learning in sets, pick it up and adopt the process the facilitator begins to share the process with the students. The responsibility of the teacher/facilitator is not removed, more that responsibility is cooperatively shared with the student set members as they take on more responsibility for the process.

An action learning set also starts with the individual set member presenting her issues, ideas and problems from her starting point – where she is *coming from*. The format recognizes that students have their own personal stance (see Chapter 4) and difference that will be intrinsic to their learning, reaching out from subjective, particular experience to that which is 'out there' and more objective and general so that students are able to 'construct' their meanings, understandings and knowledge in context with others.

Again the approach recognizes that learning beyond the transmissional is a dialogical and social process – that I create meaning in my relation with the world. 'Some learning is undertaken on our own but for us learning means making sense of and changing meaning in a social context' (McGill and Beaty, 1995).

An academic course, which incorporates action learning, may not, therefore exclude more traditional format and resources.

Action learning sets provide a strong basis upon which to build a variety of teaching and learning experiences. Action learning sets support the link between ideas and action. The action, for the most part, takes place outside the set . . . The function of the set is to enable members to learn the link between ideas and experience; to generalise from the past and to plan for the future.

(McGill and Beaty, 1995)

Using action learning for student learning and staff development

We recognize the increasing work burdens placed upon teachers in higher education. Action learning may convey, initially, an impression of an addition to that burden. However, in considering the examples below, our concern is to emphasize the potential for students in using action learning as well as the possibility of effective uses of staff time.

Projects

Projects whether, 'live' or library based will have content, research and 'how' elements at whatever level the student's programme. Projects have the advantage of linking knowledge and self experience in a social and applied context that more traditional formats of essays and unseen examinations may not.

Students may be given the task of undertaking a project and some formal inputs on how to conduct and progress the project which will be valuable. However, the reality of doing a project will involve dimensions (such as the example given earlier) which cannot be anticipated by prior information about the planning, implementation, review and writing up. In other words, knowledge *about* projects will be useful to acquire but will not be sufficient itself. The experience of *doing* the project will present blocks and realizations in the students progress as well as in her learning. Bringing the issues to a set provides the student with means to explore the 'blocks', to work through them and to reflect upon and learn from the experience for this and other situations. Further, while not directly experiencing the same situation, other members of the set may gain in understanding from the situation as well as contributing to the presenter's learning as well as their own.

In terms of staff time, the teacher, by facilitating a group of students collectively rather than meeting students individually will possibly make a saving in net time and meet a greater variety of needs and experience brought to the set. The teacher ceases to be the all-knowing person and becomes one of a group who can contribute to the presenter's learning. Once the students are familiar with the process they can become self-facilitating.

Placements

Placements can absorb significant teacher resources. The one to one relationship between tutor and student can place a heavy burden on staff and course resources. Students on placement can be grouped in sets according to geographical location and the tutor can serve a group of students meeting on, say a monthly basis, to review their placement progress and experience. The set meetings can also be used to review the students' placement action plans.

Research

Research degrees tend to be individualistic, as the learner may not be on a course but is engaged in a search for a contribution to knowledge. While it is essential to have supervisor support, action learning sets can be used to share what will be common to research in terms of the process and organization of the research. We explore in Chapter 13 the contribution that facilitating learning can make to effective supervision.

Staff development

Teachers in higher education are necessarily engaged in their continuing professional development. Research and scholarly activity have been recognized traditionally as the primary source of development. However, professional development now extends more widely to include activities that derive from the experience of practising as a teacher – as a teacher, researcher, manager, mentor, course leader to name a few of the roles over a career cycle.

Until recently, new roles were 'bolted on' to a teaching post simply by doing it. It was and still can be an individual and isolating experience. It is still important to get into doing it. In addition, teachers will wish as reflective practitioners, to question and evaluate their own practice. Peer support can be achieved through the use of action learning sets where teachers bring key issues relating to emergent and existing roles at the frontier of their work rather than working on them in isolation. Such peer sets can be voluntary in being created by staff themselves or may be supported as part of a staff development programme (McGill and Beaty, 1995).

The emerging requirement for accreditation of teaching in higher education necessitates in-house professional programmes, particularly for new staff. Existing accredited programmes frequently use learning sets as the primary vehicle for learning and development, drawing up their own dove-tailed programme and learning contract which they pursue in and between set meetings. The practice gained by teachers in the action learning process has relevance to the use of this exemplar with students.

The role of facilitator

We concentrate here on the significance of the role of facilitator in relation to action learning. The justification for facilitation and the skills required are considered more widely in Chapters 9, 10 and 11.

The primary purpose of the facilitator of a learning set is to enable each set member to work on and with their own issues. In this role the facilitator encourages each set member to take responsibility for clarifying their issues, and working towards some resolution and action as well as reflecting upon their learning. The facilitator models how to *give* support to the set member who is presenting and enables the set member as presenter to *receive* support from other set members.

A secondary but important purpose to achieve the above is the role of the facilitator in ensuring that the set works and functions as a set. Maintaining the set as functioning group is crucial to the primary purpose.

As set members become aware of the process that underlies action learning – how the set works – set members begin to model the facilitator and integrate the facilitation and process skills into their own repertoire of set practice. Set members will bring their own personal, interpersonal and group process skills to the learning set with varying levels of sophistication. The fairly structured nature of action learning fosters the acquisition and enhancement of these skills.

Thus the facilitator's 'expertise' in facilitating is acquired by set members. This is important for it may enable the facilitator to reduce her presence or to withdraw from the set once the set can become self-facilitating.

The facilitator has to keep in balance the needs of the individual set member and the maintenance of the group. These needs can be addressed in two ways. First, through the qualities and skills that a facilitator brings as a person to the set. We detail the qualities and skills in Chapters 9, 10 and 11. Secondly, the facilitator creates a learning and developmental climate for the set as a whole.

Creating a learning climate

What climate is the facilitator endeavouring to create in the set? By climate we mean the most effective conditions for learning by set members. Such a climate enables:

- each set member to achieve whatever tasks they bring to the set; the set makes a difference
- each set member is able to reflect upon their learning
- set members acquire and enhance their personal, interpersonal and group facilitation skills

- the set becomes collectively an effective learning group
- (optionally), the set seeks to become an effective self-facilitating set.

What are the characteristics that are conducive to creating a learning climate in a set? Here we can draw upon and adapt Hawkins and Shohet (1989). A learning climate is evident through facilitation where:

- A set can take any learning opportunity that is relevant to the set member and create the conditions for learning.
- Problems and crises are seen as important opportunities for learning and development. Major crises are seen as growth points, and the culture of the set is one where it is safe to take risks. Failure is seen as an event to be learnt from, rather than to be depowered by.
- Good practice emerges not from reaction to crises but from set members balancing all parts of an activity, from action, to reflection, to new thinking, to planning and then back to action.
- Individual set members take time out to reflect on their learning and development. This becomes a cooperative process rather than an individual one or one that happens rarely for the individual.
- The set encourages feedback from each other.
- Time and attention is given to individuals. The starting point is where they are coming from recognizing their individual needs.
- Learning and development are seen in the set as active concerns which results in action and further learning.
- The facilitator and set members explicitly draw attention to the process – how the set is working as well as the content that each set member brings.

The conditions set out above for a learning climate or culture in action learning are the espoused conditions. We can say that these are the conditions that should prevail. Whether they do or not will be up to the facilitator in the first instance and as the set gathers experience the whole set will embrace it by putting the above desirable conditions into action. It is the difference between *saying* what should happen and actually *doing* it (Argyris and Schön, 1978).

Reflection and review

Finally, the facilitator has a responsibility to ensure that the set engages in a reflection and review of learning at a number of levels, as follows:

Reflection, evaluation and feedback at the end of a presenter's time

Here the presenter will engage in reflection and learning about their learning as described in Chapter 5. The presenter may ask for feedback about how he reflected upon his issue. He may also convey to the group which questions and interventions were more or less helpful. Over time, set members may have shifted their perspectives through critically reflective learning.

Review of a set meeting at the end of the meeting

Set meetings usually concentrate on each set member and the time allocated to each. It is appropriate to spend 10–15 minutes near the end of the set meeting reviewing how the set has been for set members. A set review can include the following headings for consideration:

• What have I gained from being in the set today?
• What have I gained/learned about the way the set works?
• Something I would like the set to consider that I am not yet sure about.
• Something I want to share that I have difficulty with when I am presenting and/or when I am a set member giving support to another.
• Something I want to say about the set, myself, the set advisor, another set member.

These headings are a suggested range from which a facilitator can select or indeed add to. They are not intended for use all at once and certainly would be overwhelming and not containable in the time allocated above.

The feedback to the set will provide positive impressions of what is being gained and learned by set members. It will also provide the set and the facilitator with an indication of the impact that the set is having upon set members. In the early life of the set it is better to engage in the doing of action learning than to discuss what action learning is supposed to be about. The 'doing' of action learning will very soon provide a huge resource from which to review and reflect. The practice and doing emerges before reflection and will begin to influence reflection in action (Chapter 5).

Periodic review of the set after a period and series of meetings

When the set has been in operation for a period of meetings it is appropriate to review the process of the set. This is an opportunity to enable the set to reflect more broadly upon how it is working as a group. Each individual can reflect on the set's contribution to their own learning. The set can examine how the conditions are being observed and what norms have emerged that influence the way in which the set works.

How is action learning different from other types of group?

This question is often asked, particularly when the questioner has not experienced the process of action learning.

Action learning is not a seminar. We define a seminar as a meeting of a group of interested academics and students where one of them has prepared a paper on a given subject, prior to the seminar. For students presenting the paper, usually by reading it out, the seminar will be led by the tutor for the group. The paper is complete and discussion follows about the content. Seminars can be exciting and dramatic where ideas and differences are shared. They can also be desultory occasions where the only person who has done the work is the presenting student and is in a one-to-one with the tutor. In a set, the student may be preparing such a paper and possibly have distributed it beforehand for reading among other set members. The difference is that the presenting student will be invited by colleagues to consider what helped and hindered him in preparing the paper; what did he learn over and above the content; what were the struggles he had to/is trying to overcome.

Sets are not like formal meetings with fixed agendas where all at the meeting are progressing through the agenda in order to come to decisions about future actions usually common to all.

Sets are not discussion groups that have a theme common, deliberated upon and conclusions come to. Such discussions tend to be 'objective' and 'out there'. In learning sets the individual is central when presenting and starts with a narrative that emanates from the individual. Dialogue that follows is centred upon the individual's working through of the issue. Learning is centred on the individual though the set members may draw their collective and individual reflections from the issue.

A set is not a counselling or therapy group! A set member presenting their issue to the set can expect to be listened to and receive comments aimed at supporting and challenging. A set will be a place where emotions and feelings can be expressed as these are as significant as the cognitive and conative aspects that contribute to our learning. However, a learning set is not the place to explore the origins of emotions, say in childhood. Initially, learning sets may have the label: 'This is like a counselling or therapy group' applied to them as a pejorative. This may denote a person's concerns about expressing feelings.

Misuses of learning sets!

We have known sets to be used as a means of 'sending off students' into small groups to discuss an issue or progress their projects. These are then given the title 'learning sets'. The result is often a travesty of action learning as well as creating resentment among students who are perfectly aware that there is totally inadequate preparation for such group activity or attention to process that is appropriate to the task. Such 'self-directed' learning also lets staff avoid taking responsibility for creating the conditions for reflective learning.

Another potential misuse is for the facilitator to treat the set meeting as an opportunity to lecture! Learning sets are places for dialogue in which learning is the potentiality. Monologue is not appropriate in a set.

Voluntary nature of action learning

A key value of action learning is that it is a voluntary endeavour. Being a member of a set cannot be compulsory or imposed. This also applies to being a facilitator. We refer to the important condition for teaching and learning in respect of personal stance that any teacher and learner brings to the teaching and learning situation (see Chapter 4). Resentment at being in a set as an imposition will soon affect the working and effectiveness of a set. Involuntary membership will act as a block on the set member's willingness to engage in the working of the set.

Commitment is derived from this key value once there is recognition of the potentiality of the way in which a set can work, that in turn is derived from doing action learning.

Potential set members may come to sets with some scepticism. Given the models of teaching and learning most experience in their prior education this is understandable. But this is different from hostility deriving from imposition. A sceptical set member will have thoughts, questions and feelings which may be allayed through a *description* of how sets work. *Doing* some introductory work with action learning which defers making a commitment until some experience is gained will help allay concerns.

What of programmes where action learning is a key component of the course? This situation is no different to other requirements of courses. The course design and requirements should be made clear to potential students at the outset. Entry to the course will place an expectation upon the student to engage with the core content and process elements of the programme. An example would be a placement requirement on a sandwich degree programme.

Introducing action learning

Careful introduction of the processes involved in action learning will be invaluable in creating the conditions for effective set working. The teacher–student workshop on reflective dialogue set out in Chapter 8, will prepare students for learning sets. The key activity is the work undertaken in trios (triads) where students each take one of three roles in turn. These can be interpreted in action learning terms as follows:

- The *presenter* in the triad is identical to the role of presenter in learning sets.
- The *enabler* in the triad is similar to the role undertaken by the facilitator and other set members when working with the presenter.
- The *reporter* in the triad gains experience in recording the interactions and how the interaction is working (process) and then reporting back to the enabler and presenter after their dialogue. The reporter's process role in the triad is similar to the role undertaken in a learning set by the

facilitator and other set members. Whilst they are attending to the presenter's issues they are also attending (usually implicitly) to process to ensure that they are making the set work for the presenter as effectively as possible.

The experience by the reporter embodied in the work of the facilitator and set members is very useful when the set reviews its own process. In addition, if for some reason the facilitator or a set member thinks that a process matter needs to be made explicit then it may be appropriate to ask the set to stop for a moment (on the presenter's content) while the process issue is considered after which the set proceeds again. An example would be where the presenter is being overwhelmed with questions and cannot find the space to consider any one question appropriately.

The triad experience will thus have a twofold value in introducing students to reflective dialogue which can then be applied in a number of contexts including learning set work.

Beyond the above students could then work in sets where there are five to six members plus a facilitator to practise set work. Alternatively, where there are say up to 20 students, staff with some experience of action learning facilitation could invite five to six students into a circle to engage in action learning with one of the students volunteering in the circle to present. The remaining students sit in a circle outside the inner circle and observe that process (like reporters in the triads). On completion of the presenter's time, the whole group form one circle and the facilitator leads a discussion on the process that has been experienced and observed (McGill and Beaty, 1995).

In summary, action learning sets can become an important part of the repertoire of approaches to reflective dialogue that promotes critically reflective learning. Sets create the conditions for integrating, knowledge, self and action in the world.

13

Academic Supervision

In this chapter we consider the role of academic supervision in developing reflective learning in higher education. We begin with a brief résumé of available meanings of supervision, then we explore the historical roots of supervision, identifying three sources of modern practice. We draw on generic characteristics from each model to inform our approach to reflective dialogue in academic supervision, a facilitative approach we have called 'metavision'.[1] We include two stories of supervision which readers may like to compare with good practice. Finally, we offer some ideas for academic supervisors and a structure for individual and group supervision.

The origins and meanings of supervision

Supervision has been called the 'impossible' profession (Zinkin, 1989), mainly because of the struggle for practitioners to agree on a common understanding of what supervision is. Many begin with variations of the word itself, citing 'super' vision as suggestive of overseeing and management; 'extra' vision as descriptive of a broadening process; or 'consultative' supervision as a more egalitarian activity.

Hawkins and Shohet give us a definition, in the context of the helping professions (given as social work, health service, public services and teaching):

> a quintessential, interpersonal interaction with the general goal that one person, the supervisor, meets with another, the supervisee, in an effort to make the latter more effective.
>
> (Hess, 1980, quoted in Hawkins and Shohet, 1989:41)

Are academics members of a 'helping profession'? If facilitating learning is 'helping' then we base this chapter on that assumption. Committed teachers are often passionate about their role as enablers of learning, and, we suggest, belong to what may be termed a helping profession.

The first universities formed an academic community where students learned by contact with experts in liberal arts subjects. The term supervisor did not exist then, students being attached to the 'master' or 'doctor', who was expert in the subject concerned, these titles being enshrined in higher degrees today. The 'master' connotation links the learning in universities with the craft guilds, where master journeyman and apprentice worked together, the latter learning from the master by working alongside him over time.

The term 'supervisor' originates in the factory system of production, with the perceived need to control and monitor or 'oversee' the work of employees, referred to as 'hands'.

Professional counsellors are normally 'in supervision', a practice which ensures the safety of their clients, and monitors their activities in their essentially private work with vulnerable individuals. The counselling supervisor is normally an experienced counsellor themselves, mirroring the academic supervisor, who is an expert in the discipline concerned.

The roots of modern supervision methods lie in these three sources; academia, industry and therapy. We seek to use generic elements from each to inform our facilitative approach to reflective dialogue in supervision.

Clearly, this chapter is about academic supervision, but we will draw on the other two sources for very different purposes. We intend to differentiate the reflective practice of supervision from the monitoring function of industrial command and control supervision, which much of academic supervision mimics, with supervisors 'chasing' their students for work and checking up on their progress in a managerial way (Salmon, 1992:19). However, when we list the tasks of supervision we will be preserving some of the planning and evaluating functions of traditional workplace supervision. In addition, we draw on the therapeutic context to illustrate the generic nature of reflective practice, as counselling supervision, using facilitative methods is one of the few 'live' examples of reflective practice in action.[2]

The three sources of supervision

Universities and supervision

Academic supervision has its roots in the Greek academy where pupil philosophers learnt by attending upon the masters. Medieval crafts and guilds developed apprentices through journeyman schemes where the learner accompanied and observed the craft master at work. In recent times violin makers in Europe would charge an apprentice a fee to work with the master craftsman, in recognition of the value of what would be learnt. The medieval university mirrored both systems, with students being free to take part in academic discussions with senior academics, respected in their field in order to learn from the master. The ideal picture of lengthy one-to-one sessions with an academic tutor in his book-lined study has its roots in history and is unfamiliar to most university students today. The one-to-one sessions remain for students registered for higher degrees and the nature of such sessions will be discussed below. However, increasingly academic staff are being required to supervise other activities like projects in rather different contexts, e.g. industrial placements.

Industry and supervision

The earliest use of the term was devised as a system of control of workers in the factory system of production, where, with the industrial revolution of the eighteenth century, for the first time, workers were gathered together under one roof. The factory owner/managers perceived the need for:

- activities to be controlled
- tasks to be assigned
- output to be measured
- times of attendance to be checked.

The need to control workers as above, led to the appointment of a special group to oversee the labour process, i.e. the supervisors. They became powerful figures in the factory community and were known as labour masters, later evolving into the foreman, equally the master in the workplace and a key figure in labour management. In modern times supervisors have lost the power to hire, fire and fix wages, as the role has been absorbed by middle management. Recently the term tends to be subsumed under 'leadership' which is increasingly used to describe an important aspect of the managerial role.

Counselling and supervision

The historical roots of supervision in therapeutic contexts lie in Freudian analysis and the training of analysts. In order to complete a training in psychoanalysis, trainees were obliged to engage in personal analysis, training and supervision, very much along the lines first found in the original Freudian circle. The distinction between supervision and personal analysis was a subject of disagreement in the early 1930s and remains so to this day, with a continuing debate about the tasks of supervision, i.e. how much of it is teaching and how much therapy. The assumption implied in definitions of supervision, especially in literature emanating from the United States, that supervision is in effect *trainee* supervision, has its origins in the early practice and development of psychoanalysis.

The development of *consultative* or *practitioner* supervision has coincided in the USA and in the United Kingdom, with the emergence of counselling as a profession in its own right. The British Association for Counselling insists that practitioner members are in supervision, however experienced

they may be, and this applies to accomplished practitioners as well as trainees, and many practitioners have supervisory relationships with practitioners who are their equals in training, experience and seniority.

Recent recognition of the range of tasks in supervision, particularly for
trainee supervision, has brought developmental models of supervision into
mainstream practice in the UK, as well as acknowledgement of social role
models, where generic tasks in supervision relate to the roles adopted by
supervisor and supervisee, e.g. teacher/pupil, worker/client, manager/staff
member and we suggest, academic/student. A particular model, the cyclical
model, designed for use in a range of contexts, incorporating development,
tasks and reflection will be offered as a structure for academic supervision
in this chapter.

Models of supervision which are relevant in higher education

We draw on models from social and academic contexts to inform our
approach to supervision in higher education.

In the caring professions, a classic source for aspiring supervisors remains
Joan Mattinson's *The Reflective Process in Casework Supervision* published in
1975, based on social work practice. The contribution of Proctor and Inskipp
in the early 1980s provided a functional basis for supervision in the *formative, normative* and *restorative* functions, (respectively meeting the educative,
administrative and supportive needs of the supervisee), together with the
developmental stages of supervision and associated supervisor interventions
(Inskipp and Proctor, 1993). A typical developmental model was provided
by Stoltenberg and Delworth in 1987. The idea of developmental stages is
an application of learning theory to the supervisory process, and mirrors a
similar model in the mentoring process (see Chapter 14). The double-
matrix model of supervision, introduced by Hawkins and Shohet, offered a
range of foci for analysis of the supervision process (Hawkins and Shohet,
1989). More recently, a cyclical model of supervision has been offered by
Page and Wosket (1994), giving a generic structure for supervisory sessions,
and this will form the basis of our recommended structure.

Academic supervision has been lightly researched with little or no evidence on which to draw for an understanding of theory or practice. Recent
concerns, triggered by financial audits in research councils have stimulated
investigations into 'low rates of completion' as these represent, crudely, a
waste of resources. Results reveal that a sizeable proportion of students are
'seriously dissatisfied' with their experience of supervision (Rudd, 1975),
and that perceptions of supervision as given by students and supervisors can
be somewhat different (Winfield, 1987). Experienced supervisors have also
offered quite different analyses of the supervision process and these will be
explored below (Phillips and Pugh, 1987; Salmon, 1992).

Academic supervision, previously offered to students engaged in research, has now become a key part of academic life, with teachers in higher education being required to supervise undergraduates doing projects, either live or simulated, postgraduates on taught courses preparing dissertations, as well as the traditional supervision of masters and doctorate students carrying out original research. Supervised work experience appears as part of 29 per cent of undergraduate courses (Barnett, 1990) and is likely to be a requirement on more courses (Dearing, 1997). Postgraduate supervision includes Diploma projects and Masters dissertations on taught courses, where the supervisor is likely to have a teaching connection with students. The traditional supervision of research students covers achievement of a Masters by pure research, MPhil students, qualifying for a doctorate programme, and PhD students, some of whom may be funded by one of the research councils. We believe that, although contexts and models vary, the basic tasks of supervision remain as generic core elements in every supervisory relationship.

Postgraduate supervision in the UK

We will concentrate on the traditional role of supervisor in a British university, i.e. the supervision of a student registered for a higher degree.

The funding of research in UK universities is a nationalized allocation according to a formula which differentiates between research and teaching. The link between research and teaching in higher education is a contentious issue, which we will not discuss here but the status quo reflects the view that the fundamental link is sustainable (Horlock, 1991). Nevertheless, the British university (unlike its North American counterpart) is, in the main, organized around the undergraduate student, and because it is generally small, postgraduate work may be marginalized and 'lack the social integration of either undergraduates or academic staff' (Whiston and Geiger, 1992:148). Postgraduate research students are carefully chosen, by a double selection process, first at undergraduate entry, and then in the classification of degrees, thus ensuring what has been called a 'pure thin stream of excellence' in postgraduate studies (ibid.). How much more important then to retain the stream intact to completion? The reality suggests that the thin stream is reduced by a dramatic drop-out rate, the details of which are known in the humanities and social science and can be guessed at in science.

The increasing concern in research councils about 'low rates of completion' of doctoral students has stimulated investigation and the ESRC report in 1987 revealed that only 4 per cent of funded full-time students completed within the recommended three-year period, and 25 per cent within five years (Winfield, 1987), and on enquiry these figures are replicated (informally) by other research councils. Nearly a quarter of students are dissatisfied with the supervision they receive (Cox, 1988) and many are pushed into using methodologies which do not suit them (Murray, 1988). Rudd (1985) has researched the extent of postgraduate dropout, failure or late completion of theses (completion after 5 years is defined as failure) and lists the following as the most common problems:

- inadequate or negligent supervision
- personal problems
- isolation
- methodological difficulties in the research
- poor project planning and management
- writing up.

These problem areas correspond with the seven tasks of supervision which we discuss below, but research suggests that the presence of one or more of the list above may contribute to the 'failure to complete' (Rudd, 1985).

We note the emphasis in much of the existing literature on the shortcomings of students, the 'problematizing' of students, partly because they were perforce the 'subjects' of the research studies in question, and supervisor data was not available. We do recognize that students may be fallible but researchers admit that ex-students, whether they have passed or failed, have little reason to prevaricate about their experience in supervision, and separate accounts were often validated by cross-referencing (Rudd, 1985). However the reluctance to admit to supervisor inadequacy is marked and may account for the lack of response to the issue, first identified in a government report (Robbins, 1963).

Naturally, if the students are perceived to be the problem then something must be done, at selection, in training, and so on, and responses to a series of expensive reports and advisory documents (Rudd, 1975, 1985; Welsh, 1979; Winfield, 1987) have consisted of research council sanctions directed at departments where completion rates are regarded as unsatisfactory, and advocating provision of postgraduate training (Christopherson, 1982).

The training solutions adopted (like training in methodology for doctoral students) – often disregarding the students' own views – have so far made little impact on the problem, indeed: 'as yet no answers have been found to the widespread and well-documented problems of failure, dropout and low morale amongst PhD students' (Salmon, 1992:4).

So what, apart from attributions of student laziness and incompetence, might contribute to the problem of 'failure' in postgraduate research? We find one answer in a document offering advice to supervisors, where it is stated clearly that: 'the responsibility for completion clearly lies with both student and supervisor' (Christopherson, 1982:8). The same document declares that: 'academic departments are after all full of experienced supervisors who do not need guidance on how to do their job' (p. 10), but notes that: 'the response of students to questions about supervision suggests that they may have rather different views of the matter' (p. 10).

In fact, we find that student expectations of their supervisor and what the supervisor expects are disturbingly different, apart from the expectation of professional expertise which they share. For instance, students expect their supervisor to show interest and enthusiasm, to have a genuine concern for the all-round welfare of the student, give help on non-academic matters, and: 'willingly to spend time with him and to be readily available' (Welsh, 1979:42).

In contrast, supervisors expect to take the role of 'guide philosopher and friend', offering guidance, advice, constructive criticism, opportunities for discussion, disciplining and pushing, instigating ideas, and if that is not enough: 'willing to make regular contact with his students *if required*' (p. 42, italics added).

Supervisor expectations focus mainly on transmission, with minimal suggestion of dialogue, and reservations about a commitment to making and working with a relationship (op cit.). The student expectations clearly include the elements of a learning relationship, which we identified earlier as underpinning transformational learning, and which has been identified as the key factor in a research journey (Salmon, 1992).

So what kind of supervisor does contribute to successful completion of a higher degree? Brown and Atkins (1988) explored the supervisor (rather than the student for once) and found that structured supervision with emotional warmth, was more effective than emotional distance and liberality (meaning lack of boundaries). Some of the roles required for good academic supervision identified by Brown and Atkins (1988:120) have been adapted in the list below:

- *facilitator* – enabling a process of developing ideas
- *teacher* – teaching study skills and research methods, as well as subject material
- *assessor* – giving critical and constructive feedback
- *counsellor* – i.e. using counselling skills by listening and giving emotional support
- *colleague* – sharing a similar interest in the subject
- *manager* – setting guidelines, deadlines, boundaries
- *advisor* – making suggestions, proposing topics, sources, etc.

These roles correspond with the seven tasks of supervision we identified and these are discussed below.

Academic supervisors have traditionally been an expert and active researcher in the chosen field of study. This of course implies a publication record and therefore an interest in potential publication, sometimes the pay-off for the hard-pressed supervisor. He or she is not chosen for her facilitation skills and this has been a difficulty for many students. The typical supervisory pair are likely to draw on the supervisor's academic knowledge only, leaving the domains of action and affect untouched, so that the doing of the research and the student's feelings about it are ignored. The reality of the student's situation, shortage of funds, perhaps in a new institution, with little idea about how to proceed, often places the feeling and doing as prime (at least temporarily) and they will 'get in the way' of any cognitive activity. Students who are not managing their time, and are disorganized and who feel ill-equipped, will struggle to tangle with complex ideas. Supervisors who are absent or unreliable present poor models and add to the student's difficulties. An understanding of this is where good supervision experience differs from a poor one (Salmon, 1992).

The personally creative nature of a doctorate journey with its required innovative and original outcome demands support which is more than a bit of academic advice. We believe, with Cox (1988) that, as in all learning, the relationship between student and supervisor is at the heart of the work. The supervisor–student relationship 'carries' the student throughout the journey of research. The reciprocal nature of relationship (discussed in Chapter 9) is not recognized in the one-way practice of 'allocating' students to supervisors on the basis of the latter's academic expertise. For encouragement and support the relationship will need to include trust, sympathy and mutuality, i.e. a two-way process.

Overseas students (a sizeable proportion of doctoral students) are particularly vulnerable to isolation. They come to Britain with high expectations and many are disappointed. Homesickness and unwelcoming systems can lead to loneliness and resentment, while cultural differences and financial problems may exacerbate difficulties. Many overseas students, and indeed students within Britain, experience racism on a day-to-day basis, in verbal attacks or discriminatory behaviour (Lago and Thompson, 1996).

Supervisors almost always act as personal tutors because many postgraduate research students are not allocated a personal tutor. The supervisor may be the only member of staff with whom the student has contact; hence the relationship between supervisor and student is viewed by both as being important professionally *and* personally (Welsh, 1979).

Thus to support our thin stream of carefully chosen postgraduate students supervision will need to include particular skills over and above the academic knowledge and expertise traditionally associated with a supervisor of research. In order to support the supervisor–supervisee relationship, and identify the best ways of ensuring 'good steady and satisfactory progress' in research (Christopherson, 1982), we identify the seven tasks of supervision, drawing on the three sources we have identified.

Functions and tasks of supervision

Supervisors who carry an understanding of their own theory and practice as well as the research models being pursued by supervisees are likely to be effective, providing that they carry out the tasks of supervision. Supervision tasks arise out of the three functions of supervision, linked to the needs of a supervisee, and these functions have been identified as *formative* (to meet the supervisee's educative needs), *normative* (to meet the supervisee's need to take administrative control of their research), and *restorative* (to meet the needs of supervisees for emotional support) (Inskipp and Proctor, 1988). The three functions relate to the three domains of learning identified in Chapter 3, namely, cognitive (knowing or leading to knowledge), conative (acting or interacting with the world) and affect (emotion or feeling in self and in relation to others) as follows:

Function	*Needs of supervisee*	*Domain of learning*
formative	educative	cognitive/knowing/knowledge
normative	administrative	conative/doing/world
restorative	supportive	affective/feeling/self

Supervision which covers all three domains is likely to include:

1. a willingness on the part of the supervisor to share expertise relating to the discipline concerned (formative function – educative need)
2. a firm arrangement for contact, clear records, including a contract stating boundaries and commitment on both parts (normative function – administrative need)
3. a willingness to receive and respond to emotional material, and self-disclose where appropriate (restorative function – supportive need).

Supervision and learning models

Traditionally, counsellors 'learnt their trade' through their supervising analyst, absorbing from the supervision process, an understanding of theory and practice. This tradition, where the supervisor adopts the key focus of their theoretical model, in preference to others, implies a philosophy of learning, often embedded in the process.

Similarly, academic supervisors have passed on *their* theory and practice in much the same way, and supervision in universities can be similarly paradigm-bound, with undeclared assumptions, e.g. empiricism, positivism, hidden in the process. Therefore a supervisor may need to reflect upon her own philosophies and models in order to become aware of what is being passed on to the student implicitly. In particular, the supervisor's way of offering supervision will come from a particular model of learning and development, based on her understanding of how people learn and may not cover all three domains as above.

In order to cover the three learning domains and their related functions in supervision, the supervisor we suggest will need to attend to the seven tasks of supervision, arising out of the three functions, as given below:

Tasks of Supervision (based on Inskipp and Proctor, 1988 and Carroll, 1996)

Function	*Tasks*
formative (educative)	teaching evaluating monitoring professional/ethical issues
normative (administrative)	administrating, structure and organization consulting
restorative (supportive)	relating counselling (using counselling skills)

In academic supervision, as in the other contexts we have mentioned, there is no agreement on what tasks should form part of the supervision process, and the tasks of teaching and evaluating have dominated, particularly in academic supervision. The roles of teacher, consultant and counsellor (using counselling skills) appear in most approaches to supervision, but there is a lack of definition regarding the proper emphasis for each task and function. We offer some findings from doctoral students (Rudd, 1985; Salmon, 1992) in relation to the tasks we have identified, and we emphasize that, although priorities may vary, these seven tasks are likely to form part of effective supervision in other contexts, e.g. industrial placement, undergraduate projects, postgraduate dissertations and masters' theses.

The seven tasks of supervision

1. Teaching and learning
2. Evaluating
3. Monitoring professional/ethical issues
4. Administrating, structure and organization
5. Consulting
6. Relating
7. Using counselling skills.

Teaching and the learning

Academic supervisors may assume a traditional formal teaching role but comments from those being supervised state a preference for informal experiential methods and supervisees particularly seek modelling of research behaviour as a source of learning. The preferred learning relationship, to release creativity and encourage innovation, as noted above, is mutual and two-way:

> Originally I thought I needed academic support . . . but this is very far from the truth . . . An academic mentor can only lead a student along a well-trodden path. It takes a different sort of mentor to encourage a student to take risks, to follow hunches and to hang on to the passionate interest that started the whole exercise in the first place.
>
> (Salmon, 1992:96)

Welsh's research (1979) revealed that relationship factors were as important to students as teaching functions and that supervisors who adopted a primarily transmission role were not helping their students. Moreover, if their learning model is one of transmission from a safe distance – an unassailable position, then supervision presents a situation where the teacher is no longer the unquestioned authority – an insecure position. The natural reaction for a supervisor who is feeling hesitant about his role is to revert to a traditional transmissive mode, or avoid supervision as much as possible. The persistence of transmission roles in supervision suggests that teachers are asked to become supervisors without the necessary skills for developing a learning relationship.

To fulfil the teaching task in supervision we recommend the skills of reflective dialogue, particularly that of socratic questioning, described in Chapter 11. We recommend that supervisors begin by using the basic skills of facilitation, namely listening, responding and offering empathy, which are described in Chapters 10 and 11. We do recognize that there will be a time and place for transmission when the relationship is healthy and mutuality is established, but suggest that this comes later, otherwise a hierarchical boundary is immediately created, which may limit the potential for dialogue and therefore, reflective learning.

Evaluating

Doctoral students state that they need feedback desperately. Supervisors who retain drafts for excessive periods of time have been described as 'cases of grave neglect and dereliction of duty' (Rudd, 1985:79). Students record their need for evaluation of their work as absolutely crucial to enable them to carry on. However, the traditional 'insensitive machismo blunderbuss approach' (Salmon, 1992:89) is less desired by students than a supervisor who can be 'constructively critical' (ibid.). The personal significance of presenting work for evaluation is revealed by the following: 'the research is part of me and to share the research means sharing myself. This can only be risky but also destructive, if entrusted to insensitive people' (p. 90 op cit.).

Here the skills of challenging are integral to the task, with confrontation, feedback and sometimes advanced empathy as relevant for successful evaluation and reflective dialogue. Recognition, by a trusted supervisor, of feelings of resistance, may enable a student to release a block, and we discuss the skills of recognizing and responding to feelings in Chapter 11.

Monitoring professional/ethical issues

The monitoring role may be routine, reminding students of deadlines and encouraging completion of tasks, but deeper issues can emerge: 'from her questioning and probing I am encouraged to explore and articulate my

unexamined motives, my taken-for-granted assumptions about the research'
(Salmon, 1992:97), and:

> Journeying to a place of mutual respect, empathy, clarity and success
> for us as a Black researcher and a White supervisor is worth writing
> about . . . aspects of that journey could be crucial for other Black re-
> searchers on that lonely research track in White institutions.
>
> (p. 96)

When there is no structure for professional monitoring the student's work
can be compromised: 'the supervision I've had . . . there's a sense in which
it's been catastrophic' (Rudd, 1985:92). The use of reflective dialogue skills,
listening, questioning and challenging if necessary will fulfil this task in
supervision.

Administrating, structure and organization

This task may be underrated in importance, in academic settings, but doctoral supervisors cite students' lack of organization and time management
as a factor in completion failure. Traditional administrative processes include record-keeping, appraisal profiles and draft material. The academic
supervisor may be able to learn from the planning, organizing, and struc-
turing of administrative systems and provide a powerful model for the benefit of their students, as many fall short in this matter. Example or modelling
is the best teacher here, and clear contracts with firm boundaries can only
help both parties, as students experience disorganized supervision as a problem: 'I compare my experience of her with working on shifting sands. She
vacillated; the advice given one day contradicted, forgotten or denied the
next' (Salmon, 1992:90), and: 'Students I have known wait fruitless weeks
for feedback . . . it is quite possible for a student to turn up for an appointment only to be told by a secretary that the supervisor is not available'
(p. 92); 'I was very much left to flounder by myself' (Rudd, 1985:85).

The key skill here is assertion and transmitting a clear message to students. It does not matter how much or how little time a supervisor can offer
as long as it is clear to the student. Supervisors who avoid the early contracting
stage simply confuse their students, or become sitting targets with constantly demanding students. Boundaries are a necessary condition for reflective dialogue, providing clear rules about what is to be discussed, by
whom, and when, and they don't exist psychologically until they are articulated so a clear statement of availability, limits of access, etc. (possibly in
writing) will confirm boundaries for both parties.

Consulting

As a task, consulting refers to the supervisor's awareness of the systems
within which his supervisee is working, i.e. the institution, the faculty, the

department and the research team, as well as his supervisee's membership of social systems, e.g. family and friends. Many systemic difficulties can be helped through the consulting process, with a skilled supervisor. For example, doctoral students may find it difficult to refuse to cover lectures for senior academics at short notice and in consultation with their supervisor they may be able to gain the confidence to say no.

If the supervisor is likely to be working with a near equal, in seniority or expertise (quite common with part time or mature students), then the consultant role is more appropriate, particularly where the student's subject is outside the supervisor's expertise. Such an arrangement is becoming more common in higher education as departments are realizing that: 'it should not be assumed that any member of staff can supervise a research student' (Rudd, 1985:124) and 'the relationship is a peculiarly close one. They start master and pupil and ideally end up almost as equal colleagues' (Christopherson, 1982:12).

Consulting is less a task and more a process, where the two-way relationship comes into its own. The research is owned and authored by the student and she knows it better than anyone, and the supervisor learns about it through contact with the student. A supervisor who responds to students' work with an awareness and respect for the uniqueness of what is being offered is likely to foster confidence in the learning student. Such consultation along the way will ensure that at the point of completion the candidate can speak with authority about the research in question, the supreme outcome of reflective dialogue.

Relating

Students yearn for contact with their supervisor, and complain about the lack of it: 'I didn't get enough supervisor contact' (Rudd, 1985:84). Where there is insufficient contact assumptions are made like: 'not interested in me' (ibid.). Students prefer supervisory relationships which are two way, and involve mutual trust and mutual respect. The student develops towards authorship and for this she will need to nurture and grow her autonomy and authority in the work. The need to eschew hierarchical power is stressed by students: 'Never does she tell me to do this or not to do that' (Salmon, 1992:97).

The traditional academic with answers to everything is not what is needed:

> The supervisor may see that their role is in giving answers rather than helping research students find their own solutions. The supervisor needs to be an open and confident person who can let others be the centre of attention where this is necessary.

> (p. 97 op cit.)

A relationship without overt hierarchical power overtones, can enable students to gain: 'a greater capacity for critical constructive and independent thought' (Rudd, 1985:2) and this is achieved by the facilitative behaviours implied in reflective dialogue, and described in Chapters 10 and 11.

Using counselling skills

Supervisors in all contexts are adamantly against counselling their supervisee. The academic supervisor should never attempt the role of counsellor; first, she lacks professional training and could easily damage her student; secondly, her role as academic supervisor cuts across other professional roles; and thirdly, offering counselling to a student is not an appropriate task of supervision. However, many supervisors realize, in the course of their work with students, that counselling may be appropriate for particular difficulties in the student's life. Here the skill of referral is crucial and student counsellors in recent years have worked with personal tutors, enabling them to refer students to the university counselling service or other sources of personal therapy. Personal tutors can be trapped into quasi-counselling relationships with students, as can their friends, and the contract with its built in boundaries is helpful here.

However, recognition of postgraduate learning as an activity which involves emotional development means that supervisors will need to be able to work with feelings in their supervisee. We recommend that supervisors refrain from questioning students when emotional material emerges in relation to their work, as questions may take students into areas of personal trauma in which the supervisor will feel less than confident. The use of *counselling skills* is appropriate as part of the facilitation skills described in Chapters 10 and 11. They are: *listening*; *observing*; *reflecting back*; *empathy*; *summarizing* (not questioning). Sometimes the simplest use of a simple skill like listening, is all that is required: 'I could almost have managed even though he didn't know anything about the subject, if he would *just have sat and listened* but he made it clear that he hadn't got time for it' (Rudd, 1985:87; italics added).

Using counselling skills (not questioning – see comment above) ensures that the academic tutor does not get into a therapy situation with a student. Listening, reflecting back and empathy are appropriate for dealing with the affective domain where emotion and feelings are part of the student's issue. Details of these skills are given in Chapters 10 and 11.

Summary

The seven tasks outlined above include the three learning domains as indicated. The first three, namely teaching, evaluating and monitoring provide for the formative or educative function in supervision. Administration and consulting address the normative function so that supervisor's model good organization and sound research practice. Lastly, relating to the student and using counselling skills fulfils the restorative function by giving emotional support to the student, as appropriate. The tasks imply a particular approach which we have termed facilitation, and the rationale for such an approach remains its potential for enabling reflective dialogue. Supervision is a perfect place for academic staff in higher education to engage in such dialogue with postgraduate students.

Two supervision stories

Our two contrasting stories highlight some of the issues raised above, and, we hope, illustrate the tasks and functions of supervision as well as its potential to enable reflective learning. The first story describes the supervision of one of us to submission of a masters thesis. The second story relates the experience of one of us as a contract researcher in higher education. Both supervisors worked in the same institution albeit in different departments, and we recognize that many factors affect how teachers in higher education are able to carry out their supervision duties.

Supervisor A

My first academic supervisor, A, was a senior lecturer who supported my research and the writing of my thesis, part of a programme leading to the degree of MA. He also delivered some of the taught elements of the programme, including research methods, so, by the time I was writing up I knew him well. He used a facilitative approach in his taught modules and disclosed the struggles of his own research rather than presenting himself as a 'guru'.

He had begun to develop group supervision as part of the research methods module, and many of the questions and difficulties I might have taken to him in one-to-one supervision had already been dealt with in the group supervision situation. For example, research techniques, referencing and sourcing, how to write clearly, reliability and validity.

He was highly professional as a supervisor, i.e. he established a clear contract with me at the start, with our supervision sessions arranged well in advance. It was made clear to me that these should not be altered by either of us, except in emergency. Sessions were conducted in his room, without interruption, and we both recorded the outcomes of our discussion. I knew from the start that I had a limited number of sessions with him, as he had a number of students to supervise.

Early sessions were chatty as I developed my research plan, and he listened a lot, simply replaying my own ideas back to me until I got hold of what I wanted to do. However, once written material was available, he insisted that it was presented to him in advance of our sessions and he arrived with my drafts in his hand, ready to give me his comments and feedback.

He was an astute and patient listener, using reflecting back and empathy, to support me through the depressive 'dip' which occurred about halfway through my period of writing up.

He was my junior in age and I was researching a field with which he was unfamiliar but which interested him. I had a good deal of experience in the field and I received considerable respect from him. We related as equals and our sessions were consultative in atmosphere, so that he attended to the systems within which I was working, e.g. the other students, availability of other staff for consultation, my family.

Because he had attended to me so carefully and *really* understood what I was trying to do, he was able to help me to identify a way of presenting my findings which brought all the work together in a way which made my argument clear and accessible without losing the subtlety and richness of my material.

I trusted him completely and followed our agreed plan without deviation or further support, and I presented my thesis within the specified period.

On successful completion, when I went to thank him, he was nonchalant, saying 'I never doubted it' and 'I felt totally confident from the beginning of your ability to present a masters thesis'. Then I realized that he had passed on his belief in me *to* me and I had thrived on it.

Supervisor A carried out the seven tasks of supervision by:

1. clarifying our contract and his limited availability
2. making a commitment to me
3. giving me space to be creative
4. giving me support when appropriate
5. giving me direction at the point when I needed it
6. alerting me to ethical/professional issues re confidentiality
7. encouraging me to adopt an innovative approach to the subject.

Supervisor A was for me a model of professional academic supervision and I remain indebted to him.

Supervisor B

Supervisor B, a senior lecturer, chose me to join a group of researchers in a university department, to carry out a funded project commissioned by a government agency. I was to work closely with one other research assistant on the project and we were briefed together by B. The research design involved creation of a questionnaire, administration of a field survey, collection and analysis of data.

Initially, as a self-driven researcher, I was happy to conduct a literature search, and, with my colleague, revise the research design, arrange the primary field work without much support from my supervisor and we just got on with it.

Soon, however, after a number of cancelled meetings with him, I began to feel the need for direction and support. My research partner and I were not always in agreement and this made progress difficult, as neither of us had the authority to make decisions about the project.

Supervisor B was a well-known researcher in his field, highly respected, but a bit of a maverick in the department, and perceived as innovative but eccentric by his colleagues in the university. He was valued for his ability to bring funding through research projects into the institution. He had considerable personal charm, a great sense of fun, a warm personality, and a reputation for not taking things too seriously. His approach to supervision was openly laissez-faire and he encouraged an atmosphere of dilletante-ism within his section.

He worked late, and, when project reports were due, expected his team to do the same. I was okay with this but sometimes I experienced the terror of last-minute calculations to be incorporated into reports which were finished in a right-up-to-the-wire deadline.

We completed the first phase of the project successfully, published the material and reached the analysis stage of phase 2. At this point promises of renewed funding were withdrawn and the project came to an abrupt end. Fortunately, the data was incorporated into a sister project being carried out in the department, so I felt that my work was not wasted. I was offered the opportunity to contribute to the sister project, but I chose to take up a research fellowship elsewhere, rather than embark on another period of uncertainty with B.

Supervisor B illustrates that a good relationship is not enough in supervision, just as academic knowledge is insufficient. The relationship must be *professional* as well as personal and this requires attention to all the seven tasks. He addressed the seven tasks as follows:

1. he did not clarify our contract and his availability
2. he did not make a commitment to me by keeping our appointments
3. he did give me space to be creative
4. he was not there to support me when needed
5. he failed to give me direction at the point when I needed it
6. he assumed ethical/professional issues were in hand
7. he encouraged me to adopt an innovative approach to the subject.

For many students a fun-loving and light-hearted supervisor may be just what they are looking for and the progress of the contract may be incidental. As a fledgling researcher on a short contract, I needed more than that. Supervisor B remains for me a wonderful character, full of energy and fun, creative and interesting, but sadly, a hopeless supervisor.

The structure of supervision: a road map for academic supervisors

We offer an adaptation of the cyclical model (Page and Wosket, 1994) which is based on the principles of Gerard Egan, who provided a model for skilled helpers working in a variety of settings (Egan, 1990). The cyclical model enables a reflective and/or critical dialogue to occur in relation to whatever work in which the helper is engaged. The structure lends itself to both individual and group supervision, and we offer an additional recommendation for groups. In both situations, we are recommending a facilitative approach (see Chapter 9) by the supervisor, as this is likely to sustain the reflective dialogue which will lead to productive work at postgraduate level and stimulate the creative activity of high level and high quality research.

Doing one-to-one supervision

Page and Woskett (1994) offer their model for counsellors in supervision, and we adapt it for academic supervision. Their assumptions are relevant for academic practice and particularly for supervision in higher education.

The cyclical model incorporates five stages for each session as follows:

1. *contract* – the agreement between the supervision pair about task process and boundaries
2. *focus* – the choice of focus to be agreed in each session
3. *space* – a place for exploration, reflection and challenge
4. *bridge* – the way back to the project
5. *review* – evaluation or summary so far.

The assumptions which underpin the model are humanistic in kind and professional in effect. For example, supervision is for the benefit of the supervisee; the relationship should be characterized by warmth, understanding and empathy; containing emotion will enable learning in the supervisee; supervisors should reflect on their own practice. In addition, the model recognizes that supervision may be exploratory, open-ended, reflective and also action-oriented, as well as acknowledging that learning in this way is exposing and challenging for the supervisee. The humanity of the supervisor is the most valuable contribution to the process for both, and the danger of mechanization in supervision has been highlighted by Blocher:

> the possibility always exists that an immature, inadequate, and insensitive supervisor may intimidate, bully, and even damage a supervisee. No theoretical model of supervision is idiot proof and bastard resistant. When such destructive events occur in supervision it is more likely to be due to the personal inadequacies of the supervisor than to deficiencies in any well-thought through theoretical model.
>
> (Blocher, 1983:30)

With that warning in mind we look briefly at the five stages of our cycle: contract, focus, space, bridge and review, as outlined above, and refer readers to a more detailed treatment in Page and Woskett (1994).

The supervision *contracting* process will include arrangements for meeting, frequency, duration and timing. Boundaries should be agreed, such as confidentiality, telephone contact, emergency procedure, personal/professional material. This is where the supervision pair would agree that counselling is not part of the relationship and that if personal issues arise in sessions, referral may be an option. Recontracting where relevant, may occur in later sessions, but will normally feature in the first. We have established that transparency about process is a valuable facet of facilitation leading to reflective dialogue. The safety provided by firm boundaries enables a supervisee to deal with difficult issues relating to his work, e.g. lack of understanding, survey disasters, mechanical failures of research equipment or computers. Where either party breach boundaries then facilitative confrontation may be needed.

The supervisee has the right to decide the *focus* of the session, unless there is a serious problem which justifies the supervisor overriding the autonomy of the supervisee. The choice of focus will dictate the responses of the supervisor, in deciding which task it is appropriate to address, and therefore, which facilitative skills to use. Reflective dialogue skills needed here are patience while the supervisee sorts out her desired focus, listening and responding, offering empathy where appropriate, and particularly summarizing what may have been presented in a spontaneous but possibly disordered fashion.

As noted above, early sessions will need to attend to the relationship, using the material presented to establish rapport, and deal with feelings that are getting in the way of progress for the supervisee. Here the importance of emotional facilitation is evident and empathy will be a key skill. As the relationship develops and the supervisee is enabled to get to grips with their project, other tasks of supervision can be fulfilled. The *space* provided at this stage of the cycle will allow for containment, challenge and encouragement of the supervisee, to be creative and innovative, utilizing the dialogue skills of questioning and confrontation.

The *bridge* stage of the cycle is named to indicate the link from supervision back to the actual work, so supervisors will need to question and summarize and instigate action in this stage, action relating to the supervisee's project. The need to record here is paramount.

Reviewing the session completes the cycle and leaves the supervision pair ready to renew the process in the next session. Feedback and some evaluation are important in this stage, and the opportunity for reviewing the process of the session, but the most important part of review is the winding down of the session. The supervisor's summary will effect this (and it should include agreed action points), as well as the supervisee's impressions of the session (including articulation of what has been agreed). This stage is often neglected because of avoidance by both parties, unclear goals, or basic time management. It is the supervisor's responsibility to manage session timings so as to leave sufficient time for review.

Doing group supervision

The assumption up to this point is that the supervisor–student relationship is one-to-one and so it must be at crucial points in the process, probably the most important being the writing up period when retaining focus is often difficult for the student, and swift feedback from a supervisor can avert disaster. However, hard-pressed supervisors may like to consider the advantages of group supervision for at least some of the two- or three-year period for which they are carrying responsibility for students. What do we mean by group supervision and aren't research seminars group supervision?

Part of the supervisor's role is to facilitate networking for research students, and established practice is students being 'invited' to present their ongoing work to a seminar audience of other postgraduates and staff. This is where we are told students learn about critical reflection, through a process of challenge, survival and endurance. For an academic, knowledge must be worked with robustly: 'Knowledge is the academic's working material, securing it, clarifying it, integrating it, sharing it, *destroying it*' (Ryan, 1987:189, italics added).

The idea of 'destroying' knowledge is part of academic activity, passing on methods of attacking error and ignorance, through research seminars where colleagues 'justify' their work to their peers and 'field questions' in adversarial conditions not unlike a (British) court of law. Not surprisingly when researchers present their work in such a forum, they are careful to limit the material to safe, well thought out issues, where they feel secure if challenged.

Such baptisms of fire train aspiring academics to operate under conditions of some constraint as a strategic defence, limiting their exposure unless they are really sure of the resilience of their argument, rather than exploring possibilities with others which may or may not lead to solutions. Such defensive delivery, familiar in the conference presentations of experienced academics is one example of the coping strategies developed to survive in the adversarial academy and we believe this inhibits innovation and creativity for researchers at the very start of academic careers (Heron, 1986).

The worst versions of the above leaves students feeling undermined and demoralized. This need not be the case. Our proposal for group supervision, as proposed by Salmon (1992) offers a completely different scenario where groups are used to nourish and affirm the essentially creative qualities which mark original research.

A supervision group will need to adopt a different agenda to the traditional 'reporting back' scenario. The absence of familiar routines may disturb students who have been steeped in and rewarded by traditional academic dialogue. We recommend that supervisors adopt the action learning structure outlined in Chapter 12 as a firm structure to enable a smooth changeover from traditional modes to more facilitative methods. The need for controlling boundaries is part of facilitation and many supervisors are poor at this most basic skill. The action learning structure defines a contract and articulates boundaries clearly for group members and teaches them to respect the supervisor's personal boundaries without damaging the relationship. In addition, the other parts of the cycle described above are enacted through action learning but particularly helpful is the emphasis on process review in recent approaches (McGill and Beaty, 1995).

This completes our chapter about academic supervision. We have drawn on historical, social and academic sources for contributions to our discussion, including the roles of the supervisor, the three functions and seven tasks of supervision. We have presented an adaptation of the cyclical model in five stages for supervision sessions which offers a structure for supervisors to follow.

Notes

1. For many, the association with hierarchical and/or management systems makes the word 'supervision' unacceptable. In particular, where supervision takes place between two professional practitioners of equal seniority, a not uncommon situation, described in Two Supervision Stories, pp. 245–7, the 'super' root of the word is archaic. We propose the word 'meta vision' to denote a view which suggests equality within the process, as well as implying a helicopter view.
2. We are *not* recommending academic supervision that makes a supervisor into a counsellor. The counselling profession has clearly delineated between the work of a counsellor, a particular kind of professional relationship, and the use, in many contexts, including teaching, of *counselling skills*. Where the term 'counsellor' is used in our sources we substitute 'using counselling skills' as more accurate in our academic setting.

14

Mentoring

In this chapter we relate the principles of reflective practice to mentoring in higher education. We draw from the literature on mentoring to demonstrate that true mentoring incorporates reflective dialogue, and can therefore offer a context in which a teacher in higher education may encourage reflective learning, for students and colleagues, through their role as mentor. We begin with an introduction to the concept of mentoring and some possible applications of mentoring ideas in higher education. This is followed by a brief summary of mentoring research and the key skills for mentors. We complete our chapter with some mentoring 'stories', where we seek to highlight the success factors, and the reflective nature of true mentoring. Readers may like to read the mentoring 'stories' first and put them into the context of good practice.

Many teachers in higher education are being asked to mentor newly appointed members of staff who are new to teaching, and who may lack experience of teaching in higher education. In addition, as academic and personal tutors, teachers in higher education have often found themselves becoming informal mentors to particular students. The informality of such relationships may conceal the significance for the development of students and leaves the teacher's contribution (often entirely voluntary) unacknowledged and consequently perhaps, not recognized or valued.

So what exactly is mentoring and what does the role of mentor entail in a higher education context?

A mentor has been identified as someone senior who develops and enables her/his protégé to 'take the next step in life' (Megginson, 1988). Other definitions include:

- 'an experienced and trusted advisor' (*Oxford Advanced Learner's Dictionary*).
- 'a more experienced individual, willing to share his/her knowledge with someone less experienced in a relationship of mutual trust' (Clutterbuck, 1992:7)
- 'a role model . . . a guide, a tutor, a coach and a confidant' (quoted in Clutterbuck, 1991:2)

- 'someone who has the respect of the less experienced protégé in terms of what they know, but also for what they are' (Clutterbuck, 1992:7)

Mentoring is clearly differentiated from instructing and teaching in the traditional sense (Megginson, 1988). The role of mentor, in higher education as elsewhere,[1] is neither tutor, instructor, nor primarily advisor, although advice may be given. Rather it has been described by student learners in higher education as nearer that of friend, confidante, counsellor or parent figure, who is non-directive and non-judgemental (Brockbank, 1994).

Mentoring relationships may occur naturally and informally with a mentor choosing to take a particular colleague, usually younger and junior, under his wing. Such an informal relationship relies on the chosen mentee accepting the relationship. Mentors may be formally allocated to new members of staff, sometimes giving the selecting senior person the candidate they chose to appoint at selection. Alternatively, the mentor pairs may be allocated with neither party being given a choice, an arrangement doomed to failure, but there are isolated success stories.

The person being mentored is termed the protégé or mentee, neither term a comfortable one in the English language. Where the mentored person is a student we shall substitute learner and where the mentored person is a teacher we shall substitute colleague, teacher or member of staff.

Formal mentoring for teachers and students, by teachers in higher education is likely to occur in four different situations and informal mentoring in a further two contexts:

1. Newly appointed staff, who, as a condition of their appointment must undertake a teaching qualification, a certificate of teaching, usually within their first year in the institution, and certainly within their period of probation. While following a programme of study leading to accreditation as a teacher in higher education new staff may be offered, from among academic colleagues, a suitable mentor to assist their learning and provide support throughout the duration of the course.
2. Newly appointed staff, who may or may not have experience in higher education, and who are not required as a condition of appointment to undertake a qualification, may be provided with a mentor, chosen from among academic colleagues, to support the new member of staff throughout their probationary period.
3. Newly appointed staff, with experience of higher education, who are qualified, and therefore are not required to undertake a certificate programme, may be offered a mentor, chosen from academic colleagues, throughout their probationary period. This rather formal arrangement will normally lapse on completion of probation. We recount our experience of such a mentor below in Three Mentoring Stories.
4. In addition, existing members of staff, who enrol on programmes of study within the institution, professional postgraduate diploma courses or masters, where mentoring may be offered as part of the learning environment, may encounter their colleagues as mentors, who are allocated to support the learner and assist in the learning process.

Additionally, informal mentoring arrangements may occur in two ways:

5. Relationships between staff and students, as either personal or academic tutors, and sometimes between experienced staff and less-experienced staff, which neither would call mentoring, may develop quite naturally over time. These organic relationships are probably the most effective support for staff and students in higher education.
6. Exceptionally, senior managers in higher education have elected to provide themselves with an external mentor, sometimes called an external consultant or even external supervisor. We have experience of this arrangement as both senior manager and as external consultant, and recount the story below in Three Mentoring Stories.

Is mentoring a new idea or another gimmick? The historical roots of mentoring lie in the Greek myth of Ulysses, who in preparation for his lengthy sea voyages entrusted his young son to the care of his old friend Mentor. Thereafter the name has been identified with a more experienced person who *forms a relationship* with a less experienced person in order to provide them with advice, support and encouragement (Collin, 1988). The activity of mentoring is normally linked to fostering *career success*, and it has been identified as a necessary contribution to development in any profession (Clutterbuck, 1991). Our use of italics highlight the two broad functions within mentoring, namely relationship functions and career functions (Kram, 1988).

First, career functions, including sponsorship and coaching, which enhance career advancement (for the mentee). Where career functions are the primary focus, which is often the case in formal mentoring programmes, the model tends to be knowledge-based, instrumental and carefully controlled.

Secondly, what have been termed psychosocial functions, and we prefer to call relationship functions, including friendship, counselling and role modelling were identified as enhancing a sense of competence, identity and effectiveness in a professional role. When relationship functions are primary the mentoring experience includes an intensity of emotion, the potential for self-transformation and development for both parties (Baum, 1992).

The benefits of career functions come largely from the experience, seniority and organizational ranking of the mentor, who is able to help the mentee to 'navigate effectively in the organizational world' (Kram, 1988). Relationship functions, on the other hand, rely on the quality of the interpersonal bond between mentor and mentee, and the degree of trust which exists within the relationship. Factors which influence the relationship include mutual liking, respect, exclusivity, counselling skill and the desire for intimacy (Kram, 1988).

Relationship functions, including acceptance, confirmation and affirmation, are likely to enhance a 'developmental' relationship which provides the individual with the information, support and challenge which they need to meet their development needs. The description given by Clarkson and Shaw (1992) of such a developmental alliance suggests the ideal mentoring relationship, i.e. one based on explicit, consciously chosen contractual arrangements between the mentor and the person being mentored. Active learning, where the learner takes an active part in her own learning, rather than being passively fed, is likely to emerge from such developmental relationships, where they occur, as such relationships foster autonomy and independence rather than passivity and dependence. The necessary and sufficient conditions for the freedom to learn have been identified as including the three functions described above as acceptance, confirmation and affirmation (Rogers, 1983).

The superficial learning which occurs in situations of power imbalance may occur in mentoring situations and may, therefore, adversely affect perceptions of the relationship. In particular, where the mentor has hierarchical authority over the mentee, a barrier exists, known as a hierarchical boundary, and relationship functions which support a developmental relationship may be inhibited by the power imbalance inherent in the relationship (Krantz, 1989).

Mentoring relationships, either formal or informal, are known to progress in four phases. The phases or stages of a mentoring relationship have been identified as: initiation, cultivation, separation and re-definition (Kram, 1988; Levinson *et al.*, 1978). In higher education where colleagues may be mentoring each other, an understanding of the phases may enable smooth progress through them, and a realization that the relationship is not required to continue for life!

Where staff are mentoring students the phases are likely to coincide with the students' entry to and exit from higher education. The parallel with biological phases of development has been noted as well as problems of dependency implicit in the mentoring relationship (Auster, 1984; Bushardt *et al.*, 1991). Analyses of mentoring have compared the stages of mentoring with early life stages (Baum, 1992; Kahn, 1981; Kates, 1985) and effective mentor relationships incorporate an intensity of emotion not unlike parenting or falling in love (Phillips-Jones, 1982).

Analysis of mentoring pairs, incorporating student learners in higher education, with workplace mentors, has revealed evidence of intense emotions in mentoring pairs incorporating a hierarchical boundary (Beech and Brockbank, 1999). Such a boundary would exist in higher education between teacher and student, or a senior academic and junior. Findings include reactions to authority such as dependency and counter-dependency, where the authority figure is either lionized or rebelled against; or idealization of the mentoring pair, where they and others romanticize the relationship, sometimes to the point of stimulating gossip (Beech and Brockbank, 1999; Krantz, 1989).

Mentoring activity is known to develop the mentor as well as the mentee, but the value of this is frequently unrecognized in organizations (Reich, 1986) and we noted above that informal mentors in higher education are largely invisible and almost certainly unappreciated by the institution. Mentors are often out of step with institutional norms thereby providing an important stimulant for innovation and creativity. So mentors have the potential to become powerful change agents within higher education.

There is evidence that informal mentor relationships are more productive than formal ones, informal where the mentor chooses and the mentee accepts, and formal when the mentor may or may not choose, and mentees are unlikely to be given a choice. Variations on both arrangements are possible, e.g. in the analysis mentioned above, mentoring pairs were 'allocated' after student learners in higher education were asked to choose their mentors, who were then invited to accept (Beech and Brockbank, 1999).

Formal/informal is likely to be a description of the relationship rather than the mentoring arrangements, e.g. meetings can be formally arranged between an informally created mentoring couple. Successful mentoring couples almost always incorporate some 'chemistry', with the mentor 'taking a shine' to the mentee, or the mentor being 'admired' by the mentee. In other words formal systems which impose mentor relationships are less likely to succeed than informal or more self-driven, organic, arrangements where mentoring is adopted by choice (Arnold and Davidson, 1990). Another significant finding relates to the reasons for mentoring dysfunction, which include cross-gender mentoring couples, line manager–mentor relationships, and lack of training as contributing factors to problems in mentoring (ibid.).

The difference between *instrumental* mentoring and *essential* mentoring has been emphasized by Audrey Collin (1988) and she clarifies the former as involvement at a limited objective level, while the latter she suggests is characterized by involvement of both parties in the objective *and* subjective worlds of the other (Collin, 1988: 24). We recommend below that essential mentoring relationships are appropriate in academic settings; ideally created informally, although we recognize that in the scenarios we have described this may not be possible.

Mentoring has been differentiated from instructing and coaching by virtue of its emphasis on a non-directive dialogue which mirrors the reflective dialogue we have already described in earlier chapters. In researching mentoring behaviour in the workplace, reports from staff questioned about what percentage of their manager's behaviour was instructing, coaching and mentoring revealed a discrepancy with the manager's own view, with managers under-rating their instructing behaviour, and over-rating their mentoring behaviour (ibid.). This confirms other results where managers' self-ratings are compared with their subordinates', and results reveal that managers are largely unaware of how 'directive' their behaviour is, believing themselves to be more non-directive than they are (O'Connor and Davies, 1990). We include these findings as many academics may also believe themselves to be more 'non-directive' than they actually are and we recommend reflective dialogue as a way of finding out.

The success of a mentoring relationship is likely to be influenced by the expectations of the relationship carried by both parties to it. We go on now to look at the expectations of mentoring in higher education contexts.

Expectations of mentoring and stages of mentoring

We shall explore the expectations and stages of mentoring appropriate to each group described above, and how these are played out in a typical mentoring relationship.

1. New academic staff, following a programme of study leading to accreditation as a teacher in higher education, may be offered, from among academic colleagues, a suitable mentor, often chosen for their reputation as an innovative and effective teacher, for the duration of the course. Expectations of such mentors may include: 'helping to define and clarify what they need to know, what skills are needed to become a competent teacher in higher education' (Baume, 1991:1).

Many new teachers would welcome being invited to observe their mentor in action, so that they can model their own work on good practice. This may also present the mentor with an opportunity to inspect her own theories-in-use and check out their allegiance to her espoused theory. We refer readers to Chapter 3 for details of espoused theory and theory-in-use.

The initiation stage of the mentoring relationship is likely to be facilitated by the programme or course tutors, possibly through induction sessions, and the cultivation stage is then left to the mentoring couple to manage themselves. At this early stage, many mentors expect their new colleague to take the initiative, never dreaming that fear and lack of confidence may inhibit an approach, and mentors may feel disappointed and underused. The new member of staff, who is still finding his way around the campus, is not usually in a position to make a move, and often welcomes a structured approach by his mentor. A regular weekly slot, in the first term, where the mentor offers information, teaching advice and relationship support, can make a huge difference to new teachers.

The end of the course for the new teacher signals the separation stage and this is unconsciously avoided by many mentors, as an embarrassment and unnecessary. It is the mentor's responsibility to provide a proper ending of the particular *mentoring* relationship. If the cultivation stage has included regular meetings and these will no longer be on offer, the new teacher has a right to be told this, and be given time to re-define the relationship. Typically the new teacher has acquired some ideas of his own, and these, together with the advice he has received and the practice he has observed, enables him to define his own professional practice in teaching. The mentoring pair may choose to continue the relationship, if it has been productive, incorporating reflective dialogue, as the new teacher works out his probationary period.

2.   New staff who are not required to undertake a certificate of qualification may carry similar expectations of mentoring to the new staff who are so
doing, and the mentoring arrangement may not recognize these needs as
the mentor role may be loosely defined. Some new members of staff may be
very experienced in higher education and confident, while others, experienced or not, may be fearful and lacking in confidence.

Handling the cultivation stage of this less-defined mentoring relationship
can be problematic, unless a very clear initiation stage is managed at induction. Academic staff are often given this mentoring duty to perform without
anyone having the slightest idea of what is entailed. In order to manage
either of the two scenarios above, considerable skill is needed. Both require
high order relationship support but in different ways. For instance, the new
member of staff who needs to 'know the ropes' can be encouraged to
approach his mentor when needed, and will probably have the confidence
to do so. The less confident new teacher may benefit from a tight contract,
with regular structured meetings, rather like a newly accredited teacher,
and plenty of opportunity for reflective dialogue about his work. The structure outlined in Chapter 7 could be adapted in such a mentoring arrangement. There is obvious potential for difficulties in qualified staff being
allocated as mentors to staff who are not required to undertake a qualification and we welcome recommendations that all new staff in higher education should be required to undertake the accreditation procedure (Dearing,
1997).

3.   New staff who are qualified teachers, and experienced in higher education, but new to the institution, are likely to carry more traditional expectations, often mirroring industrial or commercial patterns of mentoring. For
example, expectations might include: assistance at induction, particularly
with the informal and formal structure of the institution; know-how when
tricky issues or situations arise, e.g. rooms double-booked, photocopying
provision or how to get expenses. We note that expectations by new staff in
higher education do not usually include the traditional career functions to
be found in industrial mentoring relationships, e.g. staff in higher education are unlikely to expect: 'career advice and advancement resulting from
a raised profile in the organisation' (Clutterbuck, 1992:5).

Handling the cultivation stage of this likely to be loosely defined mentoring
relationship is often problematic, as our story below suggests, for a variety
of reasons. The relationship, with initiation again facilitated at induction, is
usually tied to a probationary period and is therefore limited in time. The
new member of staff may be very experienced and need very little help in
teaching strategies, but may need a lot of support in 'negotiating the institution' and learning the informal rules and regulations, which can make
life tolerable. Alternatively, the mentor may have to deal with a teacher who
is far from confident, but is not required to attend the accreditation course,
as they are technically qualified. As the end of the probationary period
approaches, the confident teacher should be alerted to the ending of the
loose mentoring arrangement, so that he knows he is now on his own,
and this re-defines the relationship. The less confident teacher should be

prepared for the ending of the mentoring support he has been used to, and a re-definition of the relationship agreed. Either relationship may continue, but each new agreement should be articulated clearly as mentoring relationships which fizzle out leave both partners disappointed and unhappy (Beech and Brockbank, 1999).

4. For staff enrolling as students within the institution, where mentoring is part of the programme package, expectations of colleagues tend to focus on relationship functions, and include the following: availability, patience, understanding, diplomacy, innovative, interested, well-organized, advice, trusted, constructive, sympathetic, a good listener, etc. (Race, 1991).

Colleagues who either choose or are given their mentors in a formal arrangement tend to have high expectations as above, and mentors need to define their availability very carefully at initiation. Here the skill of contracting assertively, i.e. clarifying availability and the boundaries of the mentoring role, will pay dividends for both partners, particularly the need to manage time and keep boundaries, as these are factors which may lead to mentor dysfunction (Brockbank, 1994). The cultivation stage may happen naturally but again experience suggests that a formalized method of meetings, etc. will nurture a healthy mentoring partnership. The separation stage should be articulated in time for the ending of the course, so that re-definition is in place on completion. For instance, when the student/staff member submits his final coursework/portfolio or thesis, the mentor meeting may include visions of the future, as well as the usual hand-wringing which takes place in such circumstances. The mentor will ensure that the vision recorded at that meeting includes a re-definition of the relationship, whether it is continuing or not. Again the student/staff member has the right to have the situation made clear, to have a say, and, if possible, have their needs met.

5. Where mentoring relationships are created informally, mentee expectations are minimal, as she is often taken by surprise to be chosen, and grateful for any support she receives. The mentor, usually senior, who initiates the relationship, tends to define boundaries, and these are accepted by the mentee. For example, a personal or academic tutor, whilst wholly enthusiastic in mentoring students, may necessarily control his availability, in response to the competing demands of academic life. Mentoring is likely to continue throughout a student's attendance up to graduation and beyond. The separation stage may be accompanied by actual separation, as in the story below, or may not occur at all as many mentoring pairs remain in touch with each other throughout their lives. When re-definition is not attended to the separation stage can be painful for either or both (Beech and Brockbank, 1999).

6. Where external mentors are sought as consultants the expectations of both will normally be clarified at the commissioning stage. As external mentor/consultants we would ensure from the outset that the purpose of mentor sessions is clear, that boundaries are well established, and that separation and re-definition (often called an ending) is achieved.

We believe that reflective dialogue in mentoring pairs can contribute to the relationship functions of mentoring, and nurture developmental relationships between colleagues in higher education (Clarkson and Shaw, 1992), thereby promoting their personal and professional development as teachers in higher education. Such an arrangement, where mentor and mentored are relating as equals, removes the difficulties inherent in many mentoring couples, i.e. the hierarchical boundary, described above. Even in 'equal' mentoring arrangements it is essential to negotiate a contract at the start, so that each partner is clear about what is agreed between them. Such a 'contract' should include, not only times and meeting arrangements, but boundaries like casual contact and the limits of relationship support, e.g. mentoring pairs may agree that if personal material emerges in mentor sessions this will be taken to a competent expert. Mentors should never agree to be counsellors, and we discuss this below.

Mentoring skills

This brings us to the skills required by mentors to enable the developmental relationship, and these are described above as those which provide information, support and challenge, i.e. the conditions for facilitating reflective dialogue. Such skills have been described in detail in Chapters 10 and 11, and we outline them here in the context of mentoring:

- active and accurate listening
- observing and reflecting back
- empathy
- giving information
- questioning
- challenging by:
  - advanced empathy
  - immediacy
  - confronting
- feedback and summarizing.

Active and accurate listening are key skills for mentors as they are engaging in reflective dialogue and the support of a mentor reflecting back in dialogue is especially powerful, as are empathic responses where a colleague may be struggling with a new and frightening possibility. The facilitative behaviours of listening, responding and empathy are described in detail in Chapters 10 and 11.

The skilful provision of relevant information about the institution and higher education generally is a matter of timing and delivery, i.e. being able to offer information when it is appropriate and timely. This is a familiar skill for teachers in higher education. For reflective dialogue in mentoring, listening and responding are likely to be more useful initially, as these build the all-important learning relationship.

Astute questioning is part of a mentor's stock-in-trade, particularly the challenging questions about purpose and intention, as they are likely to uncover discrepancies between espoused theory and theory-in-use. Where necessary an effective mentor is prepared and able to confront and/or offer feedback to their partner. Other aspects of challenge may involve holding boundaries, e.g. not extending sessions under pressure, sticking to agreed arrangements. Questioning and challenging skills are discussed in Chapter 11.

There is confusion, as in supervision, about how much a mentor should take the role of counsellor. The mentor relationship remains a professional one, and, as such, should never stray into the realms of therapy, quite apart from the danger of unqualified attempts in such a sensitive arena. The mentor, as the supervisor, will need *counselling skills* and these were identified in Chapter 13 and we repeat them here: listening, observing, reflecting back, empathy, summarizing (not questioning).

Questioning when emotional material is being presented, may lead the session into areas of personal trauma where the mentor may not feel confident. The ability to refer to qualified help is a key function of good supervision and mentoring, and indeed, personal tutoring. Many student counselling centres offer academic staff guidance and training in what to do when they begin to feel out of their depth with personal material being presented by students, or indeed a colleague.

In summary then, the mentoring relationship offers the potential, through its relationship functions, to provide a ready-made place for reflective dialogue to occur. The skills of reflective dialogue deployed by the mentor are likely to enhance relationship functions within the mentoring pair, and cultivate the development sought. We recommend that colleagues operate informally, choosing to mentor or be mentored on the basis of personal inclination. Although created informally, mentoring pairs, using the reflective practice structure outlined in Chapter 7, may choose to record their activities as evidence for professional development, appraisals and quality assurance.

Three mentoring stories

In order to highlight some of the skills and qualities identified above we recount three personal mentoring 'stories' – these are true-life accounts of mentoring relationships in our academic life, where one of us was being mentored. The first story describes a mentor relationship between a research fellow and a supervisor. In the second story one of us was a qualified and experienced university lecturer starting in a new post. The third story is an account of mentoring as crucial external support for one of us in a senior management role at a difficult time.

Mentor A

Mentor A was my allocated research supervisor and professor, actively researching his field, but also enthusiastic about teaching a new and emerging discipline. I was selected by him so I knew he wanted me from the start. He had been trained as a manager by a blue-chip company before coming into higher education and he was exceptionally skilled interpersonally, listening and responding in a way I had never experienced before, either as a student or member of staff in higher education. I was placed in a room adjoining his and he was available to me on a daily basis informally and we also arranged formal sessions for supervision. So the mentoring was organic, occurring as part of the working day.

We completed a research project, published the material, and he supported my application for a full time position. He was able to utilize both career functions and relationship functions in the mentoring relationship and recognized from the start that we could learn from each other (he was my junior in age). He frequently affirmed me in public, mentioning some of what he had gained from the relationship. He encouraged me to inaugurate research seminars in the new discipline and applauded the collaborative model I introduced for the seminars, a complete departure from the adversarial bear fight previously experienced by my colleagues. Staff came to our seminars from other departments as guests and guest speakers. Mentor A insisted that I chair them from the start, and I modelled myself on him, using non-directive chairing skills, later to be adopted by the institution for validation panel chairpersons.

We became firm friends with successful periods of conflict, where we were able to confront issues and resolve them to a compromise, and the relationship matured as I became more confident and respected in my own right. He moved on to other positions but we kept in touch until I moved away. We moved through the stages of the mentoring relationship in classic form, and we both mourned the ending of it.

Mentor B

As a new member of staff, qualified and experienced in higher education, I was allocated mentor B, slightly senior in position, but not in age, who would act for the year of probation, but having no part in the probationary report, that being completed by the head of department.

The relationship was uncomfortable from the start as we both realized that my mentor was not in a position to enable me to develop, as I had developed ideas about teaching which were new to him, and threatening. I was self-driven, efficient and full of energy and ideas, which he routinely rubbished, and I learnt to keep them to myself. I felt throughout that I could have mentored him more effectively than he me, and I noticed his relief when the year was over.

Although superficially appropriate as a mentor, being at the forefront of teaching and learning improvements in the university, mentor B seemed reluctant to risk further reflection on his practice. Mentoring activity with me offered an opportunity for challenge by engaging in dialogue with me.

I regret that he never took that opportunity so we both lost a chance. Institutions which seek to encourage innovation may need to be alert to 'gatekeepers' of this kind, with the power to stifle the new shoots of enthusiasm before they reach maturity.

Mentor C

This was an external consultant who I sought initially as a substitute for mentor B, and subsequently, while acting as head of department with senior management responsibility. I found the interactions with mentor B disheartening and was prone to lose confidence in what I was trying to do. In sessions with my mentor/consultant I was able to identify what behaviours I found disturbing in mentor B, and raise the issue with her. She found my direct style of confrontation (so productive with mentor A) difficult and she withdrew in some confusion.

With mentor C (my external consultant) I worked through my level of commitment to the institution and decided to stay when offered a senior position. Subsequent work in mentoring sessions dealt entirely with strategies for survival in a difficult line-quasi-academic management situation – an increasingly familiar story in academic life. He helped me to identify the implicit power dynamics of the faculty and ultimately to see that another 'gatekeeper' was in place. Fortunately, I was in a position to choose to leave the field and did so at the earliest opportunity.

How did A, B and C mentor?

The outstanding characteristic of both mentors A and C was their ability and willingness to listen. Mentor B appeared to listen, but his body language was closed and he almost never used 'my' language. He was preoccupied with his own difficulties around what I was saying and was therefore unable to give his full attention to me. Although my room was near to mentor B's there was no offer of the regular debriefing that I had enjoyed with mentor A. I would have liked the informality I had enjoyed with mentor A.

All three mentors made contracts with me and carried them out professionally. Meetings were fixed and rarely altered without notice, and this was important for a new member of staff. As well as listening to me and reflecting back to me a lot of what I said, A and C offered me empathic responses and this developed enormous trust in both relationships. When I was asked about A as a mentor I said 'he made me believe I could do anything'. The trust I had in both mentors enabled me to be challenged by them. Mentor A used questioning and confrontation as challenging skills, while Mentor C used advanced empathy and immediacy, and both enabled me to reflect on what I was trying to do. Challenging skills have been described in detail in Chapter 11. Mentor B tried to challenge me but, as there had been little empathy between us, and the trust was absent, I was unable to take his challenge on board, suspecting then as I do now, that it was motivated by his need rather than my benefit. His challenges were adversarial and not 'owned' by him, which made me lose respect for him rapidly. So the lack of facilitation skills actually caused the relationship to deteriorate making the prospect of benefits to me as a mentee even more remote. (We do recognize the possibility that mentor B's style may suit other protégées, whose expectations did not include high order relationship functions.)

The stages of mentoring were well handled by mentor A as we celebrated the ending of our mentorship overtly and sadly with a party. Mentor B alerted me to the ending by one day just refusing to engage on the grounds that the year was over. With mentor C the separation involved a redefinition as I was changing my career, and the new re-defined relationship did not continue for geographical reasons. What I retain is the memory of mentors A and C as wonderful and important mentors who influenced my life for the better.

Summary

We have recommended in Chapter 7 that academic staff engage in reflective practice through a process of peer review, engaging in reflective dialogue, before, during and after their teaching events, with a trusted colleague. The skills of reflective dialogue, developed in collaboration with colleagues are exactly the skills needed for effective mentoring. Mentoring may be formal or informal, incorporating choice or not. Mentors may be senior in age or experience or even in the position they hold in relation to the learner/colleague. We note that power imbalance creates a hierarchical boundary, as described above, and academics may wish to make their choice of mentor with such power issues in mind.

The skills of facilitation, described in Chapters 10 and 11 give further detail of the mentoring skills needed for *essential* mentoring, and these can be developed and enhanced through reflective dialogue with colleagues. We have described *essential* mentoring as a non-directive and non-judgemental relationship which respects the subjective world of the learner/colleague, while remaining in touch with their shared 'objective' world. The skills of reflective dialogue, transported into a mentoring situation, provide the conditions for such a relationship.

We noted the expectations which colleagues and students may bring to the mentoring relationship as well as the developmental stages through which the mentoring pair progress.

Our mentoring stories reveal the importance of such expectations of mentoring in both parties, the stages through which a mentoring relationship proceeds, and the significance of reflective dialogue for supporting relationship functions in the situations described.

We have suggested how mentoring can be handled successfully in academic life, noting the difficulties inherent in the process, and the potential for personal development, in a professional context, given the willingness of colleagues to mentor others and to be mentored themselves.

Note

1. The term 'preceptor' used in nursing education, while it identifies tutorial and guidance responsibilities, also stresses the nurturing role of preceptorship to encourage self-discovery in the trainee (see Kitchen, 1993).

15

Conclusion

When we started thinking and writing about our experience in what has become this book we felt strongly that we wanted to convey, tangibly, the core of what it is like to be in situations where we were fortunate to share with learners those points and transitions where they moved significantly in the way in which they saw the world. We did not realize how tough it would be to articulate and realize our experience. What has been chastening has been trying to do justice to the writers who have pushed the limits of learning in higher education and to those teachers who have put their experience on the line to include the transmissional yet move beyond it to approaches to learning that becomes a part of the person.

Working as a facilitator is more risky and vulnerable than teaching through a didactic format. We do show more of ourselves. In showing more of ourselves we are also being more transparent and potentially authentic. In engaging in this way we are doing no more than we are asking of the learners who come into higher education. This is not to suggest that facilitation implies a flabby, self-indulgent and unstructured approach to working with students. Facilitators have a distinct and rigorous role in taking responsibility for creating the conditions conducive to critically reflective learning. Hence our attention to such detail earlier. Recent research supports the view that rigorous facilitation is necessary if learners are to benefit from reflective dialogue:

> It has become clear that learning from experience is difficult without expert, coordinated facilitation, and our programmes need to ensure structures which promote meaningful professional dialogue in order that the students can begin to construct their individual meanings.
>
> (Terrell and Venn, 1997:19)

We are also aware that some of the language we use is still unfamiliar to many in higher education. The terms, facilitator and facilitating, reflection and reflective, emotional and enabling, often induce embarrassment or unease covered by humour or laughter. This is partly because of the still infrequent use of such terms. More significant is that the terms themselves imply a different relationship, as yet unfamiliar, with learners.

What effects would adoption of facilitative methods have on higher educational institutions? If this book is taken seriously, what kind of alumni will emerge from them? The prospect of encouraging autonomous yet interdependent critically reflective learners as diplomates, graduates and postgraduates, can be realized if those responsible for policy and action at institutional levels, are prepared to support facilitative methods. We have suggested a few markers in Chapter 6 rather than laying down universalist solutions.

We will briefly go beyond higher education. There is a danger in a book with our title to be insulated as if what we are writing is only relevant to higher education as a closed system. We write as participants within and across social institutions and organizations and we are party to changes in the way people relate and work together. We note that there is a distinct move, in such milieu, towards autonomy and interdependence, collaboration and creativity and a move away from dependent, authoritarian, narrowly defined roles and rigid relationships. Alongside this move is the tendency to greater uncertainty and the consequent need for a capacity to live and work with ambiguity and continuous transition. This applies to knowledge, selves and action, alone and with others. Thus we consider our writing and practice to be relevant not only to that significant proportion of society who journey in, and become, the alumni of universities and colleges, but also for learners in any context who seek to know themselves and influence society.

Finally, we have given significant emphasis to the process by which critically reflective learning can be promoted. Inherent in that process are values of respect for difference, collaboration and connectedness, with I-Thou defining relationship rather than the instrumental objectification of the other. This we wish to be our contribution.

Bibliography

Abercrombie, M.L.J. (1960) *The Anatomy of Judgement*. London: Hutchinson.

Abercrombie, M.L.J. (1974) *Aims and Techniques of Group Teaching*, 3rd edn. London: SRHE.

Abercrombie, M.L.J. (1984) Changing higher education by the application of some group-analytic ideas. Paper to 8th International Conference of Group Psychotherapy, Mexico City.

Anderson, G., Boud, D. and Sampson, J. (1996) *Learning Contracts: A Practical Guide*. London: Kogan Page.

Argyle, M. (1975) *Bodily Communication*. London: Methuen.

Argyris, C. and Schön, D. (1974) *Theory in Practice: Increasing Professional Effectiveness*. London: Jossey-Bass.

Argyris, C. and Schön, D. (1978) *Organisational Learning: A Theory of Action Perspective*. Reading, Mass.: Addison-Wesley.

Arnold, V. and Davidson, M. (1990) Adopt a mentor: The new way ahead for women managers? *Women in Management Research and Abstracts*, 1, 10–18.

Ashby, W.R. (1952) *Design for a Brain*. New York: John Wiley.

Assiter, A. (ed.) (1995) *Transferable Skills in HE*. London: Kogan Page.

Atkins, S. and Murphy, K. (1993) Reflection: A review of the literature, *Journal of Advanced Nursing*, 18, 1188–92.

Ausubel, D. (1975) Cognitive structure and transfer. In N. Entwistle and D. Hounsell *How Students Learn*, Lancaster: Institute for Research and Development in Post Compulsory Education.

Auster, D. (1984) Mentors and protégés: Power-dependent dyads, *Social Inquiry*, 54 (2), 142–53.

Baddeley, J. and James, K. (1991) The power of innocence: From politeness to politics, *Management Learning*, 22 (2), 106–18.

Back, K. and Back, K. (1982) *Assertiveness at Work: A Practical Guide to Handling Awkward Situations*. London: McGraw-Hill.

Barnett, R. (1990) *The Idea of Higher Education*. Buckingham: SRHE/Open University Press.

Barnett, R. (1992a) *Improving Higher Education*. Buckingham: SRHE/Open University Press.

Barnett, R. (ed.) (1992b) *Learning to Effect*. Buckingham: SRHE/Open University Press.

Barnett, R. (1994) *The Limits of Competence*. Buckingham: SRHE/Open University Press.

Barnett, R. (1997) *Higher Education: A Critical Business*. Buckingham: SRHE/Open University Press.

Bateson, G. (1973) *Steps Towards an Ecology of Mind*. London: Paladin.

Baum, H.S. (1992) Mentoring, *Human Relations*, 45 (3), 223–45.

Baume, C. (1991) *Mentoring and Individual Development Plans for New Members of Academic Staff*. St Albans: Calibre Training Ltd.

Beard, R., Healey, E.G. and Holloway, P.J. (1968) *Objectives in Higher Education*. London: SRHE.

Beaty, L. and McGill, I. (1995) *Developing Reflective Practice: Observing Teaching as a Component of Professional Development*. Brighton: University of Brighton.

Beck, V., Giddens, A. and Lasch, E. (1994) *Reflexive Modernisation*. Cambridge: Polity Press.

Beech, N. and Brockbank, A. (1999) Power/knowledge and psycho-social dynamics in mentoring, *Management Learning*, 30 (1), 7–25.

Belenky, M.F., Clinchy, B.M., Goldberger, N.R. and Tarule, J.M. (1986) *Women's Ways of Knowing: The Development of Self, Voice and Mind*. New York: Basic Books.

Berg, L. (1968) *Risinghill: The Death of a Comprehensive School*. Harmondsworth: Penguin.

Berger, P.L. and Luckmann, T. (1966) *The Social Construction of Reality*. Harmondsworth: Penguin.

Biggs, J. (1976) Dimensions of study behaviour: Another look at ATI, *British Journal of Educational Psychology*, 22, 287–97.

Bion, W. (1961) *Experiences in Groups*. London: Tavistock.

Blocher, D. (1983) Towards a cognitive developmental approach to counseling supervision, *The Counseling Psychologist*, 11 (1), 27–34.

Bloom, B.S. (ed.) (1956) *Taxonomy of Educational Objectives, Vol. I, Cognitive Domain* New York: McKay.

Bloom, B.S. (ed.) (1964) *Taxonomy of Educational Objectives, Vol. II, Affective Domain*. New York: McKay.

Biggs, J. (1979) Individual differences in study processes and the quality of learning outcomes, *Higher Education*, 8, 381–94.

Bligh, D. (1978) Are teaching innovations in post-secondary education irrelevant? In M. Howe (ed.), *Adult Learning: Psychological Research and Applications*. Chichester: John Wiley.

Bohm, D. (1996) *On Dialogue*. L. Nichol (ed.). London: Routledge.

Boud, D., Keogh, R. and Walker, D. (1985) *Reflection: Turning Experience into Learning*. London: Kogan Page.

Bowen, J. and Hobson, P.R. (1974) *Theories of Education*. London: John Wiley.

Bowlby, J. (1969) *Attachment*. London: Hogarth Press.

Boyatzis, R.E., Cowen, S.S., Kolb, D.A. *et al.* (1995) *Innovation in Professional Education*. San Fransisco, CA: Jossey-Bass.

Boydston, J.A. (ed.) (1969) *John Dewey. The Early Works 1882–98*, Vol. 1. Carbondale and Edwardsville: Southern Illinois University Press.

Boyer, E.L. (1990) *Scholarship Reconsidered: Priorities of the Professoriate*. Princeton, NJ: Carnegie Foundation for the Advancement of Learning.

Brockbank, A. (1994) Expectations of mentoring, *Training Officer*, 30 (3), 86–8.

Brookfield, S. (1986) *Understanding and Facilitating Adult Learning*. Milton Keynes: Open University Press.

Brookfield, S.D. (1987) *Developing Critical Thinkers.* Milton Keynes: Open University Press.

Brown, G. and Atkins, M. (1988) *Effective Teaching in Higher Education.* London: Methuen.

Buber, M. (1965) *Between Man and Man.* New York: Macmillan.

Buber, M. (1994) *I and Thou.* Edinburgh: T&T Clark.

Bull, P. (1983) *Body Movement and Interpersonal Communication.* Chichester: John Wiley.

Burley-Allen, M. (1995) *Listening: The Forgotten Skill.* New York: John Wiley.

Bushardt, S.C., Fretwell, C. and Holdnak, B.J. (1991) The Mentor/Protégé Relationship, *Human Relations*, 44 (6), 619–39.

Carkhuff, R.R. (1969) *Helping and Human Relations, Vol. 11, Practice and Research.* New York: Holt, Rinehart & Winston.

Carkhuff, R.R. and Berenson, B.G. (1967) In search of honest experience: Confrontation in counselling and life. In *Beyond Counselling and Therapy.* New York: Holt Rinehart & Winston.

Carroll, M. (1996) *Counselling Supervision: Theory Skills and Practice.* London: Cassell.

Charleton, M. (1996) *Self-directed Learning in Counsellor Training.* London: Cassell.

Christopherson, Sir D. (1982) *Research Student and Supervisor.* Swindon: SERC.

Chodorow, N. (1974) Family structure and feminine personality. In M.Z. Rosaldo and L. Lamphere (eds), *Woman, Culture and Society.* Stanford: Stanford University Press.

Clarkson, P. and Shaw, P. (1992) Human relationships at work in organisations, *Management Education and Development*, 23 (1), 18–29.

Clutterbuck, D. (1986) Mentoring, *Industrial and Commercial Training*, 18 (6), 13–14.

Clutterbuck, D. (1991) *Everyone Needs a Mentor.* London: IPM.

Clutterbuck, D. (1992) *Mentoring.* Henley: Henley Distance Learning.

Collier, K.G. (1968) *New Dimensions in Higher Education.* London: Longmans Green.

Collin, A. (1988) Mentoring, *Industrial and Commercial Training*, March–April, 23–7.

Cooper, C.L. (1983) *Stress Research: Issues for the 80s.* London and New York: John Wiley.

Cooper, C. and Payne, R. (eds) (1988) *Causes, Coping and Consequences of Stress at Work.* Chichester: John Wiley.

Cox, R. (1988) Characteristics of the Training Process and those undergoing research training. In Postgraduate Research Training: Reviews of the Literature and Data Sources for the ESRC, unpublished report. London: Centre for Higher Education Studies.

Cozby, Paul C. (1973) Self-Disclosure: A Literature Review, *Psychological Bulletin*, 79: 73–91.

Dainow, S. and Bailey, C. (1988) *Developing Skills with People.* Chichester: John Wiley.

Daniel, J. (1975) Learning styles and strategies: The work of Gordon Pask. In N. Entwistle and D. Hounsell (eds), *How Students Learn.* Lancaster: Institute for Research and Development in Post Compulsory Education.

Davies, S. and Sang, B. (1997) Perfect Strangers: An Account of Process Innovation in Participatory Democracy: Learning from Citizen's Juries in the NHS, unpublished report. London: Kings Fund.

Dearing, R. (1997) National Committee of Inquiry into Higher Education (Dearing Report). Higher Education in the Learning Society, Report of the National Committee. Norwich: HMSO.

Descartes, R. (1955) Discourse on Method. In *The Philosophical Works of Descartes, Vol.*

I, trans. and ed. E.S. Haldane and G.R.T. Ross. New York: Dover Publications, p. 121.

Dewey, J. (1916) *Democracy and Education*. London: Macmillan.

Dickson, A. (1982) *A Woman in Your Own Right*. London: Quartet Books.

Dwyer, B. (1995) Preparing for the 21st century: A paradigm for our times. *Innovations in Education and Training International*, 32 (3), August, 269–77.

Easlea, B. (1981) *Science and Sexual Oppression: Patriarchy's Confrontation with Woman and Nature*. London: Weidenfeld & Nicolson.

Ekman, P. and Freisen, W. (1975) *Unmasking the Face*. Englewood-Cliffs, NJ: Prentice-Hall.

Egan, G. (1973) *Face to Face: The Small Group Experience and Interpersonal Growth*. Monterey, CA: Brookes/Cole.

Egan, G. (1976) *Interpersonal Living, A Skills/Contract Approach to Human Relations Training in Groups*. Monterey, CA: Brooks/Cole.

Egan, G. (1977) *You and Me*. Monterey, CA: Brooks/Cole.

Egan, G. (1990). *The Skilled Helper: A Systematic Approach to Effective Helping*. 4th edn Pacific Grove, CA: Brooks/Cole.

Elbow, P. (1973) *Writing Without Teachers*. London: Oxford University Press.

Entwistle, N. (1981) *Styles of Learning and Teaching*. London: John Wiley.

Entwistle, N. and Wilson, J.D. (1977) *Degrees of Excellence: The Academic Achievement Game*. London: Hodder & Stoughton.

Entwistle, N. and Hounsell, D. (1975) *How Students Learn*. Lancaster: Institute for Research and Development in Post Compulsory Education.

Eraut, M. (1994) *Developing Professional Knowledge and Competence*. London: Falmer Press.

Erikson Erik, H. (1968) *Identity Youth and Crisis*. New York: W.W. Norton.

Fleming, W. and Rutherford, D. (1984) Recommendations for Learning: rhetoric and reaction. *Studies in Higher Education*, 9, 17–26.

Flynn, J.R. (1980) *Race, IQ and Jensen*. London: Routledge.

Flood, R. and Romm, N.R.A. (1996) *Diversity Management: Triple Loop Learning*. New York: John Wiley.

Foulkes, S.H. (1975) *Group Analytic Psychotherapy, Method and Principles*. London: Gordon and Breach.

Foxley, Barbara (ed.) (1969) *Emile* (first published 1792 by J.J. Rousseau). London: Everyman.

Freire, P. (1972) *Pedagogy of the Oppressed*. Harmondsworth: Penguin.

Freire, Paulo (1974) *Education: The Practice of Freedom*. London: Writers & Readers Cooperative.

Freire, P. and Shor, I. (1987) *A Pedagogy for Liberation*. London: Macmillan.

Gibbs, G. (1992) Improving the quality of student learning through course design. In R. Barnett (ed.), *Learning to Effect*. Buckingham: SRHE/Open University Press.

Gibbs, G. (1995) Changing lecturers' conception of teaching and learning through action research. In A. Brew (ed.), *Directions in Staff Development*, Buckingham: SRHE/Open University Press.

Giddens, A. (1992) *The Transformation of Intimacy*. Cambridge: Polity.

Gilligan, C. (1982) *In a Different Voice: Psychological Theory and Women's Development*. Cambridge, MA: Harvard University Press.

Griffin, V. (1987) Naming the processes. In D. Boud and V. Griffin (eds), *Appreciating Adults Learning: From the Learners' Perspective*. London: Kogan Page.

Habermas, J. (1974) *Knowledge and Human Interest.* London: Heinemann.

Harvey, L. and Knight, P. (1996) *Transforming Higher Education.* Buckingham: SRHE/ Open University Press.

Hawkins, P. and Shohet, R. (1989) *Supervision in the Helping Professions.* Milton Keynes: Open University Press.

Hawkins, P. (1997) Private communication.

Heron, J. (1986) *Six Category Intervention Analysis.* Guildford: Human Potential Research Project.

Heron, J. (1989) *The Facilitator's Handbook.* London: Kogan Page.

Heron, J. (1993) *Group Facilitation.* London: Kogan Page.

Hess, A.K. (ed.) (1980) *Psychotherapy Supervision: Theory, Research and Practice.* New York: John Wiley.

Hillman, J. (1997) *Emotion.* Evanston, IL: Northwest University Press.

Honey, P. and Mumford, A. (1992) *The Manual of Learning Styles.* Maidenhead: Peter Honey.

Horlock, J. (1991) The link between teaching and research in universities, *Science and Public Affairs,* 6 (1), 77–83.

Illich, I. (1971) *Deschooling Society.* Harmondsworth: Penguin.

Inskipp, F. and Proctor, B. (1988) Skills for Supervising and Being Supervised, private publication.

Inskipp, F. and Proctor, B. (1993) *The Art, Craft and Tasks of Counselling Supervision.* London: Cascade.

Jacoby, M. (1984) *The Analytic Encounter: Transference and Human Relationship.* Toronto: Inner City Books.

Jaques, D. (1990) *Learning in Groups.* London: Kogan Page.

Jarvis, P. (1987) *Adult Learning in the Social Context.* London: Croom Helm.

Jourard, S.M. (1971) *The Transparent Self.* New York: Van Nostrand Reinhold.

Jowett, B. (1953a) *The Dialogues of Plato Vol II Book VII The Republic.* London: Oxford University Press.

Jowett, B. (1953b) *The Dialogues of Plato Vol I Book XVII Meno.* London: Oxford University Press.

Kahn, D.G. (1981) Fathers as mentors to daughters, working paper, Radcliffe Institute.

Kates, J. (1985) In search of professionalism, *City Woman,* 8 (1), 34–42.

Kelly, G. (1955) *The Psychology of Personal Constructs.* New York: Norton.

Kitchen, S. (1993) Preceptorship in hospitals. In B. Caldwell and M.A. Carter (eds), *The Return of the Mentor: Strategies for Workplace Mentoring.* London: Falmer Press.

Knapper, C.K. and Cropley, A.J. (1991) *Lifelong Learning and Higher Education,* 2nd edn. London: Kogan Page.

Kohlberg, L. (1958) The development of modes of thinking and choices in years 10 to 16, PhD Diss., University of Chicago.

Kohlberg, L. (1981) *The Philosophy of Moral Development.* San Francisco, CA: Harper & Row.

Kolb, D. (1984) *Experiential Learning.* Englewood Cliffs, NJ: Prentice-Hall.

Korner, S. (1955) *Kant.* Harmondsworth: Penguin.

Kram, K. (1988) *Mentoring at Work.* Lanham: University Press of America.

Krantz, J. (1989) The managerial couple: Superior-subordinate relationships as a unit of analysis, *Human Resource Management,* 28 (2), 161–76.

Kuhn, T. (1970) *The Structure of Scientific Revolutions.* Chicago, IL: University of Chicago Press.

Lago, C. and Thompson, J. (1996) *Race, Culture and Counselling.* Buckingham: Open University Press.

Laurillard, D. (1993) *Rethinking University Teaching.* London: Routledge.

Leininger, M.M. (1987) Transcultural caring: a different way to help people. In P. Pederson (ed.), *Handbook of Cross-Cultural Counselling and Therapy.* London: Praeger.

Levinson, D.J. Darrow, C.N., Klein, E.F., Levinson, M.A. and McKee, B. (1978) *Seasons of a Man's Life.* New York: Alfred A. Knopf.

Luft, J. (1984) *Group Processes, An Introduction to Group Dynamics.* Mountain View, CA: Mayfield.

Makarenko, A.S. (1951) *The Road to Life.* Foreign Languages Publishing House, Moscow.

McGill, I. and Beaty, L. (1995) *Action Learning: A Guide for Professional, Management and Educational Development,* 2nd edn. London: Kogan Page.

McKeen, C.A. and Burke, R.J. (1989) Mentor relationships in organisations: issues, strategies and prospects for women, *Journal of Management Development,* 8 (6), 33–42.

McKeon, R. (1941) *Nicomachean Ethics, Book II.* New York: Random House.

Magnuson, E. (1986) A Serious Deficiency: The Rogers Commission faults NASA's flawed decision-making process, *Time, March.*

Mann, S. (1987) Knowing ourselves as learners and researchers. In John T.E. Richardson *et al.* (eds), *Student Learning.* London: SRHE/Open University Press.

Marton, F. (1975) What does it take to learn? In N. Entwistle and D. Hounsell (eds), *How Students Learn.* Lancaster: Institute for Research and Development in Post Compulsory Education.

Marton, F. (1981) Phenomenography – Describing conceptions of the world around us. *Instructional Science,* 10, 177–200.

Marton, F., Beaty, E. and Dall'Alba, G. (1993) Conceptions of learning, *International Journal of Education Research,* 19, 277–300.

Maslow, A. (1970) *Motivation and Personality.* New York: Harper Row.

Maslow, A. (1978) Goals and implications of humanistic education. In N. Entwistle and D. Hounsell (1975) *How Students Learn.* Lancaster: Institute for Research and Development in Post Compulsory Education.

Mattinson, J. (1977) *The Reflection Process in Casework Supervision.* London: Institute of Marital Studies, Tavistock Institute of Human Relations.

Mearns, D. and Thorne, B. (1988) *Person Centred Counselling in Action.* London: SAGE.

Megginson, D. (1988) Instructor, coach, mentor: three ways of helping for managers, *Management Education and Development,* 19 (1), 33–46.

Mehrabian, A. (1971) *Silent Messages.* Belmont, CA: Wadsworth.

Merquior, J.G. (1991) *Foucault.* London: Fontana Press.

Meyers, C. (1986) *Teaching Students to Think Critically: A Guide for Faculty in All Disciplines.* San Francisco, CA: Jossey-Bass.

Mezirow, J. (1990) *Fostering Critical Reflection in Adulthood.* San Francisco: Jossey-Bass.

Michelson, E. (1995) Usual suspects: experience, reflection, and the (en)gendering of knowledge, unpublished paper, Empire State College, State University of New York.

Miller, A. (1983) *For Your Own Good: Hidden Cruelty in Child-rearing and the Roots of Violence,* trans Hildegarde and Hunter Haanum. New York: New American Library.

Miller, A. (1990) *Banished Knowledge.* London: Virago.

Miller, C., Tomlinson, A. and Jones, M. (1994) *Learning Styles and Facilitating Reflection.* London: English National Board for Nursing, Midwifery and Health Visiting (ENB).

Morgan, G. (1988) *Riding the Waves of Change.* San Francisco, CA: Jossey-Bass.

Morris, D. (1977) *Manwatching.* London: Cape.

Murray, P. (1988) *Training Needs in the Social Sciences and the Effectiveness of Current Provision in Meeting those Needs.* London: ESRC.

Neill, A.S. (1967) *Talking of Summerhill.* London: Gollanz.

Neill, A.S. (1969) *Summerhill: A Radical Approach to Education.* London: Gollanz.

Nelson-Jones, R. (1986) *Relationship Skills.* London: Holt, Rinehart & Winston.

Newman, J.H. (1976) (ed. I.T. Kerr, first published 1853) *The Idea of a University.* Oxford: Oxford University Press.

Nias, J. (1993) (ed.) *The Human Nature of Learning.* Buckingham: SRHE/Open University Press.

O'Connor, A. and Davies, G. (1990) Interpersonal behaviour and effective performance in retailing: The modesty score, *Guidance and Assessment Review*, 6 (5), 6–8.

Orbach, S. (1994) *What's Really Going On Here?* London: Virago.

Page, S. and Wosket, V. (1994) *Supervising the Counsellor: A Cyclical Model.* London: Routledge.

Pask, G. (1975) *The Cybernetics of Human Learning.* London: Hutchinson.

Pask, G. and Scott, B.C.E. (1972) Learning strategies and individual competence, *International Journal of Man-Machine Studies*, 4, 217–53.

Pease, A. (1981) *Body Language.* London: Sheldon Press.

Pedler, M. (1992) *Action Learning in Practice*, 2nd edn. Aldershot: Gower.

Perry, W. (1970) *Forms of Intellectual and Ethical Development During the College Years: A Scheme*, New York: Holt, Rinehart & Winston.

Peters, R.S. (1965) (ed.) Education as initiation. In *Authority, Responsibility and Education.* London: George Allen & Unwin.

Peters, R.S. (1973) *Authority, Responsibility and Education.* London: George Allen & Unwin.

Peters, R.S. (ed.) (1977) *John Dewey Reconsidered.* London: Routledge & Kegan Paul.

Pfeiffer, J.W. and Jones, J.E. (1975) Co-facilitating. In *The 1975 Handbook for Group Facilitators.* San Diego, CA: University Associates.

Phillips-Jones, L. (1982) *Mentors and Protégés: How to Establish, Strengthen and Get the Most from a Mentor/Protégé Relationship.* New York: Arbor House.

Phillips, E. and Pugh, D. (1987) *How to Get a PhD.* Buckingham: Open University Press.

Piaget, J. (1932) *The Moral Judgement of the Child.* New York: The Free Press.

Pines, A.L. and West, L.H.T. (1986) Conceptual understanding and science learning: An interpretation of research within a sources-of-knowledge framework, *Science Education*, 70, 583–604.

Polanyi, M. (1958) *Personal Knowledge.* London: Routledge & Kegan Paul.

Polanyi, M. (1967) *The Tacit Dimension.* New York: Doubleday.

Race, P. (1991) *Mentors' Handbook: Postgraduate Certificate in Teaching and Learning.* Cardiff: Polytechnic of Wales.

Rachman, C. (1980) Emotional processing, *Behaviour Research and Therapy*, 18, 51–60.

Radley, A. (1980) Student learning as social practice. In P. Salmon *Coming to Know.* London: Routledge.

Ramsden, P. (ed.) (1988) *Improving Learning: New Perspectives.* London: Kogan Page.

Reich, M.H. (1986) The mentor connection, *Personnel*, 63 (2), 50.
Revans, R. (1980) *Action Learning: New Techniques for Action Learning*. London: Blond and Briggs.
Reynolds, M. (1997) Learning styles: a critique, *Management Learning*, 28 (2), 115–33.
Rich, A. (1979) *On Lies, Secrets and Silence: Selected Prose – 1966–78*. New York: Norton.
Robbins, Lord (1963) *Higher Education*, Cmnd 2154. London: HMSO.
Rogers, C. (1957) The necessary and sufficient conditions for therapeutic personality change, *Journal of Consultative Psychology*, 21, 95–103.
Rogers, C. (1983) *Freedom to Learn for the 80s*. New York: Merrill Wright.
Rogers, C.R. (1979) *Carl Rogers on Personal Power*. London: Constable.
Rogers, C.R. (1992) *Client Centred Therapy*. London: Constable.
Rosen, S. and Tesser, A. (1970) On Reluctance to communicate undesirable information: The MUM effect, *Sociometry*, 33, 253–63.
Rudd, E. (1975) *The Highest Education: A Study of Graduate Education in Britain*. In association with Renate Simpson. London: Routledge and Kegan Paul.
Rudd, E. (1985) *A New Look at Postgraduate Failure*. SRHE and NFER Nelson: Guildford.
Ruddick, S. (1984) New combinations: Learning from Virginia Woolf. In C. Asher, L. DeSalvor and S. Ruddick *Between Women*. Boston: Beacon Press.
Ryan, D. (1987) The impermeable membrane. In John T.E. Richardson, Michael W. Eysenck and David W. Piper (eds)(1987) *Student Learning*. Milton Keynes: SRHE/Open University Press.
Ryle, G. (1967) Teaching and training in education. In R.S. Peters (ed.) *The Concept of Education*. London: Routledge & Kegan Paul.
Ryle, G. (1983) *The Concept of Mind*. Harmondsworth: Penguin.
Saljo, R. (1979) Learning about learning, *Higher Education*, 8, 443–51.
Saljo, R. (1982) *Learning and Understanding: A Study of Differences in Constructing Meaning from a Text*. Gothenburg: Acta Universitatis Gothenburgensis.
Saljo, R. (1988) Learning in educational settings: Methods of inquiry. In P. Ramsden (ed.), *Improving Learning: New Perspectives*. London: Kogan Page.
Salmon, P. (1980) *Coming to Know*. London: Routledge.
Salmon, P. (1989) Personal stances in learning. In S.W. Weil and I.J. McGill (eds), *Making Sense of Experiential Learning*. Buckingham: Open University Press/SRHE.
Salmon, P. (1992) *Achieving Your PhD*. Stoke-on-Trent: Trentham Books.
Schön, D. (1983) *The Reflective Practitioner*. New York: Basic Books.
Schön, D. (1987) *Educating the Reflective Practitioner*. London: Jossey-Bass.
Simmel, G. (1950) The secret and the secret society. In K. Wolff (ed.), *The Sociology of George Simmel*. New York: Free Press.
Skinner, B.F. (1954) The science of learning and the art of teaching, *Harvard Educational Review*, 24 (2), 86–97.
Skynner, R. and Cleese, J. (1983) *Families and How to Survive Them*. London: Methuen.
Steiner, R. (1972) *A Modern Art of Education*. London: Rudolf Steiner Press.
Stoltenberg, D. and Delworth, U. (1987) *Supervising Counsellors and Therapists*. San Fransisco, CA: Jossey-Bass.
Svensson, L. (1977) On qualitative differences in learning III – study skill and learning, *British Journal of Educational Psychology*, 47, 233–43.
Svensson, L. (1984) Skill in learning. In F. Marton, D.J. Hounsell and N.J. Entwistle (eds), *The Experience of Learning*. Edinburgh: Scottish Academic Press.
Taylor, E. (1983) Orientations to study: A longitudinal interview investigation of students on two human studies degree courses at Surrey University, unpublished PhD Thesis, University of Surrey.

Terrell, I. and Venn, G. (1997) A critical evaluation of the use of portfolios and journals as an aid to reflection in the development of competence, a paper for the European Conference for Educational Research, Frankfurt, September 1997, Anglia Polytechnic University.

Trigwell, K. and Prosser, M. (1991) Improving the quality of student learning: The influence of learning context and student approaches on learning outcomes. *Higher Education*, 22, 251–66.

Trigwell, K. (1995) Increasing faculty understanding of teaching. In W.A. Wright, *et al.* (eds), *Teaching Improvement Practices*. Bolton, MA: Anker.

Warnock, G.J. (ed.) (1962) *George Berkeley, The Principles of Human Knowledge*. London: Fontana.

Ward, J. (1975) Psychology applied to education. In N. Entwistle and D. Hounsell (1975) *How Students Learn*. Lancaster: Institute for Research and Development in Post Compulsory Education.

Webb, G. (1996) *Understanding Staff Development*. Buckingham: SRHE/Open University Press.

Webster, R. (1995) *Why Freud Was Wrong*. London: Harper Collins.

Weil, S.W. (1992) Creating capability for change in higher education: The RSA initiative. In R. Barnett (ed.), *Learning to Effect*. Buckingham: SRHE/Open University Press.

Weil, S.W. (1996) Don't push the river? Critically reflexive experiential enquiry for responsible social and organisational learning and change, paper to International Consortium on Experiential Learning. Capetown.

Weil, S.W. and McGill, I.J. (1989) *Making Sense of Experiential Learning*. Milton Keynes: SRHE/Open University Press.

Weil, S. (1997a) Postgraduate education and lifelong learning as collaborative enquiry in action: An emergent model. In R. Burgess (ed.), *Beyond the First Degree*. Buckingham: SRHE/Open University Press.

Weil, S. (1997b) Contribution to a conversation on *Critical Reflexivity: A Multi-dimensional Conversation* (by R. Flood, N. Romm and S. Weil. Presented at the 4th Congress on Action Research, Cartagena, Columbia, 1–5 June.

Weinstein, K. (1995) *Action Learning: A Journey in Discovery and Development*. London: Harper Collins.

Welsh, J. (1979) *The First Year of Postgraduate Research Study*. Guildford: SRHE.

Whiston, T.G. and Geiger, R. (1992) *Research and Higher Education: The United Kingdom and the United States*. Buckingham: SRHE/Open University Press.

Winfield, G. (1987) *The Social Science PhD*. London: ESRC.

Yalom, I. (1980) *Existential Psychotherapy*. New York: Basic Books.

Zinkin, L. (1989) The impossible profession. In *Clinical Supervision: Issues and Techniques* (papers from the public conference, April 1988). London: Jungian Training Committee.

Index

The Society for Research into Higher Education

The Society for Research into Higher Education exists to stimulate and coordinate research into all aspects of higher education. It aims to improve the quality of higher education through the encouragement of debate and publication on issues of policy, on the organization and management of higher education institutions, and on the curriculum and teaching methods.

The Society's income is derived from subscriptions, sales of its books and journals, conference fees and grants. It receives no subsidies, and is wholly independent. Its individual members include teachers, researchers, managers and students. Its corporate members are institutions of higher education, research institutes, professional, industrial and governmental bodies. Members are not only from the UK, but from elsewhere in Europe, from America, Canada and Australasia, and it regards its international work as among its most important activities.

Under the imprint *SRHE & Open University Press*, the Society is a specialist publisher of research, having over 70 titles in print. The Editorial Board of the Society's Imprint seeks authoritative research or study in the above fields. It offers competitive royalties, a highly recognizable format in both hardback and paperback and the worldwide reputation of the Open University Press.

The Society also publishes *Studies in Higher Education* (three times a year), which is mainly concerned with academic issues, *Higher Education Quarterly* (formerly *Universities Quarterly*), mainly concerned with policy issues, *Research into Higher Education Abstracts* (three times a year), and *SRHE News* (four times a year).

The society holds a major annual conference in December, jointly with an institution of higher education. In 1995 the topic was 'The Changing University' at Heriot-Watt University in Edinburgh. In 1996 it was 'Working in Higher Education' at University of Wales, Cardiff and in 1997, 'Beyond the First Degree' at the University of Warwick. The 1998 conference will be on the topic of globalization at the University of Lancaster.

The Society's committees, study groups and networks are run by the members. The networks at present include:

Access	Mentoring
Curriculum Development	Postgraduate Issues
Disability	Quality
Eastern European	Quantitative Studies
Funding	Student Development
Legal Education	Vocational Qualifications

Benefits to members

Individual

Individual members receive

- *SRHE News*, the Society's publications list, conference details and other material included in mailings.
- Greatly reduced rates for *Studies in Higher Education* and *Higher Education Quarterly*.
- A 35 per cent discount on all SRHE & Open University Press publications.
- Free copies of the Precedings – commissioned papers on the theme of the Annual Conference.
- Free copies of *Research into Higher Education Abstracts*.
- Reduced rates for the annual conference.
- Extensive contacts and scope for facilitating initiatives.
- Free copies of the *Register of Members' Research Interests*.
- Membership of the Society's networks.

Corporate

Corporate members receive:

- Benefits of individual members, plus.
- Free copies of *Studies in Higher Education*.
- Unlimited copies of the Society's publications at reduced rates.
- Reduced rates for the annual conference.
- The right to submit applications for the Society's research grants.
- The right to use the Society's facility for supplying statistical HESA data for purposes of research.

Membership details: SRHE, 3 Devonshire Street, London
W1N 2BA, UK. Tel: 0171 637 2766. Fax: 0171 637 2781.
email: srhe@mailbox.ulcc.ac.uk
World Wide Web: http://www.srhe.ac.uk./srhe/
Catalogue: SRHE & Open University Press, Celtic Court,
22 Ballmoor, Buckingham MK18 1XW. Tel: 01280 823388.
Fax: 01280 823233. email: enquiries@openup.co.uk

USING EXPERIENCE FOR LEARNING

David Boud, Ruth Cohen and David Walker (eds)

This book is about the struggle to make sense of learning from experience. What are the key ideas that underpin learning from experience? How do we learn from experience? How does context and purpose influence learning? How does experience impact on individual and group learning? How can we help others to learn from their experience?

Using Experience for Learning reflects current interest in the importance of experience in informal and formal learning, whether it be applied for course credit, new forms of learning in the workplace, or acknowledging autonomous learning outside educational institutions. It also emphasizes the role of personal experience in learning: ideas are not separate from experience; relationships and personal interests impact on learning; and emotions have a vital part to play in intellectual learning. All the contributors write themselves into their chapters, giving an autobiographical account of how their experiences have influenced their learning and what has led them to their current views and practice.

Using Experience for Learning brings together a wide range of perspectives and conceptual frameworks with contributors from four continents, and is a valuable addition to the field of experiential learning.

Contents
Introduction: understanding learning from experience – Part 1: Introduction – Through the lens of learning: how the visceral experience of learning reframes teaching – Putting the heart back into learning – Activating internal processes in experiential learning – On becoming a maker of teachers: journey down a long hall of mirrors – Part 2: Introduction – Barriers to reflection on experience – Unlearning through experience – Experiential learning at a distance – Learning from experience in mathematics – Part 3: Introduction – How the T-Group changed my life: a sociological perspective on experiential group work – Living the learning: internalizing our model of group learning – Experiential learning and social transformation for a post-apartheid learning future – Experiential learning or learning from experience: does it make a difference? – Index.

Contributors
Lee Andresen, David Boud, Angela Brew, Stephen Brookfield, Ruth Cohen, Costas Criticos, Kathleen Dechant, Elizabeth Kasl, Victoria Marsick, John Mason, Nod Miller, John Mulligan, Denis Postle, Mary Thorpe, Robin Usher, David Walker.

208pp ·0 335 19095 2 (Paperback)

MAKING SENSE OF EXPERIENTIAL LEARNING
DIVERSITY IN THEORY AND PRACTICE

Susan Warner Weil and Ian McGill (eds)

This book appraises the multiplicity of meanings and practices associated with experiential learning in an international context. It reflects the depth, breadth and complexity of current developments, and pushes at the boundaries of theory and practice.

The editors have identified four distinct 'villages' within the global village of experiential learning. One is clearly identified round the assessment and accreditation of prior experiential learning as a means of gaining access and recognition in relation to educational institutions, employment and professional bodies. A second is the place for those who centre their activities on changing the practice, structures and purposes of post-school education. Another can be identified among those who place learning from experience as the core of education for social change mainly outside educational institutions. Finally, there is a focus on the potential and practice of personal growth and development.

Contents
A framework for making sense of experiential learning – Meaning and practice in experiential learning – Some competing traditions in experiential learning – Learning from action – The principal meaning of dialogue for the construction and transformation of reality – Experiential learning – Learner autonomy – The autobiography as a motivational factor for students – On being an educational fantasy engineer – Generating integration and involvement in learning – Coming to know – Action learning – Our faculty goes experiential – Some critical issues related to assessment and accreditation of adults' prior experiential learning – Experiential learning and professional development – Reducing student attrition – Curriculum development for long-distance itnernships – Facilitating learning for adults through participation – Media, praxis and empowerment – Learning through the heart – Personal stances in learning – Continuing the dialogue – Index.

Contributors
Amina Barkatoolah, Avtar Brah, David Boud, Richard Bawden, Tom Bourner, Costas Criticos, Paul Frost, Dwight E. Giles Jr, Jane Henry, Susan Segal-Horn, Lucy Horwitz, Jane Hoy, Miriam Hutton, Annikki Järvinen, Phyllis Marie Jensen, K.J.B. Keregero, Mary K. St John Nelson, Dave O'Reilly, Roger Packham, Shari L. Peterson, Marie Redwine, Roger Roberts, Phillida Salmon, Tara Serrao, Timothy Stanton, Danny Wildemeersch, Julie Wylde.

302pp   0 335 09713 8   (Paperback)